FROM THE LIBRARY OF

A. W. TOZER

SELECTIONS FROM WRITERS

WHO INFLUENCED HIS

Spiritual Journey

COMPILED BY

JAMES STUART BELL

INCLUDING THE WRITINGS *of* AUGUSTINE

THOMAS À KEMPIS · MARTIN LUTHER · D. L. MOODY

BETHANY HOUSE PUBLISHERS

Minneapolis, Minnesota

Published by Bethany House Publishers
11400 Hampshire Avenue South
Bloomington, Minnesota 55438

Bethany House Publishers is a division of
Baker Publishing Group, Grand Rapids, Michigan.

Printed in the United States of America

Library of Congress Cataloging-in-Publication Data

From the library of A. W. Tozer : selections from writers who influenced his spiritual journey / compiled by James Stuart Bell.
    p. cm.
    Includes bibliographical references and index.
    ISBN 978-0-7642-0862-1 (hardcover : alk. paper) 1. Christian life. 2. Tozer, A. W. (Aiden Wilson), 1897–1963—Sources. I. Bell, James S.
    BV4501.3.F77   2011
    248.4—dc22

2010038735

To Brian and Sally Oxley,
devoted to Christian classics

ACKNOWLEDGMENTS

THIS BOOK IS ALSO DEDICATED to Dave Fessenden, a man passionate about A.W. Tozer. To Sam O'Neal for his invaluable assistance, and to Kyle Duncan, David Horton, Julie Smith, Tim Peterson, and Donna Carpenter for their publishing expertise and vision for this series.

CONTENTS

FOREWORD

IT WAS NEARLY THIRTY YEARS AGO that I discovered a small orange-covered book titled *The Best of A. W. Tozer.* I began reading these excerpts from the collected works of this celebrated Christian evangelist, revivalist, prophet, and pastor and have never stopped. Indeed, I don't think a month has gone by that I have not spent time reading and rereading selections from the works of this author.

When I confessed to a friend my three-decades-long habit of drinking from the well of A.W. Tozer's books, articles, and published sermons, he suggested I might be getting into a Tozer rut. My response to this warning is simple: one cannot get into a Tozer rut. His writings first and foremost point readers to the Lord Jesus Christ and the Holy Scriptures in ways that are refreshing. Second, Aiden W. Tozer points us to the writings of men and women throughout church history who have been personally and intimately acquainted with our glorious God because they have learned to truly praise and worship Him.

Upon reflection, it occurs to me that A.W. Tozer—despite his lack of college and seminary training—has become one of the foremost Christian educators of the twentieth and early twenty-first centuries. Tozer has been and still is a teacher to men and women who long to know God with all their heart and soul. The Holy Spirit has called such people into that noble clan that Tozer dubbed "the Society of the Burning Heart." Many of us in that joyous society consider Aiden Wilson Tozer our mentor even though we never met him in person.

James Stuart Bell, a highly respected author, editor, and member of the Society of the Burning Heart, has compiled excerpts from the writings of twenty-eight men and women who "mentored" Tozer through their writing. What a marvelous collection this is. Thoughtfully organized around eight important themes, this volume promises to become a library designed for students of the deeper life. To Jim Bell, A.W. Tozer, and the Holy Spirit who inspired both of them and these anointed writers, we are in debt.

Lyle W. Dorsett
Beeson Divinity School
Samford University

INTRODUCTION

THERE IS A PHENOMENON in nature known as "the perfect storm." It occurs when a rare combination of weather patterns converge and join forces against a vulnerable region of the globe—warm air from a low-pressure system in one direction, for example, meeting cool and dry air from a high-pressure system in another, then both streams being melded and inflamed by a burst of tropical moisture. The resulting storm is said to be perfect in its power, perfect in its force and duration, perfect in its capacity for impact.

This phenomenon is not limited to the weather, however. There are times in the world of human beings when a confluence of inherent abilities, spiritual gifts, and sheer force of will transform an individual into the perfect woman for an appointed task, the perfect man to speak to his generation. These men and women never pass quietly from birth to death as a faceless member of the crowd. Rather, they stand out. They become seared in our memory. They make an impact and, if God is with them, they leave the world a better place than when they found it.

Aiden Wilson Tozer was such a man.

Tozer was gifted with all the physical tools necessary for a modern-day prophet: a commanding voice and demeanor, a precise diction, and an inherent ability to express himself clearly and powerfully. More important, those natural tools were joined by many blessings from the Holy Spirit, including a keen insight into biblical truth and an unflinching perception of the world around him. Most important, Tozer's inclinations and abilities were honed and sharpened into the pursuit of two all-important goals: to bring glory to God through a passionate pursuit of His holy presence, and to facilitate spiritual transformation in a weak and lethargic church.

As he successfully fulfilled those goals year after year, he greatly blessed the people around him, and the church he served so long and so well has never been the same.

A Short Biography

Born April 21, 1897, in the mountains of western Pennsylvania, Tozer (as he liked to be called) passed an unremarkable early life in various towns throughout the Midwest. Things changed just before his seventeenth birthday, though, when he encountered a street preacher in Akron, Ohio.

Tozer was walking home from his job at a rubber factory when he heard about having a relationship with God. "If you don't know how to be saved, just call on God," the preacher said. He invited his listeners to pray, "Lord, be merciful to me, a sinner." Tozer didn't stop and pray on the corner of that street, but the simple message that it was possible to know God stuck with him as he continued home. Upon arriving, Tozer went upstairs to his attic sanctuary in order to wrestle with the idea. When he emerged several hours later, he was a new creature—a new man. He had found the relationship that would define every day of his life from that moment on.

Tozer was mentored by the woman who later became his mother-in-law. She encouraged him to study the Bible and pray regularly—habits that eventually matured into major pillars of his spiritual life. She also encouraged him to read good books, and this, too, became a lifelong pursuit.

Five years after his conversion, Tozer received a call to pastor a small church in a small town with the charming name of Nutter Fort, West Virginia. Other pastorates followed, including flocks in Ohio and Indianapolis, which eventually led Tozer to accept an invitation to serve as pastor of the Southside Alliance Church in Chicago in 1928.

It was at Southside, where he served more than thirty years, that Tozer's influence grew across the nation, and then around the world. Attendance at Southside sharply increased after his arrival, moving from eighty members to eight hundred over the course of his pastorate, compelling the church to construct larger facilities in 1941. In 1950, Tozer was chosen as editor of the *Alliance Weekly* magazine (now called *Alliance Life*). In 1951, he began hosting a popular radio program on the Moody radio station WMBI.

It was also at Southside that Tozer wrote the material for most of his books. He published fewer than ten during the course of his life, including two that have since become spiritual classics: *The Pursuit of God* and *The Knowledge of the Holy*. After his death, material from his sermons, editorials, and other sources was compiled into dozens of posthumous publications, so that he is now recognized as the author of more than forty books.

Tozer's influence was about more than his writing and speaking, however. He was a leader during a time when the church was in desperate need of guidance and correction. As biographer James L. Snyder put it, Tozer "saw through the fog of modern Christianity, pointing out the rocks on which it might flounder if it continued its course." He has been described as a modern-day prophet—a description that was accurate during the course of his life and one that remains accurate as his words and deeds continue to guide followers of Jesus today.

Along with his wife, Ada Cecelia Pfautz, Tozer spent the final years of his life in Toronto, where he served as pastor of Avenue Road Church. Tozer passed away on May 12, 1963. The simple epitaph on his grave can still be read today: "A. W. Tozer—A Man of God."

WHY YOU SHOULD READ THIS BOOK

A.W. Tozer was famous for his reputation as a voracious reader. He applied himself regularly to mining the written word in search of powerful ideas, stories, and spiritual truths—and then meditating on the nuggets he uncovered. In addition to a deep study of the Bible, his reading list spanned several centuries of church history—from the early church fathers, to the mystics of the middle centuries, to the noted pastors and preachers of the generation that preceded him.

Throughout the pages of this book, you will find nearly two hundred excerpted readings from the men and women whose writings were instrumental in Tozer's intellectual and spiritual formation. The highlighted writers are some of the most famous and influential minds in the history of Christianity, and the excerpts provided for you in the following pages represent the pinnacle of their achievements.

So, why should you read the material provided in this book? Because A.W. Tozer read it and benefited from it. More than that—because this material played a significant role in Tozer's spiritual growth. Indeed, Tozer himself stressed again and again that these writers shaped his faith and practice from an early age. And without their words to serve as guides along the Pilgrim Way, Tozer never would have become the man of God that emerged so fortuitously for his generation and for the ones that followed.

Tozer's example continues to speak, encouraging us to drink deeply of these heroes of the faith—just as he encouraged the members of his own congregations.

How to Read This Book

This book has been divided into eight separate chapters, each of which emphasizes a major theme from Tozer's life and writings—from worship, to practicing the presence of God, to living the Christian life. The readings themselves are short in length and focus on subjects that are important to your life and devotion to God.

One way to use this book is to make it a part of your daily devotional experience. Consider reading one excerpt each day, along with a passage of Scripture. As you do, be sure to allow yourself times of silent reflection in order to think deeply about what each author is communicating (as was Tozer's custom). You may even want to read this book in concert with *The Knowledge of the Holy* or another of Tozer's masterpieces, thereby gaining a real-time understanding of how these writers influenced and guided him.

This book can also serve as an excellent educational resource. Taking a broader look at each chapter will help you learn a great deal about the essential doctrines and practices of our faith; it will also help you find wisdom for developing transformative habits and overcoming the many obstacles you'll find as you walk the path of God.

If you are not familiar with all of the authors represented in the following pages, learning a bit about their stories in the Biographies section at the back of this book will help you to better appreciate what they have to say. In addition, as you identify certain passages and writers that are especially impactful to you, consider reading the complete volumes from which those excerpts were taken. You'll find the source of each excerpt listed on the same page, and you can identify all of the books excerpted by each author using the "Excerpts Taken From . . ." section.

Aiden Wilson Tozer was a man who dedicated his life to pursuing a passionate and intimate relationship with a holy God and to helping others in the church do the same. His life stands out as remarkable because he succeeded in his dedication and achieved what he pursued. His overall book sales alone attest to that significant impact on the church.

A significant part of that success is due to Tozer's willingness to be continually discipled by the great men and women of God, the mystics, evangelists, writers, and teachers, who had preceded him through centuries of church history. His mentors had one thing in common—through Jesus Christ they sought to lose themselves in a deep union with an ineffable God, experiencing joy unspeakable and a peace that passes all human understanding. Like the apostle Paul they were willing to surrender everything for the experience of knowing his intimate embrace and deep fellowship—the Deeper Life—an experience shared by all of them but given different descriptions and circumstances.

You now have the opportunity to be similarly discipled and tremble in reverent awe in the presence of a holy God, basking in the ocean of his limitless love and mercy.

WORSHIP:

THE CHIEF END OF MAN

"I can safely say, on the authority of all that is revealed in the
Word of God, that any man or woman on this earth who is
bored and turned off by worship is not ready for heaven."

—*Whatever Happened to Worship?*

D. L. MOODY

The Ten Commandments

Philosophers are agreed that even the most primitive races of mankind reach out beyond the world of matter to a superior Being. It is as natural for man to feel after God as it is for the ivy to feel after a support. Hunger and thirst drive man to seek for food, and there is a hunger of the soul that needs satisfying, too. Man does not need to be commanded to worship, as there is not a race so high or so low in the scale of civilization but has some kind of god. What he needs is to be directed aright.

This is what the first commandment is for. Before we can worship intelligently, we must know what or whom to worship. God does not leave us in ignorance. When Paul went to Athens, he found an altar dedicated to "The Unknown God," and he proceeded to tell of Him whom we worship. When God gave the commandments to Moses, He commenced with a declaration of His own character, and demanded exclusive recognition. "I am the LORD your God, who brought you out of Egypt, out of the land of slavery. You shall have no other gods before me" (Exodus 20:2–3).

JOHN BUNYAN

Christ a Complete Savior

God is the chief good—good so as nothing is but himself. He is in himself most happy; yes, all good and all true happiness are only to be found in God, as that which is essential to his nature; nor is there any good or any happiness in or with any creature or thing but what is communicated to it by God. God is the only desirable good; nothing without him is worthy of our hearts. Right thoughts of God are able to ravish the heart; how much more happy is the man that has interest in God. God alone is able by himself to put the soul into a more blessed, comfortable, and happy condition than can the whole world; yes, and more than if all the created happiness of all the angels of heaven did dwell in one man's bosom. I cannot tell what to say. I am drowned. The life, the glory, the blessedness, the soul-satisfying goodness that is in God are beyond all expression.

It was this glory of God, the sight and visions of this God of glory, that provoked Abraham to leave his country and kindred to come after God. The reason why men are so careless of and so indifferent about their coming to God is because they have their eyes blinded—because they do not perceive his glory. God is so blessed a one that did he not hide himself and his glory, the whole world would be ravished with him; but he has, I will not say reasons of state, but reasons of glory, glorious reasons why he hides himself from the world and appears but to particular ones.

What is heaven without God? But many there be who cannot

abide God; no, they like not to go to heaven, because God is there. The nature of God lies cross to the lusts of men. A holy God, a glorious holy God, an infinitely holy God—this spoils all. But to the soul that is awakened, and that is made to see things as they are, to him God is what he is in himself, the blessed, the highest, the only eternal good, and he without the enjoyment of whom all things would sound but empty in the ears of that soul.

Methinks, when I consider what glory there is at times upon the creatures, and that all their glory is the workmanship of God, "O Lord," say I, "what is God himself?" He may well be called the God of glory, as well as the glorious Lord; for as all glory is from him, so in him is an inconceivable well-spring of glory, of glory to be communicated to them that come by Christ to him. Therefore let the glory and love and bliss and eternal happiness that are in God allure you to come to him by Christ.

FRANÇOIS FÉNELON

Maxims of the Saints

Of the love of God, there are various kinds. At least, there are various feelings which go under that name.

First, there is what may be called mercenary or selfish love. That is, that love of God which originates in a sole regard to our own happiness. Those who love God with no other love than this love Him just as the miser loves his money and the voluptuous man his pleasures—attaching no value to God, except as a means to an end; and that end is the gratification of themselves. Such love, if it can be called by that name, is unworthy of God. He does not ask it; He will not receive it. In the language of Francis de Sales, "It is sacrilegious and impious."

Second, another kind of love does not exclude a regard to our own happiness as a motive of love, but requires this motive to be subordinate to a much higher one—namely, that of a regard to God's glory. It is a mixed state, in which we regard ourselves and God at the same time. This love is not necessarily selfish and wrong. On the contrary, when the two objects of it, God and ourselves, are relatively in the right position—that is to say, when we love God as He ought to be loved and love ourselves no more than we ought to be loved—it is a love which, in being properly subordinated, is unselfish and is right.

BERNARD OF CLAIRVAUX

On Loving God

You want me to tell you why God is to be loved and how much. I answer: the reason for loving God is God Himself, and the measure of love due to Him is immeasurable love. Is this plain? Doubtless, to a thoughtful man; but I am debtor to the unwise also. A word to the wise is sufficient; but I must consider simple folk, too. Therefore I set myself joyfully to explain more in detail what is meant above.

We are to love God for Himself because of a twofold reason: nothing is more reasonable, nothing more profitable. When one asks, "Why should I love God?" he may mean, "What is lovely in God?" or "What shall I gain by loving God?" In either case, the same sufficient cause of love exists—namely, God Himself.

First, of His title to our love. Could any title be greater than this, that He gave Himself for us unworthy wretches? And being God, what better gift could He offer than Himself? Hence, if one seeks for God's claim upon our love, here is the most important: Because He first loved us (1 John 4:19).

Ought He not to be loved in return, when we think who loved, whom He loved, and how much He loved? For who is He that loved? The same of whom every spirit testifies: "You are my God: my goods are nothing unto You" (Psalm 16:2). And is not His love that wonderful charity which "seeks not her own" (1 Corinthians 13:5)? But for whom was such unutterable love made manifest? The apostle tells us: "When we were enemies, we were reconciled to God by the death of His Son" (Romans 5:10). So it was God who loved us, loved us freely, and loved us while yet we were enemies.

And how great was this love of His? St. John answers: "God so loved the world that He gave His only-begotten Son, that whosoever believes in Him should not perish, but have everlasting life" (John 3:16). St. Paul adds: "He spared not His own Son, but delivered Him up for us all" (Romans 8:32); and the Son says of Himself, "Greater love has no man than this, that a man lay down his life for his friends" (John 15:13).

THOMAS À KEMPIS

The Imitation of Christ

Lord, what is man that You are mindful of him, or the son of man that You visit him? What has man deserved that You should give him Your grace? What cause have I, Lord, to complain if You desert me, or what objection can I have if You do not do what I ask? This I may think and say in all truth: "Lord, I am nothing, of myself I have nothing that is good; I am lacking in all things, and I am ever tending toward nothing. And unless I have Your help and am inwardly strengthened by You, I become quite lukewarm and lax."

But You, Lord, are always the same. You remain forever—always good, just, and holy; doing all things rightly, justly, and holily, disposing them wisely. I, however, who am more ready to go backward than forward, do not remain always in one state, for I change with the seasons. Yet my condition quickly improves when it pleases You and when You reach forth Your helping hand. For You alone, without human aid, can help me and strengthen me so greatly that my heart shall no more change but be converted and rest solely in You. Hence, if I knew well how to cast aside all earthly consolation, either to attain devotion or because of the necessity which, in the absence of human solace, compels me to seek You alone, then I could deservedly hope for Your grace and rejoice in the gift of new consolation.

Thanks be to You from Whom all things come, whenever it is well with me. In Your sight I am vanity and nothingness—a weak, unstable man. In what, therefore, can I glory, and how can I wish to be highly regarded? Is it because I am nothing? This, too, is utterly vain. Indeed, the greatest vanity is the evil plague of empty self-glory, because it draws one away from true glory and robs one of heavenly grace. For when a man is pleased with himself he displeases You, when he pants after human praise he is deprived of true virtue. But it is true glory and holy exultation to glory in You and not in self, to rejoice in Your name rather than in one's own virtue, and not to delight in any creature except for Your sake.

Let Your name, not mine, be praised. Let Your work, not mine, be magnified. Let Your holy name be blessed, but let no human praise be given to me. You are my glory. You are the joy of my heart. In You I will glory and rejoice all the day, and for myself I will glory in nothing but my infirmities.

Let others seek the glory that comes from another. I will seek that which comes from God alone. All human glory, all temporal honor, all worldly position is truly vanity and foolishness compared to Your everlasting glory. O my Truth, my Mercy, my God; O Blessed Trinity, to You alone be praise and honor, power and glory, throughout all the endless ages of ages.

JOHANNES TAULER

Light, Life, and Love

All works which men and all creatures can ever work even to the end of the world, without the grace of God—all of them together, however great they may be, are an absolute nothing when compared with the smallest work which God has worked in men by His grace. As much as God is better than all His creatures, so much better are His works than all the works, or wisdom, or designs which all men could devise. Even the smallest drop of grace is better than all earthly riches that are beneath the sun. Yes, a drop of grace is more noble than all angels and all souls, and all the natural things that God has made.

And yet grace is given more richly by God to the soul than any earthly gift. It is given more richly than brooks of water, than the breath of the air, than the brightness of the sun; for spiritual things are far finer and nobler than earthly things. The whole Trinity—Father, Son, and Holy Ghost—give grace to the soul and flow immediately into it; even the highest angel, in spite of his great nobility, cannot do this. Grace looses us from the snares of many temptations; it relieves us from the heavy burden of worldly cares and carries the spirit up to heaven, the land of spirits. It kills the worm of conscience, which makes sins alive. Grace is a very powerful thing. The man to whom comes but a little drop of the light of grace, to him all that is not God becomes as bitter as gall upon the tongue.

Contrary to nature, grace makes all sorrows sweet, and brings it about that a man no longer feels any relish for things which formerly gave him great pleasure and delight. On the other hand, what formerly disgusted him now delights him and is the desire of his heart—for instance, weakness, sorrow, inwardness, humility, self-abandonment, and detachment from all creatures. All this is in the highest degree dear to him, when this visitation of the Holy Ghost, grace, has in truth come to him.

Then the sick man, that is to say the external man, with all his faculties, is plunged completely into the pool of water even as the sick man who had been for 38 years by the pool at Jerusalem—and there washes himself thoroughly in the exalted, noble, precious blood of Christ Jesus. For grace in manifold ways bathes the soul in the wounds and blood of the holy Lamb, Jesus Christ.

FRANCIS DE SALES

Treatise on the Love of God

If we could find any men who were in the integrity of original justice in which Adam was created, such men would not only have an inclination to love God above all things, but would naturally be able to put that inclination into execution. For as the heavenly Author and Master of nature cooperates with and lends His strong hand to fire to spring on high, to water to flow towards the sea, to earth to sink down to its centre and stay there—so having Himself planted in man's heart a natural inclination not only to love good in general, but to love in particular and above all things His divine goodness which is better and sweeter than all things—the sweetness of His sovereign providence would require that He contribute to these blessed men of whom we speak as much help as should be necessary to practice and effectuate that inclination.

This help would be on the one hand natural, as being suitable to nature and tending to the love of God as author and sovereign Master of nature. On the other hand it would be supernatural, because it would correspond not with the simple nature of man, but with nature adorned, enriched, and honored by original justice, which is a supernatural quality proceeding from a most special favor of God. But as to the love above all things which such help would enable these men to practice, it would be called natural, because virtuous actions take their names from their objects and motives, and this love of which we speak would only tend to God as acknowledged to be Author, Lord, and Sovereign of every creature by natural light only, and consequently to be amiable and estimable above all things by natural inclination and tendency.

And although now our human nature be not endowed with that original soundness and righteousness which the first man had in his creation, but on the contrary be greatly depraved by sin—yet still the holy inclination to love God above all things stays with us, as also the natural light by which we see His sovereign goodness to be more worthy of love than all things. And it is impossible that one thinking attentively upon God, yes even by natural reasoning only, should not feel a certain movement of love which the secret inclination of our nature excites in the bottom of our hearts, by which at the first apprehension of this chief and sovereign object the will is taken and perceives itself stirred up to a complacency in it.

It happens often amongst partridges that one steals away another's eggs with intention to sit on them, whether moved by greediness to become a mother or by a stupidity which makes them mistake their own. And behold a strange thing, yet well supported by testimony—the young one that was hatched and nourished under the wings of a stranger partridge, at the first call of the true mother, who had laid the egg from which she was hatched, quits the thief-partridge, goes back to the first mother, and puts herself in her brood—all from the correspondence she has with her first origin. Yet this correspondence appeared not, but remained secret, shut up, and as it were sleeping in the bottom of nature, till it met with its object; when suddenly excited, and in a sort awakened, it produces its effect, and turns the young partridge's inclination to its first duty.

It is the same with our heart, which though it be formed, nourished, and bred amongst corporal, base, and transitory things— and in a manner under the wings of nature, notwithstanding—at the first look it throws on God, at its first knowledge of him, the natural and first inclination to love God which was dull and imperceptible awakes in an instant, and suddenly appears as a spark from amongst the ashes that, touching our will, gives it a movement of the supreme love due to the sovereign and first principle of all things.

FRANCIS OF ASSISI

"The Canticle of the Sun"

Most high, omnipotent, good Lord,
Praise, glory, and honor and benediction all are Yours.
To You alone do they belong, most High,
And there is no man fit to mention You.

Praise be to You, my Lord, with all Your creatures,
Especially to my worshipful brother sun,
The which lights up the day, and through him do You
    brightness give;
And beautiful is he and radiant with splendor great;
Of You, most High, signification gives.

Praised be my Lord, for sister moon and for the stars,
In heaven You have formed them clear and precious and
    fair.

Praised be my Lord for brother wind
And for the air and clouds and fair and every kind of
    weather,
By the which You give to Your creatures nourishment.
Praised be my Lord for sister water,
The which is greatly helpful and humble and precious
    and pure.

Praised be my Lord for brother fire,
By the which You light up the dark.
And fair is he and gay and mighty and strong.

Praised be my Lord for our sister, mother earth,
The which sustains and keeps us
And brings forth diverse fruits with grass and flowers
    bright.

Praised be my Lord for those who for Your love forgive
And weakness bear and tribulation.
Blessed those who shall in peace endure,
For by You, most High, shall they be crowned.
Praised be my Lord for our sister, the bodily death,
From the which no living man can flee.
Woe to them who die in mortal sin;
Blessed those who shall find themselves in Your most
    holy will,
For the second death shall do them no ill.

Praise and bless my Lord, and give Him thanks,
And be subject unto Him with great humility.

ANSELM

The Devotions of Saint Anselm

Are not these inestimable benefits bestowed upon you by thy Creator enough for you to make you render to Him continual thanksgiving, and pay to Him your debt of love unceasing, when you consider how at the beginning of your creation He called you by His goodness out of nothing—or rather out of the dust of the earth—to so great a height of dignity? Apply to your own life the words of the Saints. Hear what is said concerning a Saint.

This, then, is the praise given to a Saint: *With all his heart he praised the Lord.* Behold that end for which you were created; behold the task which your Master has set you to do. For to what end should God have raised you up by so glorious a privilege in your creation but that He desired you to give yourself to His praises without ceasing? You were created to praise your Creator so that, being occupied in nothing else than His praises, you might here by the service of your righteousness draw nearer unto Him, and hereafter attain to the life of blessedness. For His praise makes your righteousness in this world and your happiness in the world to come.

But if you praise, praise Him from your whole heart; praise Him by loving Him. For this is the rule of praising that is given to the Saints: "With all his heart he praised the Lord and loved God that made him." Praise therefore, and praise with your whole heart, and love Him whom you praise. For he praises, but not with his whole heart, the man whom prosperity persuades to bless God;

but adversity restrains from the office of blessing. Again he praises, but loves not, who in the praises of God seeks to have anything by his praising beside God Himself.

Praise therefore, and praise worthily, so that to the utmost of your power there be in you no charge, no drought, no contemplation, no carefulness of mind that is void of the praise of God. Let no worldly prosperity divert you, nor any worldly adversity restrain you from His praise. For thus you will praise the Lord with your whole heart and with love also; you will seek from Him nothing else than Himself, that He may Himself be the goal of your desire and the reward of your labors—your consolation in this life of shadows and your possession in the blessed life to come.

NICHOLAS OF CUSA

The Vision of God

O Lord God, Helper of those who seek You, I see You in the garden of Paradise, and I do not know what I see, because I see no visible thing. I know only the following: that I know that I do not know, and never can know, what I see.

Moreover, I do not know how to name You, because I do not know what You are. And if someone tells me that You are named by this or that name, then by virtue of the fact that he names, I know that this is not Your name. For the limit of every mode of signification that belongs to names is the wall beyond which I see You. And if anyone expresses any concept whereby, allegedly, You can be conceived, I know that this concept is not a concept of You. For every concept reaches its limit at the wall of Paradise.

Moreover, if anyone expresses any likeness and maintains that You are to be conceived in accordance with it, I know as well that this likeness is not a likeness of You. Similarly, if anyone recounts his understanding of You, intending to offer a means for Your being understood, he is still far away from You. For You are separated by a very high wall from all these methods of apprehending. For this wall separates from You whatever can be spoken of or thought of, because You are free from all the things that can be captured by any concept.

Hence, when I am very highly elevated, I see that You are Infinity. Consequently, You are not approachable, not comprehensible, not nameable, not manifold, and not visible.

ANONYMOUS

Theologica Germanica

God says, "I will not give My glory to another" (Isaiah 42:8). This is as much as to say that praise and honor and glory belong to no man, but to God only. But now, if I call any good thing my own—as if I were it, or of myself had power or did or knew anything, or as if anything were mine or of me, or belonged to me, or were due to me—I take unto myself honor and glory. And by doing so, I do two evil things.

First, I fall and go astray, as mentioned before. Secondly, I touch God in His honor and take unto myself what belongs to God only. For all that must be called good belongs to none but to the true eternal Goodness, which is God only. And whoever takes it unto himself commits unrighteousness and is against God.

Certain men say that we ought to be without will, wisdom, love, desire, knowledge, and the like. But this does not mean that there is to be no knowledge in man, and that God is not to be loved by him, nor desired and longed for, nor praised and honored—for that would be a great loss, and man would be like the beasts and the brutes that have no reason. Rather, it means that man's knowledge should be so clear and perfect that he should acknowledge a truth that in himself he neither has nor can do any good thing, and that none of his knowledge, wisdom, art, will, love, and good works come from himself, nor of any man, nor of any creature. But these are all of the eternal God, from whom they all proceed. As Christ Himself said, "Without Me, ye can do nothing" (John 15:5).

NICHOLAS OF CUSA

On Loving God

And now let us consider what profit we shall have from loving God. Even though our knowledge of this is imperfect, still that is better than to ignore it altogether. I have already said (when it was a question of wherefore and in what manner God should be loved) that there was a double reason constraining us: His right and our advantage. Having written as best I can, though unworthily, of God's right to be loved, I have still to treat of the recompense which that love brings. For although God would be loved without respect of reward, yet He wills not to leave love unrewarded.

True charity cannot be left destitute, even though she is unselfish and seeks not her own (1 Corinthians 13:5). Love is an affection of the soul, not a contract: it cannot rise from a mere agreement, nor is it so to be gained. It is spontaneous in its origin and impulse, and true love is its own satisfaction. It has its reward, but that reward is the object beloved.

For whatever you seem to love, if it is on account of something else, what you do really love is that something else, not the apparent object of desire. St. Paul did not preach the Gospel that he might earn his bread; he ate that he might be strengthened for his ministry. What he loved was not bread, but the Gospel. True love does not demand a reward, but it deserves one. Surely no one offers to pay for love; yet some recompense is due to one who loves, and if his love endures he will doubtless receive it.

On a lower plane of action, it is the reluctant, not the eager, whom we urge by promises of reward. Who would think of paying a man to do what he was yearning to do already? For instance, no one would hire a hungry man to eat, or a thirsty man to drink, or a mother to nurse her own child. Who would think of bribing a farmer to dress his own vineyard, or to dig about his orchard, or to rebuild his house? So, all the more, one who truly loves God asks no other recompense than God Himself. For if he should demand anything else it would be the prize that he loved, and not God.

JOHN MILTON

Paradise Lost

Of man's first disobedience, and the fruit
Of that Forbidden Tree, whose mortal taste
Brought death into the world, and all our woe,
With loss of Eden, till one greater Man
Restore us, and regain the blissful Seat,
Sing Heavenly Muse, that on the secret top
Of Oreb, or of Sinai, did inspire
That Shepherd, who first taught the chosen Seed
In the beginning, how the Heavens and Earth
Rose out of chaos: Or if Sion Hill
Delight thee more, and Siloa's Brook that flowed
Fast by the Oracle of God; I thence
Invoke your aid to my adventurous Song,
That with no middle flight intends to soar
Above the Aonian Mount, while it pursues
Things unattempted yet in prose or rhyme.

And chiefly Thou O Spirit, that dost prefer
Before all Temples the upright heart and pure,
Instruct me, for Thou knowest; Thou from the first
Was present, and with mighty wings outspread
Dove-like sat brooding on the vast Abyss
And made it pregnant: What in me is dark
Illumine, what is low raise and support;
That to the height of this great argument
I may assert the Eternal Providence,
And justify the ways of God to men.

G. CAMPBELL MORGAN

From the Sermon, "The Holy Spirit Through
Christ, in the Church, for the World"

What, then, is the Church in the world? It is God's institute of
praise, God's institute of prayer, and God's institute of prophecy.
The whole Church is, first of all, an institute created to praise
God. . . . The Christian Church exists to reveal God and to utter
forth His praise, to make God known to men who know Him not,
that in the presence of the revelation they may be filled with awe,
and wonder, and amazement—to make God known, that God shall
be attractive to humanity. Whether we are prepared to accept the
declaration or not, the experience abides. Men of the world can
know God only as God is revealed to them through His people.
The Word of God can be powerful only as it is incarnate. Is not
that the meaning of the central mystery of our holy religion? God
came no nearer to humanity when Jesus was born in Bethlehem,
but He came into visibility, into manifestation. In proportion as in
this Church of Jesus Christ His life is reproduced, God is being
revealed anew.

Our first business is that of praising Him, praising Him with
lip and with life, in the actual songs we sing, in the hallelujahs we
lift; praising Him by all the habits of our life, by the perpetual
testimony of our ways as they announce the fact of His being, the
fact of His love. That was the first effect the Church produced.
Filled with life, light flashed from the eyes of the disciples, songs
were on their lips, they magnified the mighty works of God, and

the city was compelled to listen. In that hour of Pentecost, God created for Himself by the coming of the Spirit through Christ a people for His own praise and glory, a kingdom of priests that they might offer to Him sacrifices of praise and thanksgiving. Unless Pentecost produces in our life fullness of joy and makes us a people filled with praise, we are failing sadly. The first function of the Christian Church is that she should be to the praise of God.

In that hour, moreover, God created in the world a great institute of prayer. For the function of the priesthood is not only Eucharistic, it is intercessory. By the coming of the Spirit He created a people able to pray. Surely this is what the apostle meant in his Roman letter when he spoke of creation groaning and travailing in its pain, and then spoke of the Church in the midst of the groaning creation, the Church groaning and travailing together with creation in pain; and at last declared that "the Spirit makes intercession for us with groanings that cannot be uttered." The Spirit of God, understanding the pain of creation, is grieved thereby, sorrow is caused in the very heart of God by the agony of humanity; that Spirit indwelling a company of people interprets to them the agony of creation, so that they enter into a new compassionate sympathy with all the suffering of the world, and thus in the midst of the groaning creation they constitute an institute of prayer.

No man can pray for the world unless the Spirit interpret to him the world's agony, and the Spirit cannot interpret the world's agony to any man unless that man live in the midst of the world's agony. Not by retirement from the world, not by hiding away within a monastic institution, not by seeking to develop my own spiritual life by removing myself from the agony of the world, can I ever pray for the world; but because I live every day in the midst of its busy life, am close to it and know it, and because the Spirit of God in me leads me into the secret of the deepest meaning of the world's agony and pain so that I no longer treat it as a superficial disease that can be dealt with by the nostrums of humanity, but as a great heart trouble that needs blood and sacrifice to deal with it, am I able to pray. Out of that revelation of the meaning of the world's agony created by the Spirit in the hearts of believing men they are able to pray. The Church of God in the economy of God was created an institute of prayer.

But more, not for praise alone was the Church created, not alone for prayer, but also for prophecy—in the highest use of the great word, for proclamation. As with lip and life the saints praise, so by lip and life the saints should preach. The Spirit came uniting these men to the Lord, disannulling orphanage and canceling distance to make the risen and ascended Christ a living bright reality. By so doing He enabled these men to speak to the Lord familiarly as those who have constant comradeship with Him, and by so doing enabled them to reveal the Lord of Whom they spoke in tone and temper and habit and speech, and in all activity. Reverently and superlatively, He came to multiply and unite in the perfect Humanity of Nazareth all the scattered members of the one great Christ over all the earth.

FRANCIS OF ASSISI

Admonitions

Hail, queen wisdom! May the Lord save you with your sister holy, pure simplicity! O Lady, holy poverty, may the Lord save you with your sister holy humility! O Lady, holy charity, may the Lord save you with your sister holy obedience! O all you most holy virtues, may the Lord, from whom you proceed and come, save you!

There is absolutely no man in the whole world who can possess one among you unless he first die. He who possesses one and does not offend the others, possesses all; and he who offends one possesses none and offends all; and every one confounds vices and sins.

Holy wisdom confounds Satan and all his wickednesses. Pure, holy simplicity confounds all the wisdom of this world and the wisdom of the flesh. Holy poverty confounds cupidity and avarice and the cares of this world. Holy humility confounds pride and all the men of this world and all things that are in the world. Holy charity confounds all diabolical and fleshly temptations and all fleshly fears. Holy obedience confounds all bodily and fleshly desires and keeps the body mortified to the obedience of the Spirit and to the obedience of one's brother and makes a man subject to all the men of this world—and not to men alone, but also to all beasts and wild animals, so that they may do with him whatsoever they will, insofar as it may be granted to them from above by the Lord.

2

PRAYER AND CONTEMPLATION

"We need never shout across the spaces to an absent God.
He is nearer than our own soul,
closer than our most secret thoughts."

—*The Pursuit of God*

ANSELM

The Devotions of Saint Anselm

Now, Love that is the bond of the Godhead, You who are the holy Love which is between the Father Almighty and His most blessed Son, You Almighty Spirit—the Comforter, the most merciful Consoler of them that mourn—do enter by Your mighty power into the innermost sanctuary of my heart, and of your goodness dwell within, making glad with the brightness of Your glorious light the neglected corners inside, and making fruitful by the visitation of Your abundant dew the fields that are parched and barren with long continued drought.

Pierce with the arrows of Your love the secret chambers of the inner man. Let the entrance of Your healthful flames set the sluggish heart alight, and the burning fire of Your sacred inspiration enlighten it and consume all that is within me, both of mind and body. Give me drink of Your pleasures as out of the river so that I may take no pleasure hereafter in the poisonous sweetness of worldly delights. Give sentence with me, God, and defend my cause against the ungodly people. Teach me to do the thing that pleases You, for You are my God. I believe that in whomever You dwell, You make there an habitation for the Father and for the Son. Blessed is he who shall be counted worthy to entertain You, because by You the Father and the Son shall make their abode with him.

Come, O come, most gracious Consoler of the soul in sorrow, You refuge in due time of trouble. Come, You cleanser from sin,

You healer of wounds. Come, You strength of the weak, You lifter up of them that fall. Come, You teacher of the lowly and destroyer of the proud. Come, You gracious father of the fatherless, You gentle defender of the cause of the widows. Come, You hope of the poor and cherisher of the sick. Come, You star of the seafarer, You haven of the shipwrecked. Come, You that are the only glory of them that live, the only salvation of them that die.

Come, most holy Spirit. Come and have mercy upon me, and fit me to receive You. Graciously grant to me that my littleness may be pleasing to Your greatness, my weakness to Your strength, according to the multitude of Your mercies, through Jesus Christ my Savior, who lives and reigns with the Father in the Unity that is of You, world without end. Amen.

G. CAMPBELL MORGAN

From the Sermon, "Prayer or Fainting"

"They ought always to pray, and not to faint" (Luke 18:1).

Before laying further emphasis upon the "always," let me take the terms of my text in order to understand Christ's philosophy of life for His own disciples. What is the real suggestiveness of this word "pray"? If you take it as to its first simplicity and intention, it means—and this is not complete but it will help us to reach the complete thought—to wish forward, to desire toward the ultimate; or if you will have that interpreted by the language of the apostle in one of his greatest epistles, that to the Colossians, it means the seeking of things which are above.

That does not at all suggest that the Christian is forevermore to be sighing after heaven, and expressing his discontent with the present world, and longing to escape from it; but rather that the Christian is to seek the upper things, setting his mind upon them, and everywhere and everywhen he is to be hoping for, and endeavoring after, the ultimate. That is the simple meaning of prayer: reaching forward, wishing forward, desiring forward, seeking the upper, the higher, the nobler.

So that in prayer there is included—first, always first—the thought of worship and adoration, that content of the heart with the perfection and acceptability and goodness of the will of God which bows the soul in worship. That is the first attitude of prayer. To pray is forevermore to set the life in its inspiration and in all its endeavor toward that ultimate goal of the glory of God. "Being justified by faith, let us have peace with God through our Lord Jesus Christ; through whom also we have had our access by faith into this grace wherein we stand; and let us rejoice in hope of the glory of God." That is the first quantity of quality of prayer: the vision of the ultimate with a corresponding attitude of life toward it, which is that of perpetual endeavor after it.

This means not merely that, in the midst of battle and strife and din and smoke and wounding and blood and tears, we see a better day, a golden age; but that the soul, seeing that golden age as in the will of God, and realizing that the supreme fact of the vision is that of God Himself, the supreme attitude of the life becomes that of submission, and the supreme effort of the life is that of cooperation with God toward the ultimate upon which His heart is set. That is prayer.

Prayer is not merely position of body, or of mind. Prayer is not merely asking for something in order that I may obtain it for myself. Prayer forevermore says when it asks for anything, "Not my will, but Thine be done." Which means, if the thing I ask for—however much I desire it, however good it seems to me to be—will hinder or postpone, by a hair's breadth or a moment, the ultimate victory, it will be denied to me. Those who know the real secret of the prayer life have discovered the fact that denial is over and over again the graciousness of overwhelming answer.

To pray is to desire forward, to seek forward, to endeavor after. It is to have a new vision of God and of the ways of God, to be overwhelmingly convinced of the perfection of God, of the perfection of all He does, of the certainty of His ultimate victory, and then to respond to the profound and tremendous conviction by petition, by praise, and by endeavor. And so men "ought always to pray" and to "pray without ceasing."

GEORGE MUELLER

Answers to Prayer

How to Ascertain the Will of God:

I seek at the beginning to get my heart into such a state that it has no will of its own in regard to a given matter. Nine-tenths of the trouble with people generally is just here. Nine-tenths of the difficulties are overcome when our hearts are ready to do the Lord's will, whatever it may be. When one is truly in this state, it is usually but a little way to the knowledge of what His will is.

Having done this, I do not leave the result to feeling or simple impression. If so, I make myself liable to great delusions. Rather, I seek the Will of the Spirit of God through, or in connection with, the Word of God. The Spirit and the Word must be combined. If I look to the Spirit alone without the Word, I lay myself open to great delusions. If the Holy Ghost guides us at all, He will do it according to the Scriptures and never contrary to them.

Next, I take into account providential circumstances. These often plainly indicate God's Will in connection with His Word and Spirit. And I ask God in prayer to reveal His Will to me aright.

Thus, through prayer to God, the study of the Word, and reflection, I come to a deliberate judgment according to the best of my ability and knowledge, and if my mind is thus at peace, and continues so after two or three more petitions, I proceed accordingly. In trivial matters, and in transactions involving most important issues, I have found this method always effective.

FRANCIS DE SALES

Introduction to the Devout Life

Prayer opens the understanding to the brightness of Divine Light, and the will to the warmth of Heavenly Love—nothing can so effectually purify the mind from its many ignorances, or the will from its perverse affections. It is as healing water that causes the roots of our good desires to send forth fresh shoots, which washes away the soul's imperfections and allays the thirst of passion.

But especially I commend earnest mental prayer to you, more particularly such as bears upon the Life and Passion of our Lord. If you contemplate Him frequently in meditation, your whole soul will be filled with Him, you will grow in His Likeness, and your actions will be molded on His. He is the Light of the world; therefore in Him, by Him, and for Him we shall be enlightened and illuminated. He is the Tree of Life, beneath the shadow of which we must find rest. He is the Living Fountain of Jacob's well, wherein we may wash away every stain.

Children learn to speak by hearing their mother talk, and stammering forth their childish sounds in imitation; and so if we cleave to the Savior in meditation, listening to His words, watching His actions and intentions, we shall learn in time, through His Grace, to speak, act, and will like Himself. Believe me, my daughter, there is no way to God save through this door. Just as the glass of a mirror would give no reflection save for the metal behind it, so neither could we here below contemplate the Godhead were it not united to the Sacred Humanity of our Savior, whose life and death are the best, sweetest, and most profitable subjects that we can possibly select for meditation. It is not without meaning that the Savior calls Himself the Bread come down from Heaven; just as we eat bread with all manner of other food, so we need to meditate and feed upon our dear Lord in every prayer and action.

Give an hour every day to meditation before dinner—if you can, let it be early in the morning, when your mind will be less cluttered and fresh after the night's rest. Do not spend more than an hour thus, unless specially advised to do so by your spiritual father. If you can make your meditation quietly in church, it will be well, and no one—father or mother, husband or wife—can object to an hour spent there. And very probably you could not secure a time so free from interruption at home.

Begin all prayer, whether mental or vocal, by an act of the Presence of God. If you observe this rule strictly, you will soon see how useful it is. It may help you to say the Creed, Lord's Prayer, and so on in Latin, but you should also study them diligently in your own language, so as to thoroughly gather up the meaning of these holy words, which must be used fixing your thoughts steadily on their meaning, not striving to say many words so much as seeking to say a few with your whole heart. One Our Father said devoutly is worth more than many prayers hurried over.

The Rosary is a useful devotion when rightly used, and there are various little books to teach this. It is well, too, to say pious litanies, and the other vocal prayers appointed for the Hours and found in Manuals of devotion. But if you have a gift for mental prayer, let that always take the chief place, so that if, having made that, you are hindered by business or any other cause from saying your vocal prayers, do not be disturbed, but rest satisfied with saying the Lord's Prayer, the Angelic Salutation, and the Creed after your meditation.

If, while saying vocal prayers, your heart feels drawn to mental prayer, do not resist it, but calmly let your mind fall into that channel without troubling because you have not finished your appointed vocal prayers. The mental prayer you have substituted for them is more acceptable to God, and more profitable to your soul. I should make an exception of the Church's Offices, if you are bound to say those by your vocation—in such a case these are your duty.

If it should happen that your morning goes by without the usual meditation, either owing to a pressure of business or from any other cause (which interruptions you should try to prevent as far as possible), try to repair the loss in the afternoon—but not immediately after a meal, or you will perhaps be drowsy, which is bad both for your meditation and your health. But if you are unable all day to make up for the omission, you must remedy it as far as may be by ejaculatory prayer, and by reading some spiritual book, together with an act of penitence for the neglect, together with a steadfast resolution to do better the next day.

TERESA OF AVILA

The Life of Saint Teresa of Jesus

So, then, going on from pastime to pastime, from vanity to vanity, from one occasion of sin to another, I began to expose myself exceedingly to the very greatest dangers: my soul was so distracted by many vanities that I was ashamed to draw near unto God in an act of such special friendship as that of prayer.

As my sins multiplied, I began to lose the pleasure and comfort I had in virtuous things—and that loss contributed to the abandonment of prayer. I see now most clearly, O my Lord, that this comfort departed from me because I had departed from Thee.

It was the most fearful delusion into which Satan could plunge me—to give up prayer under the pretence of humility. I began to be afraid of giving myself to prayer because I saw myself so lost. I thought it would be better for me, seeing that in my wickedness I was one of the most wicked, to live like the multitude—to say the prayers which I was bound to say, and that vocally; not to practice mental prayer nor commune with God so much, for I deserved to be with the devils and was deceiving those who were about me, because I made an outward show of goodness. And therefore the community in which I dwelt is not to be blamed, for with my cunning I so managed matters that all had a good opinion of me. . . .

It was rather a heavy affliction to me that I should be thought so well of, for I knew my own secret.

FRANCIS OF ASSISI

Prayers of Saint Francis

Our Father, most holy—our Creator, Redeemer, and Comforter.

Who art in heaven, in the angels and in the saints illuminating them unto knowledge, for You, O Lord, are light; inflaming them unto love, for You, O Lord, are Love; dwelling in them and filling them with blessedness, for You, O Lord, are the highest Good—the eternal Good from whom is all good and without whom is no good.

Hallowed be Your Name: may Your knowledge shine in us that we may know the breadth of Your benefits, the length of Your promises, the height of Your majesty, and the depth of Your judgments.

Your Kingdom come, that You may reign in us by grace and may make us come to Your Kingdom, where there is the clear vision of You, the perfect love of You, the blessed company of You, and the eternal enjoyment of You.

Your will be done on earth as it is in heaven, that we may love You with the whole heart by always thinking of You; with the whole soul by always desiring You; with the whole mind by directing all our intentions to You and seeking Your honor in all things and with all our strength, by spending all the powers and senses of body and soul in the service of Your love and not in anything else; and that we may love our neighbors even as ourselves, drawing to the best of our power all to Your love; rejoicing in the good of others as in our own and showing compassion in troubles and giving offense to no one.

Give us this day—through memory and understanding and reverence for the love which He had for us and for those things which He said, did, and suffered for us—*our daily bread*, Your Beloved Son, our Lord Jesus Christ.

And forgive us our trespasses, by Your ineffable mercy in virtue of the Passion of Your Beloved Son, our Lord Jesus Christ, and through the merits and intercession of the most Blessed Virgin Mary and of all Your elect.

As we forgive those that trespass against us, and what we do not fully forgive, do You, O Lord, make us fully forgive, that for Your sake we may truly love our enemies and devoutly intercede for them with You; that we may render no evil for evil, but in You may strive to do good to all.

And lead us not into temptation, hidden or visible, sudden or continuous.

But deliver us from evil—past, present, and to come. Amen.

RICHARD ROLLE

The Mending of Life

O sweet and delectable Light that is my Maker unmade, enlighten the face and sharpness of my inward eye with clearness unmade so that my mind, cleansed from uncleanness and made marvelous with gifts, may swiftly flee into the high mirth of love—and kindled with Your savor may I sit and rest, joying in You, Jesus. Going as it were ravished in heavenly sweetness, and made stable in the beholding of things unseen, never, save by godly things, shall I be gladdened.

O Love everlasting, enflame my soul to love God so that nothing may burn in me but His embraces. O good Jesus, who shall grant me to feel You who may neither be felt nor seen? Shed Yourself into the entrails of my soul. Come into my heart and fill it with Your clearest sweetness. Moisten my mind with the hot wine of Your sweet love so that, forgetful of all ills and all scornful visions and imaginations, and only having You, I may be glad and take joy in Jesus my God. Henceforward, sweetest Lord, go not from me, but continually bide with me in Your sweetness. For Your presence only is solace to me, and Your absence only leaves me heavy.

O Holy Ghost that gives grace where You will, come into me and ravish me to Yourself; change the nature that You have made with Your honeyed gifts so that my soul, fulfilled with Your liking joy, may despise and cast away all things in this world. Ghostly gifts she may take of You, the Giver, and going by songful joy into unseen light she may be all melted in holy love. Burn my reins and my heart with Your fire that on Your altar shall endlessly burn.

O sweet and true Joy, I pray for you to come! Come, O sweet and most desired! I pray for You to come! Come, O sweet and most desired! Come my Love, you that are all my comfort! Glide down into a soul longing for You and after longing after You with sweet heat. Kindle with Your heat the wholeness of my heart. With Your light enlighten my inmost parts. Feed me with honeyed songs of love as far as I may receive them by my powers of body and soul.

WILLIAM LAW

A Serious Call to a Devout and Holy Life

We naturally conceive some abhorrence of a man that is in bed when he should be at his labor or in his shop. We cannot tell how to think anything good of him, who is such a slave to drowsiness as to neglect his business for it. Let this therefore teach us to conceive how odious we must appear in the sight of Heaven if we are in bed, shut up in sleep and darkness, when we should be praising God; if we are such slaves to drowsiness as to neglect our devotions for it.

For if he is to be blamed as a slothful drone that chooses the lazy indulgence of sleep, rather than to perform his proper share of worldly business; how much more is he to be reproached that would rather lie folded up in a bed than be raising up his heart to God in acts of praise and adoration!

Prayer is the nearest approach to God, and the highest enjoyment of Him, that we are capable of in this life. It is the noblest exercise of the soul, the most exalted use of our best faculties, and the highest imitation of the blessed inhabitants of Heaven. When our hearts are full of God, sending up holy desires to the throne of grace, we are then in our highest state, we are upon the utmost heights of human greatness; we are not before kings and princes, but in the presence and audience of the Lord of all the world, and can be no higher till death is swallowed up in glory.

On the other hand, sleep is the poorest, dullest refreshment of the body, so far from being intended as an enjoyment that we are forced to receive it either in a state of insensibility, or in the folly of dreams. Sleep is such a dull, stupid state of existence that even amongst mere animals, we despise them most which are most drowsy. He, therefore, that chooses to enlarge the slothful indulgence of sleep rather than be early at his devotions to God, chooses the dullest refreshment of the body before the highest, noblest employment of the soul; he chooses that state which is a reproach to mere animals rather than that exercise which is the glory of Angels.

FRANCIS DE SALES

Introduction to the Devout Life

Such meditations as these, my daughter, will help you; and having made them, go on bravely in the spirit of humility to make your general confession. But I entreat you: be not troubled by any sort of fearfulness. The scorpion that stings us is venomous, but when his oil has been distilled, it is the best remedy for his bite. Even so, sin is shameful when we commit it, but when reduced to repentance and confession, it becomes salutary and honorable. Contrition and confession are in themselves so lovely and sweet-savored, that they efface the ugliness and disperse the ill savor of sin.

Simon the leper called Magdalene a sinner, but our Lord turned the discourse to the perfume of her ointment and the greatness of her love. If we are really humble, my daughter, our sins will be infinitely displeasing to us, because they offend God—but it will be welcome and sweet to accuse ourselves thereof because, in so doing, we honor God; and there is always something soothing in fully telling the physician all the details of our pain.

When you come to your spiritual father, imagine yourself to be on Mount Calvary, at the Feet of the Crucified Savior, whose precious Blood is dropping freely to cleanse you from all your sin. Though it is not his actual Blood, yet it is the merit of that out-poured Blood which is sprinkled over His penitents as they kneel in Confession. Be sure then that you open your heart fully, and put away your sins by confessing them, for in proportion as they are put out, so will the precious merits of the passion of Christ come in and fill you with blessings.

Tell everything simply and with straightforwardness, and thoroughly satisfy your conscience in doing so. Then listen to the admonitions and counsels of God's minister, saying in your heart, "Speak, Lord, for Thy servant heareth." It is truly God to whom you hearken, forasmuch as He has said to His representatives, "Whoso heareth you, heareth Me" (Luke 10:16). Then take the following protest, as a summary of your contrition, having carefully studied and meditated upon it beforehand; read it through with as earnest an intention as you can make.

MADAME GUYON

A Short and Easy Method of Prayer

What a dreadful delusion has prevailed over the greater part of mankind in supposing that they are not called to a state of prayer! All are capable of prayer, and are called thereto, as all are called to and are capable of salvation.

Prayer is the application of the heart to God and the internal exercise of love. Paul has enjoined us to "pray without ceasing" (1 Thessalonians 5:17), and our Lord says, "I say unto you all, watch and pray" (Mark 13:33). All therefore may, and all ought to, practice prayer. I grant that meditation is attainable but by few, for few are capable of it; and therefore, my beloved brethren who are athirst for salvation, meditative prayer is not the prayer which God requires of you, nor which we would recommend.

But let all pray. We should live by prayer, as we should live by love. "I counsel you to buy of me gold tried in the fire, that you may be rich" (Revelation 3:8)—this is much more easily obtained than we can conceive. "Come, all you that are athirst, to these living waters"; nor lose your precious moments in "hewing out cisterns, broken cisterns that will hold no water" (John 7:37; Jeremiah 2:13).

Come, you famished souls who find nothing whereon to feed; come, and you shall be fully satisfied! Come, you poor afflicted ones who groan beneath your load of wretchedness and pain, and you shall find ease and comfort! Come, you sick, to your Physician, and be not fearful of approaching Him because you are filled with diseases; expose them to His view and they shall be healed! Children draw near to your Father, and He will embrace you in the arms of love! Come, you poor, stray, wandering sheep—return to your Shepherd! Come, sinners, to your Saviour! Come, you dull, ignorant, and illiterate, you who think yourselves the most incapable of prayer. You are more peculiarly called and adapted to it!

Let all without exception come, for Jesus Christ has called all.

Yet let not those come who are without a heart; they are not asked, for there must be a heart that there may be love. But who is without a heart? O come, then, give this heart to God, and here learn how to make the donation. All who are desirous of prayer may easily pray, enabled by those ordinary graces and gifts of the Holy Spirit which are common to all men.

Prayer is the guide to perfection and the sovereign good; it delivers us from every vice and obtains us every virtue. For the one great means to become perfect is to walk in the presence of God. He Himself has said, "Walk in my presence and be ye perfect" (Genesis 17:1). It is by prayer alone that we are brought into this presence, and maintained in it without interruption.

You must then learn a species of prayer which may be exercised at all times; which does not obstruct outward employments; and which may be equally practiced by princes, kings, prelates, priests, magistrates, soldiers, children, tradesmen, laborers, women, and sick persons. It cannot, therefore, be the prayer of the head, but of the heart—not a prayer of the understanding alone, which is so limited in its operations that it can have but one object at one time, but the prayer of the heart which is not interrupted by the exercises of reason. Indeed nothing can interrupt this prayer but irregular and disordered affections, and when once we have tasted of God, and the sweetness of His love, we shall find it impossible to relish anything but Himself.

Nothing is so easily obtained as the possession and enjoyment of God, for "in him we live, move, and have our being" (Acts

17:28), and He is more desirous to give Himself into us than we can be to receive Him. All consists in the manner of seeking Him; and to seek aright is easier and more natural to us than breathing. Though you think yourselves ever so stupid, dull, and incapable of sublime attainments, yet, by prayer, you may live in God Himself with less difficulty or interruption than you live in the vital air. Will it not then be highly sinful to neglect prayer? But this I trust you will not, when you have learnt the method, which is exceedingly easy.

GEORGE MUELLER

The Life of Trust

The question "What is meant by the prayer of faith?" is beginning to arrest, in an unusual degree, the attention of Christians. What is the significance of the passages both in the New Testament and the Old which refer to it? What is the limit within which they may be safely received as a ground of practical reliance? Were these promises limited to prophetical or apostolical times, or have they been left as a legacy to all believers until the end shall come?

Somehow or other, these questions are seldom discussed either from the pulpit or the press. I do not remember to have heard any of them distinctly treated of in a sermon. I do not know of any work in which this subject is either theoretically explained or practically enforced. It really seems as if this portion of Revelation was, by common consent, ignored in all our public teachings. Do not men believe that God means what he appears plainly to have asserted? Or, if we believe that he means it, do we fear the charge of fanaticism if we openly avow that we take him at his word?

The public silence on this subject does not, however, prevent a very frequent private inquiry in respect to it. The thoughtful Christian, when in his daily reading of the Scriptures he meets with any of those wonderful promises made to believing prayer, often pauses to ask himself: *What can these words mean? Can it be that God has made such promises as these to me, and to such men as I am? Have I really permission to commit all my little affairs to a God of infinite wisdom, believing that he will take charge of them and direct them according to the promptings of boundless love and absolute omniscience? Is prayer really a power with God, or is it merely an expedient by which our own piety may be cultivated? Is it not a transcendent power, accomplishing what no other power can, overruling all other agencies, and rendering them subservient to its own wonderful efficiency?* I think there are few devout readers of the Bible to whom these questions are not frequently suggested. We ask them, but we do not often wait for an answer. These promises seem to us to be addressed either to a past or to a coming age, but not to us, at the present day.

Yet with such views as these the devout soul is not at all satisfied. *If an invaluable treasure is here reserved for the believer*, he asks, *why should I not receive my portion of it?* He cannot doubt that God has in a remarkable manner, at various times, answered his prayers; why should he not always answer them? And why should not the believer always draw near to God in full confidence that he will do as he has said? He may remember that the prayer which has been manifestly answered was the offspring of deep humility, of conscious unworthiness, of utter self-negation, and of simple and earnest reliance on the promises of God through the mediation of Christ. Why should not his prayers be always of the same character? With the apostles of old he pours out his soul in the petition, "Lord, increase our faith."

And yet it can scarcely be denied that the will of God has been distinctly revealed on this subject. The promises made to believing prayer are explicit, numerous, and diversified. If we take them in their simple and literal meaning, or if in fact we give to them any reasonable interpretation whatever, they seem to be easily understood. Our difficulty seems to be this: the promise is so "exceeding great" that we cannot conceive God really to mean what he clearly appears to have revealed. The blessing seems too vast for our comprehension; we "stagger at the promises, through unbelief," and thus fail to secure the treasure which was purchased for us by Christ Jesus.

ANSELM

Saint Anselm's Book of

Meditations and Prayers

O heavenly Father, I beseech You, look upon the ever flowing fountain of Your compassion—which, as a flood of cleansing, a flood precious beyond all price and full of life, gushed from Your dearest and only-begotten Son for the cleansing of the world, by the death of Whom Your goodness has been even pleased to give us life, and also to wash us with His Blood. Nay, more. You have consigned Your dearest Son to men as a shield of Your good will; a shield with which to shelter themselves from Your wrath—He receiving in Himself the death they fear, He presented as a shield to Your justice and Your all-just anger. More, it pleased Your mercy that not only should He bear the brunt of Your wrath, but endure our death as well. It was so indeed; Your Son, Your Only-begotten, has alone borne our death.

"Remember, O Lord, Your bowels of compassion, and Your mercies that are from the beginning of the world" (Psalm 25:6), and stretch out Your hand to Your creature that stretches forth to You. Help the weakness of him that struggles after You. Draw me, for You know that I cannot come to You, except You, the Father, draw me with the cords of love and desire. Make me a servant acceptable and pleasing unto You, for You know that I cannot please You else. Give me, I pray, those holy gifts with which alone I may please You that gives good gifts to them that ask. Grant, I pray, that my sole love and sole desire may be Yourself; my sole love and only fear, Yourself. Take me wholly for Your own, You who know that to You I owe all that I am, all that I have, all that I know, and all my powers. Convert me wholly to Your praise and glory, I that owe myself wholly to Your praise. Deliver not, I pray, Your creature to Your enemies; keep me for Yourself, whose alone I am entirely, and perfect in every part what You have begun, and confirm what You have wrought.

I beseech you hear my prayer, You who gives and inspires it even before I thought to call to You. Look upon Your suppliant, You Who when I had a mind to pray did even then deign to look upon me. Not in vain, O Lord of mercy, did You deign to inspire my prayer, not for nothing did You give it me. Nay, for this very end did You deign to give it, that You might listen to me; for this did You grant it to me, that I might implore You to have mercy on me a sinner. So thus having given me an earnest glimpse of Your mercy, give me the rest. Rescue me, O Lord my God, and snatch me out of the hands of my enemies; for they too are Yours, they are the subjects of Your almighty power; and they hate nothing of good works in me except what You have given me. There is nothing in me that they hate, but only that I love You. And they scheme with all their endeavors—with all their might, with all their craft—to prevent my loving You, glorifying You, and ever seeking You.

Therefore let not the enemies of Your glory be too strong for me, but let them be the more confounded as they see that I, bent on praising You and glorifying You, am seeking with all best endeavors that peace and glory of You, which they are intent upon diminishing. O Lord, I beseech You, let not their so unholy and execrable design concerning me—nay, against me—be brought to pass; but enlarge my soul, O Lord, for telling forth Your praise and heralding Your glory, that I may henceforth live altogether according to Your great glory, and that my whole life may glorify You. And my example invite and incite many of Your predestined to glorify You. Let the presence of Your light and the sweetness of Your glory—a glory which they can not bear—drive away from me the vile, unclean, and hateful spirits of darkness.

O break my chains asunder and take me out of durance; out of the horrible, black, and gloomy prison; out of the lake of misery and the mire of dregs; out of the abyss of death and darkness—and lead me forth into liberty and Your marvelous light.

MIGUEL DE MOLINOS

The Spiritual Guide
Which Disentangles the Soul

You should know that there are two sorts of prayer—the one tender, delightful, amicable, and full of sentiments; the other obscure, dry, desolate, tempted, and darksome. The first is for beginners, the second for proficients who are in the progress to perfection. God gives the first to gain souls, the second to purify them. With the first He uses them like children; with the second He begins to deal with them as with strong men.

This first way may be called the Animal Life, and it belongs to those who go in the tract of devotion through the senses, which God gives to beginners to the end that—being endowed with that small relish, as the natural man is with the senses—they may addict themselves to the spiritual life. The second way is called the Life of Men, and it belongs to those who, not focusing on the pleasures of the senses, fight and war against their own passions so that they may conquer and obtain perfection, which is the proper employment of men.

Also, be aware that dryness or aridity in prayer is an instrument for your good. It is nothing else but a lack of the senses that puts a stop to the flight of almost all spiritual men and makes them even draw back, and leave off prayer. This may be seen in many souls that only persevere while they taste consolation through their senses.

But know that the Lord makes use of the Veil of Dryness

so that we may not know what he is working in us, and so be humble—because if we feel and understand what he is working in our souls, satisfaction and presumption would get in, imagining that we were doing some good thing and reckoning our selves very near to God. This would be our undoing.

AUGUSTINE OF HIPPO

Confessions

Oh! That I might repose on you! Oh! That you would enter into
my heart and inebriate it, that I may forget my ills and embrace
you, my sole good! What are you to me? In your pity, teach me
to utter it. Or what am I to you that you demand my love, and
if I give it not, are wroth with me and threaten me with grievous
woes? Is it then a slight woe to love you not? Oh! For your mercies' sake, tell me, O Lord my God, what you are unto me. Say
unto my soul, "I am your salvation." So speak, that I may hear.
Behold, Lord, my heart is before you; open you the ears thereof,
and say unto my soul, "I am your salvation." After this voice let
me haste, and take hold on you. Hide not your face from me. Let
me die—lest I die—only let me see your face.

Narrow is the mansion of my soul; enlarge it, that you may
enter in. It is ruinous; repair it. It has that within which must
offend your eyes, I confess and know it. But who shall cleanse it?
Or to whom should I cry, save you? Lord, cleanse me from my
secret faults, and spare your servant from the power of the enemy.
I believe, and therefore do I speak. Lord, you know. Have I not
confessed against myself my transgressions unto you, and you,
my God, have forgiven the iniquity of my heart? I contend not
in judgment with you, who are the truth; I fear to deceive myself,
lest my iniquity lie unto itself. Therefore I contend not in judgment with you; for if you, Lord, should mark iniquities, O Lord,
who shall abide it?

MADAME GUYON

The Autobiography of Madame Guyon

A lady, an exile, came to my father's house. He offered her an apartment which she accepted, and she stayed a long time. She was one of true piety and inward devotion. She had a great esteem for me because I desired to love God. She remarked that I had the virtues of an active and bustling life, but I had not yet attained the simplicity of prayer which she experienced. Sometimes she dropped a word to me on that subject. As my time had not yet come, I did not understand her. Her example instructed me more than her words. I observed on her countenance something which marked a great enjoyment of the presence of God. By the exertion of studied reflection and thoughts I tried to attain it but to little purpose. I wanted to have, by my own efforts, what I could not acquire except by ceasing from all efforts.

My father's nephew, of whom I have made mention before, was returned from Cochin, China, to take over some priests from Europe. I was exceedingly glad to see him, and remembered what good he had done me. The lady mentioned was no less rejoiced than I. They understood each other immediately and conversed in a spiritual language. The virtue of this excellent relation charmed me. I admired his continual prayer without being able to comprehend it. I endeavored to meditate and to think on God without intermission, to utter prayers and ejaculations. I could not acquire, by all my toil, what God at length gave me Himself, and which is experienced only in simplicity. My cousin did all he could to attach me more strongly to God. He conceived great affection for me. The purity he observed in me from the corruptions of the age, the abhorrence of sin at a time of life when others are beginning to relish the pleasures of it, (I was not yet eighteen), gave him a great tenderness for me. I complained to him of my faults ingenuously. These I saw clearly. He cheered and exhorted me to support myself, and to persevere in my good endeavors. He would fain have introduced me into a more simple manner of prayer, but I was not yet ready for it. I believe his prayers were more effectual than his words.

No sooner was he gone out of my father's house than You, O Divine Love, manifested Your favor. The desire I had to please You, the tears I shed, the manifold pains I underwent, the labors I sustained, and the little fruit I reaped from them moved You with compassion. This was the state of my soul when Your goodness, surpassing all my vileness and infidelities, and abounding in proportion to my wretchedness, granted me in a moment what all my own efforts could never procure. Beholding me rowing with laborious toil, the breath of Your divine operations turned in my favor and carried me full sail over this sea of affliction.

BROTHER LAWRENCE

The Practice of the Presence of God

You tell me nothing new: you are not the only one that is troubled with wandering thoughts during prayer. Our mind is extremely roving, but as the will is mistress of all our faculties, she must recall them and carry them to God as their last end. When the mind, for want of being sufficiently reduced by recollection at our first engaging in devotion, has contracted certain bad habits of wandering and dissipation, they are difficult to overcome. They commonly draw us, even against our wills, to the things of the earth.

I believe one remedy for this is to confess our faults, and to humble ourselves before God. I do not advise you to use multiplicity of words in prayer—many words and long discourses being often the occasions of wandering. Rather, hold yourself in prayer before God like a dumb or paralytic beggar at a rich man's gate. Let it be your business to keep your mind in the presence of the Lord. If it sometimes wander, and withdraw itself from Him, do not disquiet yourself for that; trouble and disquiet serve rather to distract the mind than to re-collect it. The will must bring it back in tranquility. If you persevere in this manner, God will have pity on you.

One way to re-collect the mind easily in the time of prayer, and to preserve it more in tranquility, is not to let it wander too far at other times. You should keep your thoughts strictly in the presence of God. And being accustomed to think of Him often, you will find it easy to keep your mind calm in the time of prayer, or at least to recall it from its wanderings.

I have told you already at large, in my former letters, of the advantages we may draw from this practice of the presence of God. Let us set about it seriously and pray for one another.

JOHN BUNYAN

Israel's Hope Encouraged

When Jacob received the name of Israel, he was found wrestling with the angel; yes, and so resolved a wrestler was he that he purposed, now he had begun, not to give out without a blessing. "I will not let you go," said he, "except you bless me" (Genesis 32:26).

Discouragements he had while he wrestled with him, to have left off, before he obtained his desire; for the angel bid him leave off. "Let me go," said he. He had wrestled all night and had not prevailed, and now the day broke upon him, and consequently his discouragement was like to be the greater, for that now the majesty and terribleness of him with whom he wrestled would be seen more apparently. But this did not discourage him. Besides, he lost the use of a limb as he wrestled with him. Yet all would not put this Israel out. Pray he did, and pray he would, and nothing should make him leave off prayer until he had obtained, and therefore he was called "Israel." "For as a prince you have power with God and with men, and have prevailed" (Genesis 32:28, 30).

A wrestling spirit of prayer is a demonstration of an Israel of God; this Jacob had, this he made use of, and by this he obtained the name of Israel. A wrestling spirit of prayer in straits, difficulties, and distresses—a wrestling spirit of prayer when alone, in private, in the night, when no eye sees but God's, then to be at it, then to lay hold of God, then to wrestle, to hold fast, and not to give over until the blessing is obtained, is a sign of one that is an Israel of God.

TERESA OF AVILA

The Way of Perfection

O sisters, those of you whose minds cannot reason for long, or whose thoughts cannot dwell upon God but are constantly wandering, must at all costs form this habit. I know quite well that you are capable of it—for many years I endured this trial of being unable to concentrate on one subject, and a very sore trial it is. But I know the Lord does not leave us so devoid of help that if we approach Him humbly and ask Him to be with us He will not grant our request. If a whole year passes without our obtaining what we ask, let us be prepared to try for longer. Let us never grudge time so well spent. Who, after all, is hurrying us? I am sure we can form this habit and strive to walk at the side of this true Master.

I am not asking you now to think of Him, or to form numerous conceptions of Him, or to make long and subtle meditations with your understanding. I am asking you only to look at Him. For who can prevent you from turning the eyes of your soul (just for a moment, if you can do no more) upon this Lord? You are capable of looking at very ugly and loathsome things—can you not, then, look at the most beautiful thing imaginable?

Your Spouse never takes His eyes off you, daughters. He has borne with thousands of foul and abominable sins which you have committed against Him, yet even they have not been enough to make Him cease looking upon you. Is it such a great matter, then, for you to avert the eyes of your soul from outward things and sometimes to look at Him? See, He is only waiting for us to look at Him, as He says to the Bride.

You will find Him. He longs so much for us to look at Him once more that it will not be for lack of effort on His part if we fail to do so.

FRANCIS DE SALES

Introduction to the Devout Life

Should it happen sometimes, my daughter, that you have no taste for or consolation in your meditation, I entreat you not to be troubled, but to seek relief in vocal prayer. Bemoan yourself to our Lord, confess your unworthiness, implore His aid, kiss His image, if it be beside you, and say in the words of Jacob, "I will not let Thee go, except Thou bless me," or with the Canaanite woman, "Yes, Lord, I am as a dog before Thee, but the dogs eat of the crumbs which fall from their master's table."

Or you can take a book and read attentively until such time as your mind is calmed and quickened; or sometimes you may find help from external actions, such as prostrating yourself, folding your hands upon your breast, or kissing your crucifix (supposing you are alone).

But if after all this you are still unrelieved, do not be disturbed at your dryness, however great it be, but continue striving after a devout attitude in God's Sight. What numbers of courtiers appear a hundred times at court without any hope of a word from their king, but merely to pay their homage and be seen of him? Just so, my daughter, we ought to enter upon mental prayer purely to fulfill our duty and testify our loyalty.

If it pleases God's Divine Majesty to speak to us and discourse in our hearts by His holy inspirations and inward consolations, it is doubtless a great honor and very sweet to our soul. But if He does not vouchsafe such favors, but makes as though He saw us not—as though we were not in His Presence—nevertheless we must not quit it. On the contrary we must remain calmly and devoutly before Him, and He is certain to accept our patient waiting and give heed to our assiduity and perseverance so that another time He will impart to us His consolations and let us taste all the sweetness of holy meditation. But even were it not so, let us, my child, be satisfied with the privilege of being in His Presence and seen of Him.

MADAME GUYON

A Short and Easy Method of Prayer

During prayer, a direct contest and struggle with distractions and temptations rather serves to augment them, and withdraws the soul from that adherence to God, which should ever be its principal occupation. The surest and safest method for conquest is simply to turn away from the evil and draw yet nearer and closer to our God.

A little child, on perceiving a monster, does not wait to fight with it. The child will scarcely turn its eyes towards it, but quickly shrinks into the bosom of its mother, in total confidence of safety. So, likewise, should the soul turn from the dangers of temptation toward God. "God is in the midst of her," says the Psalmist, "she shall not be moved; God shall help her, and that right early" (Psalm 46:5).

If we do otherwise, and in our weakness attempt to attack our enemies, we shall frequently feel ourselves wounded, if not totally defeated. But by casting ourselves into the simple presence of God, we shall find instant supplies of strength for our support. This was the succor sought for by David: "I have set," he says, "the Lord always before me: because he is at my right hand, I shall not be moved. Therefore my heart is glad, and my glory rejoices: my flesh also shall rest in hope" (Psalm 16:8–9). And it is said in Exodus: "The Lord shall fight for you, and you shall hold your peace" (Exodus 14:14).

ANSELM

Saint Anselm's Book of
Meditations and Prayers

You are my living God, my holy Christ, my merciful Lord, my great King, my good Shepherd, my Teacher of truth, my seasonable help, my Beloved beautiful beyond all men, my living Bread, my Priest for ever, my Guide and Leader to my fatherland, my true light, my heavenly Sweetness, my straight Way, my Wisdom full of illumination, my stainless Simplicity, my peace-making Reconciliation, my safe Protection, my good Portion, my everlasting Salvation, my great Compassion, my all-enduring Patience, my immaculate Victim, my holy Redemption, my unfailing Hope, my perfect Charity, my holy Resurrection, my eternal Life, my Exultation, and my most blessed Life, Who shall endure for evermore.

You I beseech, implore, and beg that You would complete the work Your mercy has begun in me. For I, the least of Your servants and not unmindful of the benefits Your tender mercy has bestowed on me, give thanks to You that, notwithstanding my unworthiness, You of Your sole compassion did cause me to be born of Christian parents, and did loose me from my original bonds by the waters of holy baptism and the Holy Spirit's renovation, and did enroll me in the company of the sons of Your adoption. For You did give me the gift of the right faith, and have evermore vouchsafed to increase and confirm it in my heart by the illumination of Your grace, and by the teachings of holy mother Church

And, O Lord, I beseech and suppliantly pray that You evermore increase this faith in me, this true and holy faith, this Catholic and orthodox faith, this most wise, far-seeing and unconquerable faith, this faith so richly adorned with all blessings and with every virtue—that it may by love work in me what is pleasing to You, and may refuse to give way amidst words of strife in time of persecution, or in the day of necessity and death.

O God, You Fount and Origin, Bestower and Preserver of all virtues, increase in me, I beseech You, true faith, unfailing hope, and perfect charity; profound humility, invincible patience, and perpetual chastity of body and of mind. Give me prudence, justice, fortitude, and temperance; give me discretion in all things and a watchful sensibility, that I may wisely make discernment between good and evil, between the right hand and the left. Therefore make me rich in holy virtues, so as by them to serve You, and by means of them to please You in truth. For by Your grace I am enamored of their beauty. Give me them for the honor and glory of Your name; make them comrades of my faith, that they may be its inseparable companions all through the period of my life.

And thus make me, I pray, by Your grace always steadfast in faith and ready to do all good works that Your faith, which my tongue professes and my writings witness to, may be publicly and openly set forth by the good behavior of an irreprovable life.

WILLIAM LAW

A Serious Call to a Devout and Holy Life

That intercession is a great and necessary part of Christian devotion is very evident from Scripture. The first followers of Christ seem to support all their love, and to maintain all their intercourse and correspondence, by mutual prayers for one another. Paul, whether he writes to churches or particular persons, shows his intercession to be perpetual for them—that they are the constant subject of his prayers.

Thus to the Philippians: "I thank my God upon every remembrance of you, always in every prayer of mine for you all making request with joy" (Philippians 1:3–4). Here we see not only a continual intercession, but one performed with so much gladness as shows that it was an exercise of love in which he highly rejoiced.

His devotion had also the same care for particular persons, as appears by the following passages: "I thank God, whom I serve from my forefathers, with a pure conscience, that without ceasing I have remembrance of thee in my prayers night and day" (2 Timothy 1:3). How holy an acquaintance and friendship was this, how worthy of persons that were raised above the world and related to one another as new members of a kingdom of Heaven!

Apostles and great saints did not only thus benefit and bless particular churches, and private persons, but they themselves also received graces from God by the prayers of others. Thus said Paul to the Corinthians: "You also helping together by prayer for us, that for the gift bestowed upon us by the means of many persons, thanks may be given by many on our behalf" (2 Corinthians 1:11).

This was the ancient friendship of Christians, uniting and cementing their hearts not by worldly considerations or human passions, but by the mutual communication of spiritual blessings, by prayers and thanksgivings to God for one another. It was this holy intercession that raised Christians to such a state of mutual love that far exceeded all that had been praised and admired in human friendship. And when the same spirit of intercession is again in the world, when Christianity has the same power over the hearts of people that it then had, this holy friendship will be again in fashion and Christians will be again the wonder of the world, for that exceeding love which they bear to one another. For a frequent intercession with God—earnestly beseeching Him to forgive the sins of all mankind, to bless them with His providence, enlighten them with His Spirit, and bring them to everlasting happiness—is the most divine exercise that the heart of man can be engaged in.

Be daily, therefore, on your knees, in a solemn deliberate performance of this devotion, praying for others in such forms, with such length, importunity, and earnestness, as you use for yourself. Do so and you will find all little, ill-natured passions die away and your heart grow great and generous, delighting in the common happiness of others, as you used only to delight in your own.

For he that daily prays to God that all men may be happy in Heaven, takes the likeliest way to make him wish for and delight in their happiness on earth. And it is hardly possible for you to beseech and entreat God to make any one happy in the highest enjoyments of His glory to all eternity, and yet be troubled to see him enjoy the much smaller gifts of God in this short and low state of human life.

GEORGE MUELLER

Answers to Prayer

As was the case with our second orphanage, so also was the case of the New Orphan House (our third): I had daily prayed for the needed helpers and assistants for the various departments. Before a stone was laid, I began to pray for this. And as the building progressed, I continued day by day to bring this matter before God, feeling assured that, as in everything else, He would graciously be pleased to appear on our behalf and help us, as the whole work is intended for His honor and glory.

At last the time was near when the house could be opened, and the time therefore near when the applications, which had been made in writing during more than two years previously, should be considered for the filling up of the various positions. It was found, however, that while there had been about 50 applications made for the various situations, some places could not be filled up because the individuals who had applied for them were married, or were, on examination, found unsuitable.

This was no small trial of faith: day by day, for years, I had asked God to help me in this particular, even as He had done in the case of the second Orphan House. I had also expected help, confidently expected help—and yet now, when help seemed needed, it was wanting.

What was now to be done, dear Reader? Would it have been right to charge God with unfaithfulness? Would it have been right to distrust Him? Would it have been right to say, "It is useless to pray"? By no means. This, on the contrary, I did: I thanked God for all the help He had given me in connection with the whole of the enlargement; I thanked Him for enabling me to overcome so many and such great difficulties; I thanked Him for the helpers He had given me for the second Orphan House; I thanked Him also for the helpers He had given me already for No. 3.

Instead of distrusting God, I looked upon this delay of the full answer to prayer only as a trial of faith, and therefore resolved that, instead of praying once a day with my dear wife about this matter, as we had been doing day by day for years, we should now meet daily *three* times to bring this before God. I also brought the matter before the whole staff of my helpers in the work requesting their prayers. Thus I have now continued for about four months longer in prayer, day by day calling upon God three times on account of this need, and the result has been that one helper after the other has been given, without the help coming too late or the work getting into confusion. And I am fully assured that the few who are yet needed will also be found, when they are really required.

SAMUEL RUTHERFORD

The Trial and Triumph of Faith

How shall we know when our prayers are answered? Hannah knew it by peace after prayer.

Paul knew it by receiving new supply to bear the want of that he sought in prayer; he is answered that is more heavenly after prayer.

Liberty and boldness of faith is also a sign of an answered prayer. The Intercessor at the right hand of God cannot lose his own work; his Spirit groans in the saints. Does not my head accept what I set my heart on work to do? (Romans 8:23, 26, 27, compared with Revelation 8:3).

We are heard and answered of God when we are not heard and answered of God. I pray for a temporal favor—victory to God's people in this battle—and they lose the day. Yet I am heard and answered, because I prayed for that victory not under the notion of victory, but as linked with mercy to the church and the honor of Christ. So, the formal object of my prayers was a spiritual mercy to the church, and the honor of Jesus Christ. Now, the Lord, by the loss of the day, has shown mercy to his people in humbling them, and glorifies his Son in preserving a fallen people. So he hears that which is spiritual in my prayers; he is not to hear the errors of them. Christ puts not dross in his censer of gold.

We are heard whenever we ask in faith; but let faith reach no further than God's will. When we make God's will our rule, he will do his own will; if he does not follow my will, it is to be noted that the creature's will divided from God's will, in things not necessary for salvation and God's glory, is no part of God's will and no asking of faith. . . .

Patience to wait on God until the vision speaks is also an answer.

Finally, some letters require no answer, but are mere expressions of the desires of the friend. The general prayers of the saints— that the Lord would gather in his elect, that Christ would come and marry the bride and consummate the nuptials—do refer to a real answer, when our husband, the King, shall come in person at his second appearance.

JOHN WESLEY

"Wesley's Covenant Prayer"

I am no longer my own, but yours.
Put me to what you will, rank me with whom you will.
Put me to doing, put me to suffering.
Let me be employed for you or laid aside for you,
Exalted for you or brought low for you.

Let me be full, let me be empty.
Let me have all things, let me have nothing.
I freely and heartily yield all things to your pleasure and
    disposal.

And now, O glorious and blessed God, Father, Son and
    Holy Spirit,
You are mine, and I am thine.

So be it.
And the covenant which I have made on earth,
Let it be ratified in heaven.
Amen.

MARTIN LUTHER

Small Catechism

Question: What is confession?

Answer: Confession has two parts: First, a person admits his sin. Second, a person receives absolution or forgiveness from the confessor, as if from God Himself, without doubting it, but believing firmly that his sins are forgiven by God in Heaven through it.

Question: Which sins should people confess?

Answer: When speaking to God, we should plead guilty to all sins, even those we don't know about, just as we do in the "Our Father." But when speaking to the confessor, only the sins we know about, which we know about and feel in our hearts.

Question: Which are these?

Answer: Consider here your place in life according to the Ten Commandments. Are you a father? A mother? A son? A daughter? A husband? A wife? A servant? Are you disobedient, unfaithful, or lazy? Have you hurt anyone with your words or actions? Have you stolen, neglected your duty, let things go, or injured someone?

AUGUSTINE OF HIPPO

Confessions

What is there in me that could be hidden from you, Lord, to whose eyes the abysses of man's conscience are naked, even if I were unwilling to confess it to you? In doing so I would only hide you from myself, not myself from you. But now that my groaning is witness to the fact that I am dissatisfied with myself, you shine forth and satisfy. You are beloved and desired, so that I blush for myself and renounce myself and choose you, for I can neither please you nor myself except in you.

To you, then, O Lord, I am laid bare, whatever I am, and I have already said with what profit I may confess to you. I do not do it with words and sounds of the flesh, but with the words of the soul and with the sound of my thoughts, which your ear knows. For when I am wicked, to confess to you means nothing less than to be dissatisfied with myself; but when I am truly devout, it means nothing less than not to attribute my virtue to myself. Because you, O Lord, bless the righteous, but first you justify him while he is yet ungodly.

My confession, therefore, O my God, is made unto you silently in your sight—and yet not silently. As far as sound is concerned, it is silent. But in strong affection it cries aloud. For neither do I give voice to something that sounds right to men, which you have not heard from me before, nor do you hear anything of the kind from me which you did not first say to me.

EXHORTATIONS AND PROPHETIC WORDS

"The vague and tenuous hope that God is too kind
to punish the ungodly has become a deadly opiate
for the consciences of millions."

—*Knowledge of the Holy*

AUGUSTINE OF HIPPO

On Christian Doctrine

It is the duty, then, of the interpreter and teacher of Holy Scripture, the defender of the true faith and the opponent of error, both to teach what is right and to refute what is wrong; and in the performance of this task to conciliate the hostile, to rouse the careless, and to tell the ignorant both what is occurring at present and what is probable in the future.

But once his hearers are friendly, attentive, and ready to learn, whether he has found them so or has himself made them so, the remaining objects are to be carried out in whatever way the case requires. If the hearers need teaching, the matter treated of must be made fully known by means of narrative. On the other hand, to clear up points that are doubtful requires reasoning and the exhibition of proofs.

If, however, the hearers require to be roused rather than instructed, in order that they may be diligent to do what they already know, and to bring their feelings into harmony with the truths they admit, greater vigor of speech is needed. Here entreaties and reproaches, exhortations and upbraidings, and all the other means of rousing the emotions, are necessary. And all the methods I have mentioned are constantly used by nearly every one in cases where speech is the agency employed.

JONATHAN EDWARDS

From the Sermon,
"Sinners in the Hands of an Angry God"

The God that holds you over the pit of hell, much as one holds a spider or some loathsome insect over the fire, abhors you, and is dreadfully provoked. His wrath towards you burns like fire. He looks upon you as worthy of nothing else but to be cast into the fire. He is of purer eyes than to bear to have you in his sight. You are ten thousand times more abominable in his eyes than the most hateful venomous serpent is in ours. You have offended him infinitely more than ever a stubborn rebel did his prince.

And yet it is nothing but his hand that holds you from falling into the fire every moment. It is to be ascribed to nothing else that you did not go to hell the last night; that you were suffered to awake again in this world after you closed your eyes to sleep. And there is no other reason to be given why you have not dropped into hell since you arose in the morning, but that God's hand has held you up. There is no other reason to be given why you have not gone to hell since you have sat here in the house of God, provoking his pure eyes by your sinful wicked manner of attending his solemn worship. Yea, there is nothing else that is to be given as a reason why you do not this very moment drop down into hell.

O sinner! Consider the fearful danger you are in: it is a great furnace of wrath, a wide and bottomless pit, full of the fire of wrath, that you are held over in the hand of that God, whose wrath is provoked and incensed as much against you as against many of the damned in hell. You hang by a slender thread, with the flames of divine wrath flashing about it, and ready every moment to singe it, and burn it asunder—and you have no interest in any Mediator, and nothing to lay hold of to save yourself, nothing to keep off the flames of wrath, nothing of your own, nothing that you ever have done, nothing that you can do, to induce God to spare you one moment.

THOMAS À KEMPIS

The Imitation of Christ

Very soon your life here will end; consider, then, what may be in store for you elsewhere. Today we live; tomorrow we die and are quickly forgotten. Oh, the dullness and hardness of a heart which looks only to the present instead of preparing for that which is to come!

Therefore, in every deed and every thought, act as though you were to die this very day. If you had a good conscience you would not fear death very much. It is better to avoid sin than to fear death. If you are not prepared today, how will you be prepared tomorrow? Tomorrow is an uncertain day; how do you know you will have a tomorrow?

What good is it to live a long life when we amend that life so little? Indeed, a long life does not always benefit us; on the contrary, it frequently adds to our guilt. Would that in this world we had lived well throughout one single day. Many count up the years they have spent in religion but find their lives made little holier. If it is so terrifying to die, it is nevertheless possible that to live longer is more dangerous. Blessed is he who keeps the moment of death ever before his eyes and prepares for it every day.

If you have ever seen a man die, remember that you, too, must go the same way. In the morning consider that you may not live till evening, and when evening comes do not dare to promise yourself the dawn. Be always ready, therefore, and so live that death will never take you unprepared. Many die suddenly and unexpectedly, for in the unexpected hour the Son of God will come. When that last moment arrives you will begin to have a quite different opinion of the life that is now entirely past and you will regret very much that you were so careless and remiss.

How happy and prudent is he who tries now in life to be what he wants to be found in death. Perfect contempt of the world, a lively desire to advance in virtue, a love for discipline, the works of penance, readiness to obey, self-denial, and the endurance of every hardship for the love of Christ, these will give a man great expectations of a happy death.

You can do many good works when in good health; what can you do when you are ill? Few are made better by sickness. Likewise they who undertake many pilgrimages seldom become holy. Do not put your trust in friends and relatives, and do not put off the care of your soul till later, for men will forget you more quickly than you think. It is better to provide now, in time, and send some good account ahead of you than to rely on the help of others. If you do not care for your own welfare now, who will care when you are gone?

The present is very precious; these are the days of salvation; now is the acceptable time. How sad that you do not spend the time in which you might purchase everlasting life in a better way. The time will come when you will want just one day, just one hour in which to make amends, and do you know whether you will obtain it?

A. B. SIMPSON

The Fourfold Gospel

In this city there is a picture hung up in a parlor and expensively framed. It is a very simple picture. It has just one word on it. On a little bit of paper—a telegraph form—is the one word: "SAVED!"

It was framed by the lady of that mansion, and it is dearer to her than all her works of art. One day when the awful news came to her through the papers that the ship on which her husband had sailed was a perfect wreck, that little telegram came to her door and saved her from despair. It came across the sea. It was the message of that rescued man by the electric wire, and it meant to those two hearts all that life is worth.

Oh, let such a message go up today to yonder shore. The Holy Ghost will flash it hence while I am drawing the next breath. The angels will echo it over heaven, and there are dear friends there to whom it will mean as much as their own very heaven.

I have seen another short sentence in a picture, too. It came from a woman who had been rescued from a ship where friends and family had all perished. Her dear little ones were in the slimy caves of the cruel sea. Those beloved faces had gone down forever, but she was saved, and from yonder shore she sent back this sad and weary message to her husband: "Saved alone."

So I can imagine a selfish Christian entering yonder portals. They meet him at the gates:

"Where are your dear ones? Where are your friends? Where is your crown?"

"Alas, I am saved alone."

God help you, reader, to so receive and give that you shall save yourself and others also.

JONATHAN EDWARDS

From the Sermon,

"Sinners in the Hands of an Angry God"

And now you have an extraordinary opportunity: a day wherein Christ has thrown the door of mercy wide open and stands calling and crying with a loud voice to poor sinners; a day wherein many are flocking to him and pressing into the kingdom of God. Many are daily coming from the east, west, north, and south; many that were very lately in the same miserable condition as you are now in a happy state, with their hearts filled with love to him who has loved them and washed them from their sins in his own blood, and they are rejoicing in hope of the glory of God.

How awful is it to be left behind at such a day! To see so many others feasting, while you are pining and perishing! To see so many rejoicing and singing for joy of heart, while you have cause to mourn for sorrow of heart, and howl for vexation of spirit! How can you rest one moment in such a condition? Are not your souls as precious as the souls of the people at Suffield, where they are flocking from day to day to Christ?

Are there not many here who have lived long in the world and are not to this day born again? Are there not many here who are aliens from the commonwealth of Israel, and have done nothing ever since they have lived but treasure up wrath against the day of wrath? Oh, sirs, your case, in an especial manner, is extremely dangerous. Your guilt and hardness of heart is extremely great. Do you not see how generally persons of your years are passed over and left, in the present remarkable and wonderful dispensation of God's mercy? You have need to consider yourselves and awake thoroughly out of sleep. You cannot bear the fierceness and wrath of the infinite God. And you, young men and young women, will you neglect this precious season which you now enjoy, when so many others of your age are renouncing all youthful vanities, and flocking to Christ? You especially have now an extraordinary opportunity; but if you neglect it, it will soon be with you as with those persons who spent all the precious days of youth in sin, and are now come to such a dreadful pass in blindness and hardness. And you, children, who are unconverted, do not you know that you are going down to hell, to bear the dreadful wrath of that God who is now angry with you every day and every night? Will you be content to be the children of the devil, when so many other children in the land are converted, and are become the holy and happy children of the King of kings?

And let every one that is yet out of Christ, and hanging over the pit of hell—whether they be old men and women, or middle aged, or young people, or little children—now hearken to the loud calls of God's Word and providence. This acceptable year of the Lord, a day of such great favor to some, will doubtless be a day of as remarkable vengeance to others. Men's hearts harden, and their guilt increases apace at such a day as this, if they neglect their souls; and never was there so great danger of such persons being given up to hardness of heart and blindness of mind. God seems now to be hastily gathering in his elect in all parts of the land; and probably the greater part of adult persons that ever shall be saved will be brought in now in a little time, and that it will be as it was on the great out-pouring of the Spirit upon the Jews in the apostles' days. The elect will obtain, and the rest will be blinded.

If this should be the case with you, you will eternally curse this day, and will curse the day that ever you were born, to see such a season of the pouring out of God's Spirit, and you will

107

wish that you had died and gone to hell before you had seen it. Now undoubtedly it is, as it was in the days of John the Baptist, that the axe is in an extraordinary manner laid at the root of the trees, that every tree which brings not forth good fruit may be hewn down and cast into the fire.

Therefore, let every one that is out of Christ, now awake and fly from the wrath to come. The wrath of Almighty God is now undoubtedly hanging over a great part of this congregation. Let every one fly out of Sodom: "Haste and escape for your lives; look not behind you, escape to the mountain, lest you be consumed."

MARTIN LUTHER

From a Letter to Melanchthon

If you are a preacher of mercy, do not preach an imaginary mercy, but the true mercy. If the mercy is true, you must therefore bear the true, not an imaginary sin. God does not save those who are only imaginary sinners.

Be a sinner, and let your sins be strong; but let your trust in Christ be stronger, and rejoice in Christ who is the victor over sin, death, and the world. We will commit sins while we are here, for this life is not a place where justice resides. We, however, says Peter (2 Peter 3:13), are looking forward to a new heaven and a new earth where justice will reign.

It suffices that through God's glory we have recognized the Lamb who takes away the sin of the world. No sin can separate us from Him, even if we were to kill or commit adultery thousands of times each day. Do you think such an exalted Lamb paid merely a small price with a meager sacrifice for our sins?

Pray hard, for you are quite a sinner.

FREDERICK FABER

Church Doctrine,
a Witness Against Worldly Times

We live in very worldly times. No one can doubt this who hears or reads ever so little of what is going on around him. The times are very worldly. We are wiser than our forefathers, but only in the ways of getting riches. Trade and noise, ships, railways, roads, changes here and changes there; all sorts of wild plans and dreams, we hear of them continually; we hear of nothing else. The world speaks of nothing else, thinks of nothing else.

Men of business, from sunrise to sunset, are making money. Their hours are all spent in writing letters, in keeping accounts, in going to public meetings, and so on. Men in power are struggling to keep their enemies out of power—planning, scheming, debating, and toiling continually. Then, for people who have less to do, there are theatres, races, balls, gambling houses, and a hundred other sinful pleasures. All these are the sort of things newspapers are so full of. We might almost think the world was going to last for ever, and that people never died—only we read there the names of people who have just died, and thus the world in its own newspapers witnesses against itself.

Now when we read or hear of all these things—of all this early rising and taking late rest, and eating the bread of carefulness—it must sometimes come across us to ask: "When do these people find time to save their souls? When do they pray? When do they repent? When do they hate the world? When do they despise its honors? When do they neglect its gold and silver, or sell all they have and give unto the poor? When do they find time to be Christians? How strange to be sure it all seems; I wonder what the end of it all will be!" Or in another way, we may fancy an angel looking down upon London or one of our great cities and, seeing the ways of living among the people, their greediness and avarice and worldliness and sin, would he be easily brought to believe that all those men were in the middle of a hot battle, of a deadly fight against the world, the flesh, and the devil?

Really it is fearful to see how the world goes on—so high, so careless, so proud, so antichristian, as if there were no Holy Trinity, no Heaven, no Cross, no Angels, no Dead Men, no Churches. It is fearful. But there will be an end of it all; and that end will be more fearful still. God give us grace to hate it with deep and perfect hatred! It is His enemy.

CHARLES SPURGEON

The Sword and the Trowel

When we were in Venice, we purchased a few curiosities. And finding them burdensome, we thought of sending them home by one of the English vessels lying in the Canal. We went out in a gondola with our box, and having asked for the captain of one of the vessels, we put to him the question: "Will you take a box for us to London, and what is the charge?" His reply was very ready, "I can't say till I know what's in it, for I don't want to get into trouble." A very commonsense answer indeed; we admired its caution and honesty.

What a pity that men do not exercise as much care in spiritual matters, as to what they will receive or reject. Dear reader, in these times there are thousands of bad books published and herds of bad teachers sent forth to deceive the unwary; you must be on your guard, lest you be led into error. Take nothing for granted, enquire into things for yourself, and try every new doctrine—and professedly old doctrine, too—by the Word of God. You may take contraband goods on board before you are aware of it; keep both eyes open, watch and examine, and when a thing is pressed upon you, find out what's in it. Do not believe all a man says because he is a clergyman, or eloquent, or learned, or even because he is kind and generous. Bring all to the bar of Holy Scripture, and if they cannot stand the test, receive them not, whatever their bold pretences.

But reader, is your own present religion good for anything?

Do you know what's in it, and what it is made of? May it not be mischievous and false? Search yourself, and do not take a hope into your soul till you know what it is made of. The devil and his allies will try to trick you into carrying their wares, but be warned in time, and reject their vile devices. The finished work of Jesus received by faith is "a good hope through grace," and there is no other. Do you have it? Or are you foolishly looking to another? The Lord lead you away from all else to Jesus. Whatever may be the ground of trust which men may offer you, take care to *know what's in it* before you accept it.

WILLIAM LAW

A Serious Call to a Devout and Holy Life

It may now be reasonably inquired how it comes to pass that the lives even of the better sort of people are thus strangely contrary to the principles of Christianity? But before I give a direct answer to this, I desire also to inquire how it comes to pass that swearing is so common a vice among Christians? It is indeed not yet so common among women as it is among men. But among men this sin is so common that perhaps there are more than two in three that are guilty of it through the whole course of their lives.

Now I ask: how can it be that two in three of the men are guilty of so gross and profane a sin as this is? There is neither ignorance nor human infirmity to plead for it; it is against an express commandment, and the most plain doctrines of our blessed Savior. But if you find the reason why the generality of men live in this notorious vice, then you will also have found the reason why the generality even of the better sort of people live so contrary to Christianity.

Now the reason of common swearing is this: it is because men have not so much as the intention to please God in all their actions. For let a man but have so much piety as to intend to please God in all the actions of his life, as the happiest and best thing in the world, and then he will never swear more. It will be as impossible for him to swear, while he feels this intention within himself, as it is impossible for a man that intends to please his prince to go up and abuse him to his face.

It seems but a small and necessary part of piety to have such a sincere intention as this, and that he has no reason to look upon himself as a disciple of Christ who is not this far advanced in piety. And yet it is purely for want of this degree of piety that you see such a mixture of sin and folly in the lives even of the better sort of people. It is for want of this intention that you see men that profess religion, yet live in swearing and sensuality; that you see clergymen given to pride and covetousness and worldly enjoyments. It is for want of this intention that you see women that profess devotion, yet live in all the folly and vanity of dress, wasting their time in idleness and pleasures, and in all such instances of state and equipage as their estates will reach. For let but a woman feel her heart full of this intention and she will find it as impossible to patch or paint as to curse or swear; she will no more desire to shine at balls or assemblies, or to make a figure amongst those that are most finely dressed, than she will desire to dance upon a rope to please spectators. She will know that the one is as far from the wisdom and excellency of the Christian spirit as the other.

It was this general intention that made the primitive Christians such eminent instances of piety, and made the goodly fellowship of the saints and all the glorious army of martyrs and confessors. And if you will here stop and ask yourselves why you are not as pious as the primitive Christians were, your own heart will tell you that it is neither through ignorance nor inability, but purely because you never thoroughly intended it. You observe the same Sunday worship that they did, and you are strict in it, because it is your full intention to be so. And when you as fully intend to be like them in their ordinary common life, when you intend to please God in all your actions, you will find it as possible to be strictly exact in the service of the Church.

And when you have this intention to please God in all your actions, as the happiest and best thing in the world, you will find in you as great an aversion to everything that is vain and impertinent in common life, whether of business or pleasure. You will be as fearful of living in any foolish way, either of spending your time or your fortune, as you are now fearful of neglecting the public worship.

JOHN BUNYAN

Solomon's Temple Spiritualized

I take the pinnacles on the top of the temple to be types of those lofty, airy notions with which some delight themselves while they hover like birds above the solid and godly truths of Christ. Satan attempted to entertain Christ Jesus with this type and antitype at once when he set him on one of the pinnacles of the temple and offered to thrust him upon a false confidence in God, by a false and unsound interpretation of a text (Matthew 4:5–6; Luke 4:9–11).

You have some men who cannot be content to worship in the temple, but must be aloft; no place will serve them but pinnacles—pinnacles that they may be speaking in and to the air, that they may be promoting their heady notions, instead of solid truth—not considering that now they are where the devil would have them be. They strut upon their points, their pinnacles; but let them look to it: there is difficult standing upon pinnacles. Their neck, their soul, is in danger. We read that God is in his temple, not upon these pinnacles (Psalm 4; Habakkuk 2:20).

It is true, Christ was once upon one of these; but the devil set him there with intent to dash him in pieces by a fall, and yet even then told him that if he would venture to tumble down, he should be kept from dashing his foot against a stone. To be there, therefore, was one of Christ's temptations; consequently one of Satan's stratagems: nor went he there of his own accord, for he knew that there was danger; he loved not to clamber pinnacles.

This should teach Christians to be low and little in their own eyes, and to forbear to intrude into airy and vain speculations, and to take heed of being puffed up with a foul and empty mind.

FRANCIS OF ASSISI

Admonitions

Blessed is the servant who does not regard himself as better when he is esteemed and extolled by men than when he is reputed as mean, simple, and despicable. For what a man is in the sight of God, so much he is, and no more. Woe to that religious person who is elevated in dignity by others, and who of his own will is not ready to descend. And blessed is that servant who is raised in dignity not by his own will and who always desires to be beneath the feet of others.

Blessed is that religious person who feels no pleasure or joy save in most holy conversation and the works of the Lord, and who by these means leads men to the love of God in joy and gladness. And woe to that religious person who takes delight in idle and vain words, and by this means provokes men to laughter.

Blessed is that servant who does not speak through hope of reward, and who does not manifest everything and is not "hasty to speak," but who wisely foresees what he ought to say and answer. Woe to that religious person who, not concealing in his heart the good things which the Lord has disclosed to him, and not manifesting them to others by his work, seeks rather through hope of reward to make them known to men by words—for now he receives his reward and his hearers bear away little fruit.

D. L. MOODY

The Ten Commandments

There has been an awful letting-down in this country regarding the Sabbath during the last 25 years, and many a man has been shorn of spiritual power, like Samson, because he is not straight on this question. Can you say that you observe the Sabbath properly? You may be a professed Christian: are you obeying this commandment? Or do you neglect the house of God on the Sabbath day and spend your time drinking and carousing in places of vice and crime, showing contempt for God and His law? Are you ready to step into the scales? Where were you last Sabbath? How did you spend it?

I honestly believe that this commandment is just as binding today as it ever was. I have talked with men who have said that it has been abrogated, but they have never been able to point to any place in the Bible where God repealed it. When Christ was on earth, He did nothing to set it aside; He freed it from the traces under which the scribes and Pharisees had put it, and gave it its true place: "The Sabbath was made for man, and not man for the Sabbath" (Mark 2:27).

It is just as practicable and as necessary for men today as it ever was—in fact, more than ever, because we live in such an intense age. The Sabbath was binding in Eden, and it has been in force ever since. The fourth commandment begins with the word *remember*, showing that the Sabbath already existed when God wrote this law on the tables of stone at Sinai. How can men claim that this one commandment has been done away with when they will admit that the other nine are still binding?

I believe that the Sabbath question today is a vital one for the whole country. It is the burning question of the present time. If you give up the Sabbath the church goes; if you give up the church the home goes; and if the home goes the nation goes. That is the direction in which we are traveling. The church of God is losing its power on account of so many people giving up the Sabbath, and using it to promote selfishness.

CHARLES SPURGEON

From the Sermon, "How to Read the Bible"

I do not wish to say much more about this, but I should like to push it home upon some of you. You have Bibles at home, I know. You would not like to be without Bibles; you would think you were heathens if you had no Bibles. You have them very neatly bound, and they are very fine looking volumes—not much thumbed, not much worn, and not likely to be so, for they only come out on Sundays for an airing, and they lie in lavender with the clean pocket handkerchiefs all the rest of the week. You do not read the Word, you do not search it, and how can you expect to get the divine blessing? If the heavenly gold is not worth digging for you are not likely to discover it.

Often and often have I told you that the searching of the Scriptures is not the way of salvation. The Lord has said, "Believe in the Lord Jesus Christ, and you shall be saved." But the reading of the word often leads, like the hearing of it, to faith. And faith brings salvation; for faith comes by hearing, and reading is a sort of hearing. While you are seeking to know what the gospel is, it may please God to bless your souls.

But what poor reading some of you give to your Bibles. I do not want to say anything which is too severe because it is not strictly true—let your own consciences speak. But still, I make bold to enquire: Do not many of you read the Bible in a very hurried way? Just a little bit, and off you go? Do you not soon forget what you have read and lose what little effect it seemed to have?

How few of you are resolved to get at its soul, its juice, its life, its essence, and to drink in its meaning. Well, if you do not do that, I tell you again your reading is miserable reading, dead reading, unprofitable reading. It is not reading at all; the name would be misapplied. May the blessed Spirit give you repentance touching this thing.

SAMUEL RUTHERFORD

The Trial and Triumph of Faith

The truly humble person is the most thankful soul that is; yet unthankfulness is one of the sins of the age we live in. It flows from:

1. Condemning and despising God's instruments. The valor of Jephthah is no mercy to Israel, because the elders hate and despise a bastard (Judges 11:1, 2, 6). The curing of Naaman's leprosy is not looked on as a mercy. Why? Because washing in Jordan must do it, and there be better rivers in his own land, in Damascus. Not only God, but all his instruments that he works by must be eye-sweet to us and carry God and omnipotency on their foreheads, else the mercy is no mercy to us.

2. Mercies cease to be mercies when they are smoked and blackened with our apprehensions. David (2 Samuel 18–19) receives a great victory and is established on his throne, which had been reeling and staggering of late. But there is one sad circumstance in that victory—his dear son Absalom was killed, and the mercy no mercy in David's apprehension. "Would God I had died for Absalom!" So a little cross can wash away the sense of a great mercy. The want of a draught of cold water strangles the thankful memory of God's wonders done for his people's deliverance out of Egypt, and his dividing the Red Sea.

What a price would the godly in England have put on the

removal of that which indeed was but a mass book, and the burdensome ceremonies, within these few years? But because this mercy is not molded and shaped according to the opinion of many, with such and such reformation and church-government, I am afraid there is fretting in too many instead of the return of praise—and hating of these, for whom they did sometimes pray. God grant that the sufferings of the land, and this unnatural bloodshed, may be near an end!

Except the land be further humbled, I fear the end of evils is not yet come. This is a directing of the Spirit of the Lord, to teach God how to shape and flower his mercies toward us. Is it not fitting there be water in our wine and a thorn in our rose? Shall God draw the linaments and proportion of his favors after the measure of my foot? Shall the Almighty be instructed to regulate his ways of supernatural providence according to the frame of our apprehensions?

Oh, he is a wise Lord, and wonderful in counsel! Every mercy cannot be overlaid with sapphires and precious stones, nor must all our deliverances drop sweet-smelling myrrh. God knows when and how to level and smooth all his favors, and remove all their knots, in a sweet proportion to the main and principal end—the salvation of his own. There is a crook in our best desires, and a rule cannot admit of a crook even in relation to the creature; far less to him who does all things after the counsel of his own will.

JOHN CALVIN

On the Christian Life

This is the place to address those who, having nothing of Christ but the name and sign, would yet be called Christians. How dare they boast of this sacred name? None have intercourse with Christ but those who have acquired the true knowledge of him from the Gospel. The apostle denies that any man truly has learned Christ who has not learned to put off "the old man, which is corrupt according to the deceitful lusts, and put on Christ" (Ephesians 4:22).

They are convicted, therefore, of falsely and unjustly pretending a knowledge of Christ, whatever be the volubility and eloquence with which they can talk of the Gospel. Doctrine is not an affair of the tongue, but of the life; is not apprehended by the intellect and memory merely, like other branches of learning, but is received only when it possesses the whole soul and finds its seat and habitation in the inmost recesses of the heart.

Let them, therefore, either cease to insult God by boasting that they are what they are not, or let them show themselves not unworthy disciples of their divine Master. To doctrine in which our religion is contained we have given the first place, since by it our salvation commences; but it must be transfused into the breast, and pass into the conduct, and so transform us into itself, as not to prove unfruitful. If philosophers are justly offended, and banish from their company with disgrace those who, while professing an art which ought to be the mistress of their conduct, convert it into mere loquacious sophistry, with how much better reason shall we detest those flimsy sophists who are contented to let the Gospel play upon their lips, when, from its efficacy, it ought to penetrate the inmost affections of the heart, fix its seat in the soul, and pervade the whole man a hundred times more than the frigid discourses of philosophers?

TERESA OF AVILA

The Way of Perfection

God deliver us from people who wish to serve Him and yet are mindful of their own honor. Reflect how little they gain from this; for, as I have said, the very act of desiring honor robs us of it, especially in matters of precedence. There is no poison in the world which is so fatal to perfection. You will say that these are little things which have to do with human nature and are not worth troubling about. But do not trifle with them, for in religious houses they spread like foam on water, and there is no small matter so extremely dangerous as are punctiliousness about honor and sensitiveness to insult. . . .

This human nature of ours is so wretchedly weak that, even while we are telling ourselves that there is nothing for us to make a fuss about, we imagine we are doing something virtuous and begin to feel sorry for ourselves, particularly when we see that other people are sorry for us, too. In this way the soul begins to lose the occasions of merit which it had gained. It becomes weaker, and thus a door is opened to the devil by which he can enter on some other occasion with a temptation worse than the last.

It may even happen that, when you yourself are prepared to suffer an insult, your sisters come and ask you if you are a beast of burden, and say you ought to be more sensitive about things. Oh, my sisters, for the love of God, never let charity move you to show pity for another in anything to do with these fancied insults, for that is like the pity shown to holy Job by his wife and friends.

SAMUEL RUTHERFORD

A Selection From His Letters

Well-beloved sister,

I have been thinking, since my departure from you, of the pride and malice of your adversaries. You may already realize this (since you have had the Book of Psalms so often), but I am reminded of how David's enemies snuffed at him and through the pride of their heart said, "The Lord will not require it" (Psalm 10:13). I beseech you, therefore, in the bowels of Jesus, set before your eyes the patience of your forerunner Jesus, who, when He was reviled, reviled not again; when He suffered, He threatened not, but committed Himself to Him who judges righteously (1 Peter 2:23).

And since your Lord and Redeemer received many a black stroke on His glorious back with patience, and many a buffet of the unbelieving world, and says of Himself, "I gave My back to the smiters, and My cheeks to them that plucked off the hair; I hid not my face from shame and spitting" (Isaiah 50:6); follow Him and think it not hard that you receive a blow with your Lord. Take part with Jesus in His sufferings and glory in the marks of Christ.

If this storm were over, you must prepare yourself for a new wound; for, five thousand years ago, our Lord proclaimed deadly war betwixt the Seed of the Woman and the seed of the Serpent. Be upon Christ's side of it and care not what flesh can do. Hold yourself fast by your Savior, however you be buffeted, and those that follow Him. Yet a little while and the wicked shall not be. "We are troubled on every side, yet not distressed; we are perplexed, but not in despair; persecuted, but not forsaken; cast down, but not destroyed' (2 Corinthians 4:8–9). If you can possess your soul in patience, their day is coming. Worthy and dear sister, know how to carry yourself in trouble. And when you are hated and reproached, the Lord shows it to you: "All this is come upon us, yet have we not forgotten You, neither have we dealt falsely in Your covenant" (Psalm 44:17). "Unless Your law had been my delight, I had perished in mine affliction" (Psalm 119:92).

Keep God's covenant in your trials; hold you by His blessed word, and sin not; flee anger, wrath, grudging, envying, fretting; forgive a hundred pence to your fellow servant, because your Lord has forgiven you ten thousand talents. For I assure you by the Lord, your adversaries shall get no advantage against you, except that you sin and offend your Lord in your sufferings. But the way to overcome is by patience, forgiving and praying for your enemies, and in doing so you heap coals upon their heads, and your Lord shall open a door to you in your trouble. Wait upon Him, as the night watchman waits for the morning. He will not tarry. Go up to your watchtower and come not down, but by prayer and faith and hope, wait on. When the sea is full, it will ebb again; and so soon as the wicked come to the top of their pride and are waxed high and mighty, then is their change approaching; they that believe make not haste.

Now, again, I trust in our Lord, you shall by faith sustain yourself and comfort yourself in your Lord and be strong in His power; for you are in the beaten and common way to heaven when you are under our Lord's crosses. You have reason to rejoice in it, more than in a crown of gold. And rejoice and be glad to bear the reproaches of Christ. I rest, recommending you and yours forever, to the grace and mercy of God. Yours in Christ.

FRANÇOIS FÉNELON

Spiritual Letters

Your excessive distress is like a summer torrent, which must be suffered to run away. Nothing makes any impression upon you, and you think you have the most substantial evidence for the most imaginary states. It is the ordinary result of great suffering. God permits you, notwithstanding your excellent faculties, to be blind to what lies immediately before you, and to think you see clearly what does not exist at all. God will be glorified in your heart if you will be faithful in yielding to his designs. But nothing would be more injudicious than the forming of resolutions in a state of distress, which is manifestly accompanied by an inability to do anything according to God.

When you shall have become calm, then do in a spirit of recollection what you shall perceive to be nearest the will of God respecting you. Return gradually to devotion, simplicity, and the oblivion of self. Commune and listen to God, and be deaf to self. Then do all that is in your heart, for I have no fear that a spirit of that sort will permit you to take any wrong step.

But to suppose that we are sane when we are in the very agony of distress, and under the influence of a violent temptation of self-love, is to ensure our being led astray. Ask any experienced adviser, and he will tell you that you are to make no resolutions until you have re-entered into peace and recollection. You will learn from him that the readiest way to self-deception is to trust to ourselves in a state of suffering, in which nature is so unreasonable and irritated.

You will say that I desire to prevent you doing as you should if I forbid your doing it at the only moment when you are capable of it. God forbid! I neither desire to permit nor hinder: my only wish is so to advise you that you shall not be found wanting toward God. Now, it is as clear as day that you would fall in that respect if you took counsel at the hands of a self-love wounded to the quick and an irritation verging upon despair. Would you change anything to gratify your self-love, when God does not desire it? God forbid! Wait, then, until you shall be in a condition to be advised. To enjoy the true advantages of illumination, we must be equally ready for every alternative, and must have nothing which we are not cheerfully disposed at once to sacrifice for His sake.

WILLIAM LAW

A Collection of Letters

The large account you have given of yourself, is very affecting, and I hope God will turn all the variety of your past distress into means of a future solid peace and rest in his divine love. To be weary and heavy laden is to have the highest fitness to receive that rest which Christ alone can give. These are the persons that he called to him when he was upon earth. They who are content with themselves are in the utmost danger of never knowing that happiness for which they were created.

For a while, consider yourself in such solitude as if there was only God and you in the world, free from every thought but that of desiring to be wholly and solely his, and looking wholly to his goodness, to be delivered out of the misery of your fallen state. Stand firmly in this faith, that God and the kingdom of heaven are certainly within you, and within you for this only reason that they may become your salvation. As all therefore is within, so let all your care be turned inwards in loving, adoring, and praying to this God and Christ within you.

Be not too eager about much reading. Nor read anything but that which nourishes, strengthens, and establishes this faith in you of an inward Savior, who is the life of your soul. To grow up in this faith is taking the best means of attaining to the best knowledge in all divine matters.

Cast away all reflections about yourself, the world, or your past life. And let all be swallowed up or lost in this joyful thought, that you have found the Messiah, the Savior of the world, not in books, not in history, but in the birth and bottom of your own soul. Give yourself up to this birth of heaven within you—expect all from it, let it be the humble, faithful, longing desire of your heart, and desire no knowledge but that which is born of it and proceeds from it. Stand only in this thirst of knowledge, and then all that you know will be spirit and life.

MADAME GUYON

The Autobiography of Madame Guyon

Most men appear to me very unjust when they readily resign themselves to another man, and then look upon that as prudence. They confide in men who are nothing and boldly say, "Such a person cannot be deceived." But if one speaks of a soul wholly resigned to God, which follows him faithfully, they cry aloud, "That person is deceived with his resignation."

O divine Love! Do You want either strength, fidelity, love, or wisdom to conduct those who trust in You and who are Your dearest children?

I have seen men bold enough to say, "Follow me, and you shall not be misled." How sadly are those men misled themselves by their presumption! How much sooner should I go to him who would be afraid of misleading me—who, trusting neither to his learning nor experience, would rely upon God only!

Our Lord showed me, in a dream, two ways by which souls steer their course, under the figure of two drops of water. The one appeared to me of an unparalleled beauty, brightness, and purity; the other to have also a brightness, yet full of little streaks. Both were good to quench thirst—the former altogether pleasant, but the latter not so perfectly agreeable.

By the former is represented the way of pure and naked faith, which pleases the Spouse much because it is so pure, so clear from all self-love. The way of emotions or gifts is not so; yet it is that in which many enlightened souls walk, and into which they had drawn Father La Combe. But God showed me that He had given him to me to draw him into one more pure and perfect. I spoke before the sisters, he being present, of the way of faith, how much more glorious it was to God, and advantageous for the soul, than all those gifts, emotions and assurances, which ever cause us to live to self.

FREDERICK FABER

Church Doctrine,

A Witness Against Worldly Times

When we say the times are worldly, we mean that people are always thinking of and loving things they see—things seen, things temporal, things that profit them here and are not much set by in heaven. These are times when people think of riches, honor, power, happiness, and mirth; of life and health and good spirits; of elegance and comfort; of beauty, love, and prosperity; of eating and drinking, marrying and giving in marriage. These are times when people do not think of death, of judgment, of Baptism, of Bibles, of Churches, of Holy Communion, of constant prayer, of fasting and watching, of self-denial and hard penance.

Worldly times are times when all the world, but a few, seem to have agreed with each other to forget all these things, and to say nothing about them—not to take the trouble to deny them, but simply to forget them. This is worldliness.

Now, all the doctrines of the Church are opposed to worldliness. The Church herself is the world's enemy. She is set down in the earth by Christ to fight with the world and to get the better of it: which she will do because of the Holy Ghost Who is with her and in her.

BERNARD OF CLAIRVAUX

On Loving God

It is natural for a man to desire what he reckons better than that
which he has already, and to be satisfied with nothing which lacks
that special quality which he misses. Thus, if it is for her beauty
that he loves his wife, he will cast longing eyes after a fairer woman.
If he is clad in a rich garment, he will covet a costlier one; and no
matter how rich he may be, he will envy a man richer than himself.
Do we not see people every day, endowed with vast estates, who
keep on joining field to field, dreaming of wider boundaries for
their lands? Those who dwell in palaces are ever adding house to
house, continually building up and tearing down, remodeling and
changing. Men in high places are driven by insatiable ambition
to clutch at still greater prizes. And nowhere is there any final
satisfaction, because nothing there can be defined as absolutely
the best or highest. But it is natural that nothing should content
a man's desires but the very best, as he reckons it.

Is it not, then, mad folly to always be craving for things which
can never quiet our longings, much less satisfy them? No matter
how many such things one has, he is always lusting after what he
has not; never at peace, he sighs for new possessions. Discontented,
he spends himself in fruitless toil and finds only weariness in the
evanescent and unreal pleasures of the world. In his greediness,
he counts all that he has clutched as nothing in comparison with

what is beyond his grasp, and he loses all pleasure in his actual possessions by longing after what he has not, yet covets.

No man can ever hope to own all things. Even the little one does possess is got only with toil and is held in fear, since each is certain to lose what he hath when God's day, appointed though unrevealed, shall come. But the perverted will struggles towards the ultimate good by devious ways—yearning after satisfaction, yet led astray by vanity and deceived by wickedness. Ah, if you wish to attain to the consummation of all desire, so that nothing unfulfilled will be left, why weary yourself with fruitless efforts, running hither and thither, only to die long before the goal is reached?

It is so that these impious ones wander in a circle, longing after something to gratify their yearnings, yet madly rejecting that which alone can bring them to their desired end—not by exhaustion, but by attainment. They wear themselves out in vain travail, without reaching their blessed consummation, because they delight in creatures, not in the Creator. They want to traverse creation, trying all things one by one, rather than think of coming to Him who is Lord of all.

And if their utmost longing were realized, so that they should have all the world for their own? Yet without possessing Him who is the Author of all being, then the same law of their desires would make them condemn what they had and restlessly seek Him whom they still lacked—that is, God Himself. Rest is in Him alone. Man knows no peace in the world; but he has no disturbance when he is with God. And so the soul says with confidence, "Whom have I in heaven but You? There is none upon earth that I desire in comparison of You. God is the strength of my heart and my portion for ever. It is good for me to hold fast by God, to put my trust in the Lord God" (Psalm 73:25ff). Even by this way one would eventually come to God, if only he might have time to test all lesser goods in turn.

But life is too short, strength too feeble, and competitors too many for that course to be practicable. One could never reach the end, though he were to weary himself with the long effort and fruitless toil of testing everything that might seem desirable. It would be far easier and better to make the journey in imagination rather than in experiment. For the mind is swifter in operation and keener in discrimination than the bodily senses, to this very purpose that it may go before the sensuous affections so that they may cleave to nothing which the mind has found worthless. And so it is written, "Prove all things: hold fast that which is good" (1 Thessalonians 5:21)—which is to say that right judgment should prepare the way for the heart. Otherwise we may not ascend into the hill of the Lord nor rise up in His holy place (Psalm 24:3).

We should have no profit in possessing a rational mind if we were to follow the impulse of the senses, like brute beasts, with no regard at all to reason. Those whom reason does not guide in their course may indeed run, but not in the appointed race-track, neglecting the apostolic counsel, "So run that you may obtain the prize." For how could they obtain the prize who put that least of all in their endeavor and run round after everything else first?

WILLIAM BOOTH

Letters to Salvationists on
Religion for Every Day

The first topic to which I shall call your attention is your daily employment. And by that I mean the method by which you earn your livelihood. Or, supposing that having some independent means of support you are not compelled to labor for your daily bread, then I shall point out that special form of work, the doing of which Providence has plainly made to be your duty. Because it is difficult to conceive of any Salvationist who has not some regular employment for which he holds himself responsible to God.

Work is a good thing, my Comrades. To be unemployed is generally counted an evil—anyway, it is so in the case of a poor man. But it seems to me that the obligation to be engaged in some honorable and useful kind of labor is as truly devolved upon the rich as upon the poor, perhaps more so. Work is necessary to the well-being of men and women of every class, everywhere. To be voluntarily idle, in any rank or condition of life, is to be a curse to others and to be accursed yourself.

Everything in God's creation works. The stars travel round and round in space; the ocean rises, falls, and dashes itself about in storms and tempests; the winds career to and fro in the heavens; the clouds are ever receiving and pouring forth their life-giving waters. All the forces of nature are ever active in order to fulfill the bountiful purposes of their Maker.

Everything that can be said to have life works. The plants and the trees struggle into being, pushing their way upwards through all sorts of opposition, and then fighting the very elements in order to maintain their existence and bring forth their fruits. All the living creatures on the earth or in the waters work. They have to hunt for their food; in many instances, to construct their homes; and in every case, to defend themselves against their enemies—and very hard work at times they find it, I can tell you.

God works. He is the greatest Worker in the universe. No being toils with the ceaseless activity, with the unerring wisdom, the gigantic energy, the beneficent purpose of Jehovah. And the inhabitants of Heaven work. To spend eternity in the monotony of an enforced idleness would be, neither more nor less than a miserable existence. Indeed, we could not conceive of angels or saints or any other intelligent creatures being happy and contented without some form of employment.

All the best, greatest, and most useful men and women who have ever lived, in this world, have been untiring workers. They would not have been eminent in character, position, or achievement without unceasing toil. They have risen early, sat up late, redeemed the moments, begrudged the time necessary for sleep and food and the ordinary demands of life.

Work is a good thing, my Comrades. I have ever found it to be so in my own experience. And specially has it proved itself to be a blessing in these, the latter days of my life.

A. B. SIMPSON

Walking in the Spirit

What is spiritual power? First, it is the power which convicts of sin. It is the power that makes the hearers to see themselves as God sees them, and humbles them in the dust. It sends people home from the house of God not feeling better but worse; not always admiring the preacher, but often so tried that they perhaps resolve that they will never hear him again. But they know from their inmost soul that he is right and they are wrong. It is the power of conviction; the power that awakens the conscience and says to the soul, "You are the man." It is the power of which the apostle speaks in connection with his own ministry: "by manifestation of the truth, commending ourselves to every man's conscience in the sight of God."

They that possess this power will not always be popular preachers, but they will always be effectual workers. Sometimes the hearer will almost think that they are personal, and that someone has disclosed to them his secret sins. Speaking of such a sermon, one of our most honored evangelists said that he felt so indignant with the preacher under whom he was converted that he waited for some time near the door for the purpose of giving him a trashing for daring to expose him in the way he had done, thinking that somebody had informed on him. Let us covet this power. It is the very stamp and seal of the Holy Ghost on a faithful minister.

It is the power that lifts up Christ and makes Him real to the apprehension of the hearer. Some sermons leave upon the mind a vivid impression of the truth; others leave upon the mind the picture of the Savior. It is not so much an idea as a person. This is true preaching, and this is the Holy Spirit's most blessed and congenial ministry. He loves to draw in heavenly lines the face of Jesus and make Him shine out over every page of the Bible, and every paragraph of the sermon as a face of beauty and a heart of love. Let us cultivate this power, for this is what the struggling, hungry world wants—to know its Savior. "We would see Jesus" is still its cry; and the answer still is, "I, if I be lifted up from the earth, will draw all men unto me."

Next, this power leads men to decision. It is not merely that they know something they did not know before, that they get new thoughts and conceptions of truth which they carry away to remember and reflect upon, nor even that they feel the deepest and most stirring emotions of religious feeling, but the power of the Spirit always presses them to action—prompt, decisive, positive action.

The power of the Holy Ghost leads men to decide for God and to enlist against Satan, to give up habits of sin and to make great and everlasting decisions. The Lord grant us so to speak in His name, in demonstration of the Spirit and power, that the result shall be, as Paul himself expresses it on writing to the Thessalonians, "Our word came unto you not in word only, but in power, and ye turned from idols to serve the living and true God, and to wait for His Son from heaven, even Jesus, which saved us from the wrath to come."

THOMAS À KEMPIS

The Imitation of Christ

Happy is he to whom truth manifests itself—not in signs and words that fade, but as it actually is. Our opinions, our senses often deceive us and we discern very little. What good is much discussion of involved and obscure matters when our ignorance of them will not be held against us on Judgment Day? Neglect of things which are profitable and necessary, and undue concern with those which are irrelevant and harmful, are great folly.

We have eyes and do not see.

What, therefore, have we to do with questions of philosophy? He to whom the Eternal Word speaks is free from theorizing. For from this Word are all things and of Him all things speak—the Beginning Who also speaks to us. Without this Word no man understands or judges aright. He to whom it becomes everything, who traces all things to it and who sees all things in it, may ease his heart and remain at peace with God.

O God, You Who are the truth, make me one with You in love everlasting. I am often wearied by the many things I hear and read, but in You is all that I long for. Let the learned be still, let all creatures be silent before You; You alone speak to me.

The more recollected a man is, and the more simple of heart he becomes, the easier he understands sublime things, for he receives the light of knowledge from above. The pure, simple, and steadfast spirit is not distracted by many labors, for he does them all for the honor of God. And since he enjoys interior peace he seeks no selfish end in anything. What, indeed, gives more trouble and affliction than uncontrolled desires of the heart?

A good and devout man arranges in his mind the things he has to do, not according to the whims of evil inclination but according to the dictates of right reason. Who is forced to struggle more than he who tries to master himself? This ought to be our purpose, then: to conquer self, to become stronger each day, and to advance in virtue.

Every perfection in this life has some imperfection mixed with it, and no learning of ours is without some darkness. Humble knowledge of self is a surer path to God than the ardent pursuit of learning. Not that learning is to be considered evil, or knowledge, which is good in itself and so ordained by God; but a clean conscience and virtuous life ought always to be preferred. Many often err and accomplish little or nothing because they try to become learned rather than to live well.

If men used as much care in uprooting vices and implanting virtues as they do in discussing problems, there would not be so much evil and scandal in the world, or such laxity in religious organizations. On the day of judgment, surely, we shall not be asked what we have read but what we have done; not how well we have spoken but how well we have lived.

Tell me, where now are all the masters and teachers whom you knew so well in life and who were famous for their learning? Others have already taken their places and I know not whether they ever think of their predecessors. During life they seemed to be something; now they are seldom remembered. How quickly the glory of the world passes away! If only their lives had kept pace with their learning, then their study and reading would have been worthwhile.

How many there are who perish because of vain worldly knowledge and too little care for serving God. They became vain in their own conceits because they chose to be great rather than humble.

He is truly great who has great charity. He is truly great who is little in his own eyes and makes nothing of the highest honor. He is truly wise who looks upon all earthly things as folly that he may gain Christ. He who does God's will and renounces his own is truly very learned.

OUR COUNSELOR:
THE HOLY SPIRIT

"I say that a Christian congregation can survive and often
appear to prosper in the community by the exercise of human
talent and without any touch from the Holy Spirit! All that
religious activity and the dear people will not know anything
better until the great and terrible day when our self-employed
talents are burned with fire and only that which was
wrought by the Holy Ghost will stand forever!"

—*Tragedy in the Church*

JOHN KNOX

The Scots Confession

Our faith and its assurance do not proceed from flesh and blood—that is to say, from natural powers within us—but are the inspiration of the Holy Ghost, whom we confess to be God, equal with the Father and with his Son, who sanctifies us and brings us into all truth by his own working, without whom we should remain forever enemies to God and ignorant of his Son, Christ Jesus. For by nature we are so dead, blind, and perverse that neither can we feel when we are pricked, see the light when it shines, nor assent to the will of God when it is revealed, unless the Spirit of the Lord Jesus quickens that which is dead, removes the darkness from our minds, and bows our stubborn hearts to the obedience of his blessed will.

And so, as we confess that God the Father created us when we were not, as his Son our Lord Jesus redeemed us when we were enemies to him, so also do we confess that the Holy Ghost does sanctify and regenerate us, without respect to any merit proceeding from us, be it before or after our regeneration.

To put this even more plainly: as we willingly disclaim any honor and glory from our own creation and redemption, so do we willingly also disclaim any honor for our regeneration and sanctification. For by ourselves we are not capable of thinking one good thought. But he who has begun the work in us alone continues us in it, to the praise and glory of his undeserved grace.

A. B. SIMPSON

A Larger Christian Life

To be filled with the Holy Spirit is to be connected with a living Person. We are not filled with an influence; we are not filled with a sensation; we are not filled with a set of ideas and truths; we are not filled with a blessing—we are filled with a Person. This is very strange and striking. It is wholly different from all other teaching. Human systems of philosophy and religion all deal mainly with intellectual truths, moral conditions or external acts. Greek philosophy was a system of ideas; Confucianism is a system of morals; Judaism is a system of laws and ceremonies. But Christianity all centers in a living Person, and its very essence is the indwelling life of Christ Himself.

He was not only its Head and Founder, but He is forever its living Heart and Substance, and the Holy Spirit is simply the agent and channel through whom He enters, possesses, and operates in the consecrated heart. This reduces Christian life to great simplicity. We do not require to get filled in a great many compartments, and with a great many different experiences, ideas, or influences—but in the center of our being to receive Him in His personal life and fullness, and then He flows into every part and lives out His own life in all the diversified experiences and activities of our manifold life.

In the one garden we plant the living seed, and water it from the same great fountain, and lo! it springs up spontaneously with all the varied beauty and fruitfulness of the lily and the rose, the foliage plant and the fruit tree, the clinging jessamine and the spreading vine. We have simply to turn on the fertilizing spring and nature's spontaneous life bursts forth in all its beautiful variety.

This, by a simple figure, is Christ's theory of a deeper life. Our being is the soil, He is the seed, His Holy Spirit is the Fountain of living Waters, and "the fruit of the Spirit is love, joy, peace, long-suffering, gentleness, goodness, faith, meekness, temperance."

JOHN WESLEY

From the Sermon, "On the Holy Spirit"

Well may a man ask his own heart whether it is able to admit the Spirit of God. For where that divine Guest enters, the laws of another world must be observed. The body must be given up to martyrdom, or spent in the Christian warfare, as unconcernedly as if the soul were already provided of its house from heaven. The goods of this world must be parted with as freely as if the last fire were to seize them tomorrow. Our neighbor must be loved as heartily as if he were washed from all his sins and demonstrated to be a child of God by the resurrection from the dead.

The fruits of this Spirit must not be mere moral virtues, calculated for the comfort and decency of the present life, but holy dispositions, suitable to the instincts of a superior life already begun.

Thus to press forward, whither the promise of life calls him—to turn his back upon the world, and comfort himself in God—every one that has faith perceives to be just and necessary, and forces himself to do it. Every one that has hope does it gladly and eagerly, though not without difficulty. But he that has love does it with ease and singleness of heart.

FRANÇOIS FÉNELON

The Inner Life

It is certain from the Holy Scriptures that the Spirit of God dwells within us, acts there, prays without ceasing, groans, desires, asks for us what we know not how to ask for ourselves, urges us on, animates us, speaks to us when we are silent, suggests to us all truth, and so unites us to Him that we become one spirit (1 Corinthians 6:17). This is the teaching of faith, and even those instructors who are farthest removed from the interior life cannot avoid acknowledging so much.

Still, notwithstanding these theoretical principles, they always strive to maintain that in practice the external law, or at least a certain light of learning and reason, illuminates us within, and that our understanding acts of itself from that instruction. They do not rely sufficiently upon the interior teacher, the Holy Spirit, who does everything in us. He is the soul of our soul; we could not form a thought or a desire without Him. Alas! What blindness is ours! We reckon ourselves alone in the interior sanctuary, when God is much more intimately present there than we are ourselves.

What, then! you will say, *are we all inspired?* Yes, doubtless; but not as were the prophets and apostles. Without the actual inspiration of the Spirit of grace, we could neither do, nor will, nor believe any good thing. We are, then, always inspired, but we incessantly stifle the inspiration. God does not cease to speak, but the noise of the creatures without, and of our passions within, confines us and prevents our hearing. We must silence every creature, including self, that in the deep stillness of the soul we may perceive the ineffable voice of the Bridegroom. We must lend an attentive ear, for His voice is soft and still, and is only heard of those who hear nothing else!

Ah, how rare is it to find a soul still enough to hear God speak! The slightest murmur of our vain desires, or of a love fixed upon self, confounds all the words of the Spirit of God. We hear well enough that He is speaking, and that He is asking for something, but we cannot distinguish what is said—and are often glad enough that we cannot. The least reserve, the slightest self-reflective act, the most imperceptible fear of hearing too clearly what God demands interferes with the interior voice.

Need we be astonished, then, if so many people—pious indeed but full of amusements, vain desires, false wisdom, and confidence in their own virtues—cannot hear it, and consider its existence as a dream of fanatics? Alas! What would they do with their proud reasonings? Of what efficacy would be the exterior word of pastors, or even of the Scriptures themselves, if we had not within the word of the Holy Spirit giving to the others all their vitality? The outward word, even of the Gospel, without the fecundating, vivifying, interior word would be but an empty sound. "It is the letter that alone kills (2 Corinthians 3:6), and the Spirit alone can give us life."

G. CAMPBELL MORGAN

The Teaching of Christ

Looking back over these passages of Scripture connecting Jesus with the Holy Spirit, it is again evident that there was no attempt on the part of the Lord at systematic teaching. That in itself is a matter of supreme importance.

It is a dangerous thing in doctrinal teaching to argue from silence. Yet there is a value in observing the things about which Christ said practically nothing. When we find Him silent on some great matter, we may be content to be silent on that subject, too. We are always in danger of losing the supreme value of this whole fact of the ministry of the Holy Spirit when we are eager and anxious to state systematically, or even theologically, all the facts concerning the Spirit of God, and the relation of the Spirit of God to the Trinity—topics on which no final word can be said. And it is infinitely better that we should ever abide in this matter where Christ left the subject, for on the subject of the nature of the Spirit of God He made no advance upon that first mystic, suggestive, and beautiful word spoken to Nicodemus: "The wind bloweth where it listeth, and thou hearest the voice thereof, but knowest not whence it cometh, and whither it goeth."

The fact we know, but all the mystery of it we do not know, nor can we! But knowing the fact, we postpone, at least for the present, the attempt to understand the mystery, and obeying the fact we find the great force serving our purpose, and accomplishing our end. Is that not the law of the wind?

Dr. Jowett, when he wanted to preach upon this very passage, went down to Tynemouth, and sat by an old sailor—a real sailor, a man who had spent many years upon a sailing vessel—and said to him, "Do you know anything about the wind?" "Yes, sir, I know a lot about the wind." "Well, will you explain to me the phenomenon of the wind?" "I don't know what you mean, sir." "Well, how do you explain the wind: what do you know about it?" "No, sir, I don't know anything about the wind; but I know the wind, and I can hoist a sail!" That is the whole philosophy of this teaching. "The wind bloweth where it listeth, and thou hearest the voice thereof"—we know the fact; "but knowest not whence it cometh and whither it goeth"—that is the mystery; but knowing the fact we hoist the sail, and the fact becomes the force that drives our vessel across the lake, though when we get to the other side we know no more about the mystery of it than we did when we started; but our vessel has been carried over; "so is every one that is born of the Spirit."

The man born of the Spirit comes to recognition of the blowing of the wind, a voice in the soul, a vision before the eye, a new touch of power upon the life. And in effect he says, "Whence, I cannot tell; whither, I know not; what, I cannot discover; but I will hoist the sail; I will act upon the impulse suggested," and immediately the force of the Spirit enters into the life, and presently he arrives at the desired haven, because recognizing the mystery, and knowing the fact, he has been obedient to the law of the fact, and the fact has been a force cooperative with his life.

To my own mind, that great silence of Jesus, that recognition of mystery, is in itself one of the most wonderful things in all His teaching concerning the Spirit.

JOHN BUNYAN

A Treatise on the Fear of God

It is the Spirit of God, even the Holy Ghost, that convinces us of sin, and so of our damnable state because of sin. Therefore the Spirit of God, when he works in the heart as a spirit of bondage, does it by working in us by the law, for by the law is the knowledge of sin (Romans 6: 20). And he in this his working is properly called a spirit of bondage; because by the law he shows us that indeed we are in bondage to the law, the devil, and death and damnation.

He is called in his working the spirit of bondage, because he here also holds us—to wit, in this sight and sense of our bondage state—so long as it is necessary we should be so held; which to some of the saints is a longer, and to some a shorter time. Paul was held in it three days and three nights, but the jailer and the three thousand, so far as can be gathered, not above an hour; but some in these later times are so held for days and months, if not for years. But I say, let the time be longer or shorter, it is the Spirit of God that holds him under this yoke, and it is good that a man should be for his time held under it.

Now, as I said, the sinner at first is by the Spirit of God held under this bondage; that is, has such a discovery of his sin and of his damnation for sin made to him, and also is held so fast under the sense thereof, that it is not in the power of any man, nor yet of the very angels in heaven, to release or set him free until the Holy Spirit changes his ministration and comes in the sweet and peaceable tidings of salvation by Christ in the gospel to his poor dejected and afflicted conscience.

G. CAMPBELL MORGAN

The Spirit of God

The ministry of the Spirit is larger than His ministry in the Church; it is world-wide, and is always based upon the work of the Christ. Whether to the Church or to the world, the Spirit has no message but the message of Jesus Christ. To the man in the Church, and to the whole Church, He is revealing the Christ in new beauty and new glory. To the world He is revealing sin, righteousness, and judgment in their relation to the Christ. The Spirit is poured upon all flesh; and, in cooperation with the Church, He convinces of sin, and of righteousness, and of judgment.

Therein lies the heart, the centre, and the responsibility of foreign missionary work. How shall they hear without a preacher? And how shall they preach, except they be sent? The Holy Spirit is waiting in the far-distant places of the earth for the voice of anointed man to preach, in order that through that instrumentality He may carry on His work of convicting of sin, and of righteousness, and of judgment.

Beyond that, there is this other marvelous ministry which is too often lost sight of. By His presence in the world He is restraining the out-working of iniquity, and is checking, hindering, and driving back every attempted combination of the forces of evil for the swamping of the Church and the hindering of the kingdom. The Spirit's restraining work will go forward until the moment has come when the number of the elect is complete. Then shall the Spirit be withdrawn when the Church is called away, in order that iniquity may be manifested and smitten to its final doom, and the glorious kingdom of our God be set up.

The only sense in which the Spirit is withdrawn is that which characterizes His special work in this age—that, namely, of conserving the Church and preventing the progress of evil to finality. He will carry on His work of striving with men as He did prior to the Deluge, but with results more glorious.

JOHN CALVIN

Institutes of the Christian Religion

But in order to have a clearer view of this most important subject we must remember that Christ came provided with the Holy Spirit after a peculiar manner: namely, that he might separate us from the world and unite us in the hope of an eternal inheritance. Hence the Spirit is called the Spirit of sanctification because he quickens and cherishes us, not merely by the general energy which is seen in the human race, as well as other animals, but because he is the seed and root of heavenly life in us.

Accordingly, one of the highest commendations which the prophets give to the kingdom of Christ is that under it the Spirit would be poured out in richer abundance. One of the most remarkable passages is that of Joel: "It shall come to pass afterward that I will pour out my Spirit upon all flesh" (Joel 2:28). For although the prophet seems to confine the gifts of the Spirit to the office of prophesying, he yet intimates under a figure that God will, by the illumination of his Spirit, provide himself with disciples who had previously been altogether ignorant of heavenly doctrine.

Moreover, as it is for the sake of his Son that God bestows the Holy Spirit upon us, and yet has deposited him in all his fullness with the Son to be the minister and dispenser of his liberality, he is called at one time the Spirit of the Father, at another the Spirit of the Son: "You are not in the flesh but in the Spirit, if it be that the Spirit of God dwells in you. Now, if any man have not the Spirit of Christ, he is none of his" (Romans 8:9). And hence he encourages us to hope for complete renovation: "If the Spirit of him that raised up Jesus from the dead dwell in you, he that raised up Christ from the dead shall also quicken your mortal bodies by his Spirit that dwells in you" (Romans 8:11). There is no inconsistency in ascribing the glory of those gifts to the Father, inasmuch as he is the author of them, and, at the same time, ascribing them to Christ, with whom they have been deposited that he may bestow them on his people. Hence he invites all the thirsty to come unto him and drink (John 7:37). And Paul teaches that "unto every one of us is given grace, according to the measure of the gift of Christ" (Ephesians 4:7).

And we must remember that the Spirit is called the Spirit of Christ, not only inasmuch as the eternal Word of God is with the Father united with the Spirit, but also in respect of his office of Mediator; because, had he not been endued with the energy of the Spirit, he had come to us in vain. In this sense he is called the "last Adam," and said to have been sent from heaven "a quickening Spirit" (1 Corinthians 15:45), where Paul contrasts the special life which Christ breathes into his people, that they may be one with him, with the animal life which is common even to the reprobate. In like manner, when he prays that believers may have "the grace of our Lord Jesus Christ, and the love of God," he at the same time adds, "the communion of the Holy Ghost," without which no man shall ever taste the paternal favor of God or the benefits of Christ. Thus, also in another passage he says, "The love of God is shed abroad in our hearts by the Holy Ghost, which is given unto us" (Romans 5:5).

A. B. SIMPSON

Walking in the Spirit

We must ever bear in mind, in tracing the Holy Spirit's work in
the believer's heart, the distinction between purity of heart and
maturity of character. From the moment that the soul is yielded
to Christ in full surrender, and He is received as its divine and
indwelling life, we have His purity. The old, sinful self is reckoned
dead, and in no sense is it recognized as our true self. There is
a complete and eternal divorce, and the old heart is henceforth
treated as if it were not, and Christ recognized as the true I—and,
of course, a life that is essentially pure and divine.

But, although wholly separated from the old, sinful life, the
new spirit is yet in its infancy, and before it lie boundless stages
of progress and development. The acorn is as complete in its parts
as the oak of a thousand years, but not as fully developed. And
so the soul which has just received Christ as its abiding life and
sanctification is as wholly sanctified, and as completely one with
Him, as Enoch or John is today—but not as mature.

This is the meaning of Christian growth. We do not grow
into holiness, we receive holiness in Christ as a complete, divine
life; complete in all its parts from the beginning, and divine, as
Christ is. But it is like the infant Christ on Mary's bosom, and it
has to grow up into all the fullness of the stature of perfect manhood in Christ.

This is the work of the Holy Ghost as the mother and the
nurse, the teacher, educator, cherisher of our spiritual life, and it

is in this connection that we must learn to walk in the Spirit, and rise with Him into "all the good pleasure of His goodness, and the work of faith with power," until we shall have reached the fullness of His own prayer for us.

"Now the God of peace that brought again from the dead the Lord Jesus Christ, great Shepherd of the sheep, through the blood of the everlasting covenant, make you perfect in every good work to do His will, working in you that which is pleasing in His sight, through Jesus Christ; to whom be glory forever and ever. Amen."

JONATHAN EDWARDS

An Unpublished Essay on the Trinity

It is a confirmation that the Holy Ghost is God's love and delight, because the saints' communion with God consists in their partaking of the Holy Ghost. The communion of the saints is twofold: it is their communion with God and communion with one another. "That you also may have fellowship with us, and truly our fellowship is with the Father and with His Son, Jesus Christ" (1 John 1:3).

Communion is a common partaking of good, either of excellency or happiness, so that when it is said the saints have communion or fellowship with the Father and with the Son, the meaning of it is that they partake with the Father and the Son of their good—which is either their excellency and glory—"You are made partakers of the Divine nature" (2 Peter 1:4); "That we might be partakers of His holiness" (Hebrews 12:10); "And the glory which You have given Me, I have given them, that they may be one, even as we are one, I in them and You in Me" (John 17:22–23)—or of their joy and happiness: "That they might have My joy fulfilled in themselves" (John 17:13).

But the Holy Ghost, being the love and joy of God, is also His beauty and happiness, and it is in our partaking of the same Holy Spirit that our communion with God consists: "The grace of the Lord Jesus Christ, and the love of God, and the communion of the Holy Ghost, be with you all, amen" (1 Corinthians 13:14). They are not different benefits, but the same that the Apostle here wishes—meaning, in partaking of the Holy Ghost, we possess and enjoy the love and grace of the Father and the Son, for the Holy Ghost is that love and grace. We are said to have fellowship with the Son and not with the Holy Ghost, because therein consists our fellowship with the Father and the Son, even in partaking with them of the Holy Ghost.

JOHN CALVIN

Institutes of the Christian Religion

It is necessary to attend to what I lately said: that our faith in doctrine is not established until we have a perfect conviction that God is its author. Hence, the highest proof of Scripture is uniformly taken from the character of him whose Word it is. The prophets and apostles boast not their own acuteness or any qualities which win credit to speakers, nor do they dwell on reasons; but they appeal to the sacred name of God, in order that the whole world may be compelled to submission.

The next thing to be considered is how it appears not probable merely, but certain, that the name of God is neither rashly nor cunningly pretended. If, then, we would consult most effectually for our consciences, and save them from being driven about in a whirl of uncertainty, from wavering, and even stumbling at the smallest obstacle, our conviction of the truth of Scripture must be derived from a higher source than human conjectures, judgments, or reasons—namely, the secret testimony of the Spirit. It is true, indeed, that if we choose to proceed in the way of arguments, it is easy to establish, by evidence of various kinds, that if there is a God in heaven the Law, the Prophecies, and the Gospel, proceeded from him. Nay, although learned men, and men of the greatest talent, should take the opposite side, summoning and ostentatiously displaying all the powers of their genius in the discussion; if they are not possessed of shameless effrontery, they will be compelled to confess that the Scripture exhibits clear evidence of its being spoken by God, and, consequently, of its containing his heavenly doctrine. . . .

Still, it is preposterous to attempt, by discussion, to rear up a full faith in Scripture. True, were I called to contend with the craftiest despisers of God, I trust, though I am not possessed of the highest ability or eloquence, I should not find it difficult to stop their obstreperous mouths. I could, without much ado, put down the boastings which they mutter in corners, were anything to be gained by refuting their cavils. But although we may maintain the sacred Word of God against gainsayers, it does not follow that we shall forthwith implant the certainty which faith requires in their hearts. Profane men think that religion rests only on opinion, and, therefore, that they may not believe foolishly, or on slight grounds, desire and insist to have it proved by reason that Moses and the prophets were divinely inspired. But I answer that the testimony of the Spirit is superior to reason.

For as God alone can properly bear witness to his own words, so these words will not obtain full credit in the hearts of men until they are sealed by the inward testimony of the Spirit. The same Spirit, therefore, who spoke by the mouths of the prophets must penetrate our hearts in order to convince us that they faithfully delivered the message with which they were divinely entrusted. This connection is most aptly expressed by Isaiah in these words: "My Spirit that is upon you, and my words which I have put in your mouth, shall not depart out of your mouth, nor out of the mouth of your seed, nor out of the mouth of your seed's seed, says the Lord, from henceforth and for ever" (Isaiah 59:21).

SAINT JOHN OF THE CROSS

Spiritual Canticle of the Soul
and the Bridegroom Christ

That which the soul aims at is equality in love with God, the object of its natural and supernatural desire. He who loves cannot be satisfied if he does not feel that he loves as much as he is loved. And when the soul sees that in the transformation in God—such as is possible in this life, notwithstanding the immensity of its love—it cannot equal the perfection of that love with which God loves it, the soul desires the clear transformation of glory in which it shall equal the perfection of love with which it is itself beloved of God. It desires, I say, the clear transformation of glory in which it shall equal His love.

For though in this high state, which the soul reaches on earth, there is a real union of the will, yet it cannot reach that perfection and strength of love which it will possess in the union of glory— seeing that in that time, according to the apostle, the soul will know God as it is known of Him: "Now I know in part; but then shall I know even as also I am known" (1 Corinthians 13:12, KJV). That is: "I shall then love God even as I am loved by Him."

For as the understanding of the soul will then be the understanding of God, and its will the will of God, so its love will also be His love. Though in heaven the will of the soul is not destroyed, it is so intimately united with the power of the will of God, Who loves it, that it loves Him as strongly and as perfectly as it is loved of Him; both wills being united in one sole will and one sole love of God. Thus the soul loves God with the will and strength of God Himself, being made one with that very strength of love with which itself is loved of God.

This strength is of the Holy Spirit, in Whom the soul is there transformed. He is given to the soul to strengthen its love—ministering to it and supplying in it, because of its transformation in glory, that which is defective in it. In the perfect transformation, also, of the state of spiritual marriage such as is possible on earth, in which the soul is all clothed in grace, the soul loves in a certain way in the Holy Spirit, Who is given to it in that transformation.

JOHN WESLEY

From the Sermon,
"On Grieving the Holy Spirit"

We are said to grieve the Holy Spirit by our sins because of his immediate presence with us. They are more directly committed under his eye, and are, therefore, more highly offensive to him. He is pleased to look upon professing Christians as more peculiarly separated to his honor; nay, we are so closely united to him that we are said to be "one spirit with him." Therefore, every sin which we now commit, besides its own proper guilt, carries in it a fresh and infinitely high provocation. "Know ye not your own selves," says St. Paul, "that your bodies are the temples of the Holy Ghost?"

And how are they so, but by his inhabitation and intimate presence with our souls? When, therefore, we set up the idols of earthly inclinations in our hearts (which are properly his altar) and bow down ourselves to serve those vicious passions which we ought to sacrifice to his will, this must be, in the highest degree, offensive and grievous to him. "For what concord is there between" the Holy Spirit "and Belial? Or what agreement has the temple of God with idols?"

We grieve the Holy Spirit by our sins because they are so many contempts of the highest expression of his love, and disappoint him in his last remedy whereby he is pleased to endeavor our recovery. And thus every sin we now commit is done in despite of all his powerful assistances and in defiance of his reproofs—an ungrateful return for infinite lovingkindness!

. . . But if arguments of this kind are not strong enough to keep us from grieving our best friend, the Holy Spirit of God, let us consider that, by this ungrateful conduct, we shall provoke him to withdraw from us.

G. CAMPBELL MORGAN

The Spirit of God

The Holy Spirit is the Creator of beauty. He is revealed in the garnishing of the heavens, in the blue of day, and in the darkness of night with all the splendors of stars scattered in profusion across it. All these are beautiful, and they appeal to the beautiful in man; for they were born of God, as man is born of God. Not only is this true of the beauty which overawes, but also of the form of every leaf and flower and spire of grass. The stately sweep of the sea and the delicate dome of the dew-drop are alike the outworking of the wisdom and energy of the Spirit of God. Man, born of the Spirit, in the grace of transformed life gives evidence of the Spirit's power. So also, in different degree and kind, but none the less certainly, is it with the flowers of the field. Put them under microscopic test, and their exquisiteness and beauty and precision and regularity reveal the working of the Spirit of God. He in nature not only directs the order, but creates the varied and varying beauty.

Again, the Spirit is the breath of renewal. Through death He ever leads to life. That fact is revealed even in the death of the Son of God, for it is written that through the eternal Spirit He offered Himself without blemish unto God. The winter wind that beat upon Him in His dying was but the preface to the summer wind of Pentecost.

These things are to be seen everywhere in nature because the self-same Spirit who works in regeneration works also in generation.

This Spirit, the breath of renewal through death, comes with manifold glory in the spring, bringing a renewal of the earth. Winter's cold precedes spring. Autumn's fire precedes winter's cold. Through fire and cold the Spirit ever moves to new life; and the new forms of beauty, manifold and wondrous, with which the face of the earth is renewed are His.

The truth of this, almost all who have ever tasted of the good gifts of the Holy Spirit must have experienced. It is to be hoped that we have had, some time or other, so lively a sense of his holy influence upon us that when we have been so unhappy as to offend him, we could easily perceive the change in our souls—in that darkness, distress, and despondency which more especially follow the commission of willful and presumptuous sins. At those seasons, when the blessed Spirit retired and concealed his presence from us, we were justly left to a sense of our own wretchedness and misery until we humbled ourselves before the Lord, and by deep repentance and active faith obtained a return of divine mercy and peace.

And the more frequently we offend him, the more we weaken his influences in our souls. For frequent breaches will necessarily occasion estrangement between us, and it is impossible that our intercourse with him can be cordial when it is disturbed by repeated interruptions. A man will forgive his friend a great many imprudences, and some willful transgressions; but to find him frequently affronting him, all his kindness will wear off by degrees; and the warmth of his affection, even towards him who had the greatest share of it, will die away—he cannot but think that such a one does not any longer either desire or deserve to maintain a friendship with him.

JESUS CHRIST:
SAVIOR, SANCTIFIER, HEALER,
AND COMING KING

"When our Lord looked at us, He saw not only what
we were—He was faithful in seeing what we could become!
He took away the curse of being and gave us
the glorious blessing of becoming."

—*Who Put Jesus on the Cross?*

JOHN KNOX

The Scots Confession

When the fullness of time came, God sent his Son—his eternal wisdom, the substance of his own glory—into this world, who took the nature of humanity from the substance of a woman, a virgin, by means of the Holy Ghost. And so was born the "just seed of David," the "Angel of the great counsel of God," the very Messiah promised, whom we confess and acknowledge to be Emmanuel, true God and true man, two perfect natures united and joined in one person. So by our Confession, we condemn the damnable and pestilent heresies of Arius, Marcion, Eutyches, Nestorius, and such others as did either deny the eternity of his Godhead, or the truth of his humanity, or confounded them, or else divided them.

We acknowledge and confess that this wonderful union between the Godhead and the humanity in Christ Jesus did arise from the eternal and immutable decree of God from which all our salvation springs and depends. . . .

We acknowledge that our Lord Jesus offered himself a voluntary sacrifice unto his Father for us; that he suffered contradiction of sinners; that he was wounded and plagued for our transgressions; that he, the clean innocent Lamb of God, was condemned in the presence of an earthly judge so that we should be absolved before the judgment seat of our God; that he suffered not only the cruel death of the cross, which was accursed by the sentence of God, but also that he suffered for a season the wrath of his Father which sinners had deserved. But yet we avow that he remained the only, well-beloved, and blessed Son of his Father even in the midst of his anguish and torment, which he suffered in body and soul to make full atonement for the sins of his people. From this we confess and avow that there remains no other sacrifice for sin; if any affirm so, we do not hesitate to say that they are blasphemers against Christ's death and the everlasting atonement thereby purchased for us.

A. B. SIMPSON

The Fourfold Gospel

The character and life of Christ have a completeness of detail which
no other Bible biography possesses. The story has been written out
by many witnesses, and the portrait is reproduced in all its linea-
ments and features. He has traversed every stage of life from the
cradle to the grave, and represented humanity in every condition
and circumstance of temptation, trial and need, so that His example
is equally suited to childhood, youth or manhood, to the humble
and the poor, in life's lowliest path, or to the sovereign that sways
the widest scepter, for He is at once the lowly Nazarene and the
Lord of Lords. He has felt the throb of every human affection.
He has felt the pang of every human sorrow.

He is the Son of Man in the largest, broadest sense. Nay, His
humanity is so complete that He represents the softer traits of
womanhood as well as the virility and strength of manhood, and
even the simplicity of a little child, so that there is no place in the
experiences of life where we may not look back at this Pattern Life
for light and help as we bring it into touch with our need and ask,
"What would Jesus do?"

God has sent forth the life of Christ as our Example and commanded us to imitate and reproduce Him in our lives. This is not
an ideal picture to study as we would some paragon of art. It is
a life to be lived and it is adapted to all the needs of our present
existence. It is a plain life for a common people to copy, a type of
humanity that we can take with us into the kitchen and the family

room, into the workshop and the place of business, into the field where the farmer toils, and the orchard where the gardener prunes, and the place where the tempter assails, and even the lot where want and poverty press us with their burdens and their cares. This Christ is the Christ of every man who will receive Him as a Brother and follow Him as an Example and a Master. "I have given you an example," He says, "that ye should do as I have done." He expects us to be like Him. Are we copying Him and being made conformable unto His image? There is but one Pattern.

For ages God "sought for a man and found none." At last humanity produced a perfect type and since then God has been occupied in making other men according to this Pattern. He is the one original. When Judson came to America, the religious papers were comparing him to Paul and the early apostles, and Judson wrote expressing his grief and displeasure, saying: "I do not want to be like them. There is but One to copy, Jesus Himself. I want to plant my feet in His footprints and measure their shortcomings by His and His alone. He is the only Copy. I want to be like Him." So let us seek to walk even as He walked.

The secret of a Christ-like life lies partly in the deep longing for it. We grow like the ideals that we admire. We reach unconsciously at last the things we aspire to. Ask God to give you a high conception of the character of Christ and an intense desire to be like Him and you will never rest until you reach your ideal. Let us look at this Ideal.

MARTIN LUTHER

Disputation on the Divinity
and Humanity of Christ

May you preserve this article in its simplicity: that in Christ there is
a divine and a human nature, and these two natures in one person,
so that they are joined together like no other thing, and yet so that
the humanity is not divinity, nor the divinity humanity, because
that distinction in no way hinders but rather confirms the union!
That article of faith shall remain, that Christ is true God and true
man, and thus you shall be safe from all heretics, and even from
Schwenkfeld, who says that Christ is not a creature, and that others teach falsely. . . .

But I am not troubled that he thus seeks to make a name for
himself and works secretly, but more by the fact that better theologians are not moved by these frivolous calumnies to say to him:
"You, wicked man, are a liar! We do not say that Christ is merely
a creature, but that he is God and man in one person. The natures
are joined personally in the unity of the person. There are not
two sons, not two judges, not two persons, not two Jesuses, but
because of the undivided union and the unity of the two natures
there is a communication of attributes, so that what is attributed
to one nature is attributed to the other as well, because they are
one person."

If these articles are held fast, Arius falls along with all heretics,
but Schwenkfeld works secretly like the tooth of the serpent, who
bites secretly so that he cannot be accused. Therefore we are now

holding this disputation so that you may learn the substance and manner of speaking of Scripture and the Fathers.

It is an incomprehensible thing, such as not even the angels can grasp and comprehend, that two natures should be united in one person. Therefore, so that we may grasp this in some small measure, God has given us patterns of speech: that Christ is God and man in one person, and there are not two persons, but two natures are united in one person, so that what is done by the human nature is said also to be done by the divine nature, and vice versa. Thus the Son of God died and was buried in the dust like everyone else, and the son of Mary ascended into heaven and is seated at the right hand of the Father.

D. L. MOODY

The Way to God

In Ephesians 3:18, we are told of "the breadth, and length, and depth, and height" of God's love. Many of us think we know something of God's love, but centuries hence we shall admit we have never found out much about it. Columbus discovered America, but what did he know about its great lakes, rivers, forests, and the Mississippi valley? He died without knowing much about what he had discovered.

When we wish to know the love of God, we should go to Calvary. Can we look upon that scene and say God did not love us? That cross speaks of the love of God. Greater love never has been taught than that which the cross teaches. What prompted God to give up Christ—what prompted Christ to die—if it were not love? "Greater love has no man than this; that a man lay down his life for his friends" (John 15:13).

Christ laid down His life for His enemies; Christ laid down His life for His murderers; Christ laid down His life for them that hated Him; and the spirit of the cross, the spirit of Calvary, is love. When they were mocking Him and deriding Him, what did he say? "Father, forgive them, for they know not what they do" (Luke 23:34).

That is love. He did not call down fire from heaven to consume them. There was nothing but love in His heart.

FRANÇOIS FÉNELON

Maxims of the Saints

Holy souls are without impatience, but not without trouble. They are above murmuring, but not above affliction. The souls of those who are thus wholly in Christ may be regarded in two points of view, or rather in two parts—namely, the natural appetites, propensities, and affections on the one hand, which may be called the inferior part, and the judgment, the moral sense, and the will on the other, which may be described as the superior part.

As things are in the present life, those who are wholly devoted to God may suffer in the inferior part, and may be at rest in the superior. Their wills may be in harmony with the Divine will; they may be approved in their judgments and conscience, and at the same time may suffer greatly in their physical relations and in their natural sensibilities.

In this manner, Christ upon the cross, while His will remained firm in its union with the will of His heavenly Father, suffered much through His physical system. He felt the painful longings of thirst, the pressure of the thorns, and the agony of the spear. He was deeply afflicted also for the friends He left behind Him, and for a dying world. But in His inner and higher nature, where He felt Himself sustained by the secret voice uttered in His sanctified conscience and in His unchangeable faith, He was peaceful and happy.

D. L. MOODY

The Way to God

If we would know what Christ wants to be to us, we must first of all know Him as our Savior from sin. When the angel came down from heaven to proclaim that He was to be born into the world, you remember he gave His name: "He shall be called Jesus [Savior], for He shall save His people from their sins" (Matthew 1:21). Have we been delivered from sin? He did not come to save us *in* our sins, but *from* our sins.

Now, there are three ways of knowing a man. Some men you know only by hearsay; others you merely know by having been once introduced to them—you know them very slightly; others again you know by having been acquainted with them for years— you know them intimately. So I believe there are three classes of people today in the Christian Church and out of it: those who know Christ only by reading or by hearsay—those who have a historical Christ; those who have a slight personal acquaintance with Him; and those who thirst, as Paul did, to "know Him and the power of His resurrection" (Philippians 3:10).

The more we know of Christ, the more we shall love Him and the better we shall serve Him. Let us look at Him as He hangs upon the Cross, and see how He has put away sin. He was manifested that He might take away our sins; and if we really know Him we must first of all see Him as our Savior from sin.

MARTIN LUTHER

From the Sermon,
"Christ Our Great High Priest"

Christ sacrificed not goats nor calves nor birds; not bread; not blood nor flesh, as did Aaron and his posterity. He offered his own body and blood, and the manner of the sacrifice was spiritual, for it took place through the Holy Spirit. Though the body and blood of Christ were visible the same as any other material object, the fact that he offered them as a sacrifice was not apparent. It was not a visible sacrifice, as in the case of offerings at the hands of Aaron. Then the goat or calf, the flesh and blood, were material sacrifices visibly offered, and recognized as sacrifices. But Christ offered himself in the heart before God. His sacrifice was perceptible to no mortal. Therefore, his bodily flesh and blood became a spiritual sacrifice. Similarly, we Christians, the posterity of Christ, offer up our own bodies (Romans 12:1). And our offering is likewise a spiritual sacrifice, or, as Paul has it, a "reasonable service"; for we make it in spirit, and it is beheld of God alone.

Again, in the new order, the tabernacle or house is spiritual; for it is heaven, or the presence of God. Christ hung upon a cross; he was not offered in a temple. He was offered before the eyes of God, and there he still abides. The cross is an altar in a spiritual sense. The material cross was indeed visible, but none knew it as Christ's altar. Again, his prayer, his sprinkled blood, his burnt incense, were all spiritual, for it was all wrought through his spirit.

Accordingly, the fruit and blessing of his office and sacrifice, the forgiveness of our sins and our justification, are likewise spiritual. In the Old Covenant, the priest with his sacrifices and sprinklings of blood effected merely as it were an external absolution, or pardon, corresponding to the childhood stage of the people. The recipient was permitted to move publicly among the people; he was externally holy and as one restored from excommunication. He who failed to obtain absolution from the priest was unholy, being denied membership in the congregation and enjoyment of its privileges; in all respects he was separated like those in the ban today.

But with the priesthood of Christ is true spiritual remission, sanctification, and absolution. These avail before God—God grant that it be true of us—whether we be outwardly excommunicated, or holy, or not. Christ's blood has obtained for us pardon forever acceptable with God. God will forgive our sins for the sake of that blood so long as its power shall last and its intercession for grace in our behalf, which is forever. Therefore, we are forever holy and blessed before God.

SAMUEL RUTHERFORD

A Selection From His Letters

My very dear brother,

You are heartily welcome to my world of suffering, and heartily welcome to my father's house! God give you much joy of your new Master. If I have been in the house before you, I was faithful not to give the house an ill name, or to speak evil of the Lord of the family: I rather wish God's Holy Spirit (O Lord, breathe upon me with that Spirit!) to tell you the fashions of the house (Ezekiel 43:11). One thing I can say is that through waiting on, you will grow a great man with the Lord of the house. Hang on until you get some good from Christ. Take ease yourself, and let Him bear all; lay all your weights and your loads, by faith, on Christ—He can and He will bear you.

I rejoice that He has come and has chosen you in the furnace; it was even there where He and you set tryst. He keeps the good old fashion with you that was in Hosea's days (Hosea 2:14): "Therefore, behold I will allure her, and bring her to the wilderness, and speak comfortably to her." There was no talking to her heart while she was in the fair flourishing city and at ease, but out in the cold, hungry, waste wilderness He allured her; He whispered news into her ear there, and said, "You are mine." What would you think of such a bode? You may soon do worse than say, "Lord, hold all; Lord Jesus, a bargain be it, it shall not go back on my side."

You have gotten a great advantage in the way of heaven, since you have started to the gate in the morning. Like a fool, as I was,

I suffered my sun to be high in the heavens, and near afternoon, before I ever took the gate by the end. I pray you now keep the advantage you have. My heart, be not lazy; set quickly up the brass on hands and feet, as if the last pickle of sand were running out of your glass, and death were coming to turn the glass. And be very careful to take heed to your feet in that slippery and dangerous way of youth that you are walking in. Dry timber will soon take fire. Be covetous and greedy of the grace of God, and beware that it be not a holiness which comes only from the cross; for too many are that way disposed. "When He slew them, then they sought Him, and they returned and inquired early after God." "Nevertheless, they did flatter Him with their mouth, and they lied unto Him with their tongues" (Psalm 78:34, 36). It is part of our hypocrisy to give God fair, white words when He has us in His grips (if I may speak so), and to flatter Him till He win to the fair fields again. Try well green godliness, and examine what it is that you love in Christ. If you love but Christ's sunny side, and would have only summer weather and a land-gate, not a sea-way to heaven, your profession will play you a slip, and the winter-well will go dry again in summer.

Make no sport of Christ; but labor for a sound and lively sight of sin, that you may judge yourself an undone man, a damned slave of hell and of sin, one dying in your own blood—except Christ come and rescue you, and take you up. Therefore, make sure and fast work of conversion. Cast the earth deep; and down, down with the old work, the building of confusion, that was there before. Let Christ lay new work and make a new creation within you.

FRANCIS DE SALES

Treatise on the Love of God

Although our Savior's redemption is applied to us in as many different manners as there are souls, yet love is still the universal means of salvation. It mingles with everything, and without love, nothing is profitable. The Cherubim were placed at the gate of the earthly paradise with their flaming sword to teach us that no one shall enter into the heavenly paradise who is not pierced through with the sword of love.

For this cause, the sweet Jesus who bought us with His blood is infinitely desirous that we should love Him, so that we may eternally be saved—and He desires we may be saved that we may love Him eternally. His love tends to our salvation and our salvation to His love. "Ah!" said He: "I came to cast fire upon the earth; and what do I desire, if it is already kindled?" (Luke 12:49). But to set out more to the life the ardor of this desire, He in admirable terms requires this love from us. "You shall love the Lord your God with your whole heart, and with your whole soul, and with your whole mind. This is the greatest and the first commandment" (Matthew 22:37–38).

Good God! How amorous the divine heart is of our love. Would it not have sufficed to publish a permission giving us leave to love Him, as Laban permitted Jacob to love his fair Rachel, and to gain her by services? Ah no! He makes a stronger declaration of His passionate love of us, and commands us to love Him with all our power, lest the consideration of His majesty and our misery, which make so great a distance and inequality between us, or some other pretext, might divert us from His love.

In this, He well shows that He did not leave in us for nothing the natural inclination to love Him. For to the end it may not be idle, He urges us by this general commandment to employ it. And that this commandment may be effected, He leaves no living man without furnishing him abundantly with all means requisite to do so.

The visible sun touches everything with its vivifying heat, and as the universal lover of inferior things, it imparts to them the vigor necessary to produce. Even so, the divine Goodness animates all souls and encourages all hearts to its love, none being excluded from its heat. "Eternal wisdom," says Solomon, "preaches abroad, she utters her voice in the streets: At the head of multitudes she cries out, in the entrance of the gates of the city she utters her words, saying: 'O children, how long will you love childishness, and fools covet those things which are hurtful to themselves, and the unwise hate knowledge? Turn at my reproof: behold I will utter my spirit to you, and will show you my words' " (Proverbs 1:20–23). And the same wisdom continues in Ezekiel, saying: "Our iniquities and our sins are upon us, and we pine away in them: how then can we live? Say to them: 'As I live,' says the Lord God,' I desire not the death of the wicked, but that the wicked turn from his way, and live' " (Ezekiel 33:10).

See now whether God does not desire we should love Him!

JONATHAN EDWARDS

Discourse on the Excellency of Jesus Christ

There meet in Jesus Christ infinite justice and infinite grace. As Christ is a divine person, he is infinitely holy and just; hating sin, and disposed to execute condign punishment for sin. He is the Judge of the world, and the infinitely just Judge of it, and will not at all acquit the wicked or by any means clear the guilty.

And yet he is infinitely gracious and merciful. Though his justice be so strict with respect to all sin and every breach of the law, yet he has grace sufficient for every sinner, and even the chief of sinners. And it is not only sufficient for the most unworthy to show them mercy and bestow some good upon them, but to bestow the greatest good—yes, it is sufficient to bestow all good upon them, and to do all things for them. There is no benefit or blessing that they can receive so great, but the grace of Christ is sufficient to bestow it on the greatest sinner that ever lived.

And not only so, but so great is his grace that nothing is too much as the means of this good. It is sufficient not only to do great things, but also to suffer in order to it; and not only to suffer, but to suffer most extremely even unto death, the most terrible of natural evils; and not only death, but the most ignominious and tormenting, and every way the most terrible that men could inflict—yes, and greater sufferings than men could inflict, who could only torment the body. He had sufferings in his soul that were the more immediate fruits of the wrath of God against the sins of those he undertakes for.

There do meet in the person of Christ such really diverse excellencies, which otherwise would have been thought utterly incompatible in the same subject—such as are conjoined in no other person whatever, either divine, human, or angelical; and such as neither men nor angels would ever have imagined could have met together in the same person, had it not been seen in the person of Christ.

JOHANNES TAULER

The Inner Way

O God, how greatly we need Your mercy! For we are so foolish and senseless that we often allow little things to keep us back, imagining that we are pleasing God when we sing His praise with many high-sounding words; though the words used by the Savior and His dear disciples were short and simple. Or again, we think we are pleasing God and helping our neighbor by an unjustifiable waste of time and much outward sorrow. Or again, we think it is good and useful for us to carry on much unnecessary business and to delight in our fellow creatures (however holy they may be, or appear to be). . . . Or again, we think we may have and hold many things with delight, and as our own, without spiritual harm—either temporal goods, company, familiar intercourse with relations or spiritual friends—while at the same time we are pleasing our dear Lord and continuing in His love.

Though He was despised, He was sorrowful and poor, and said Himself: "There is no man that has left house, or brethren, or sisters, or father, or mother, or wife, or children, or lands for My sake, but he shall receive an hundredfold now in this time, and in the world to come eternal life." He says also in another place: "He who hates not his father and mother and wife and children, and brethren and sisters, yea, and his own life also, he cannot be My disciple."

O God! Could we but see into the depths of the loving teaching of our dear Lord, we should surely acknowledge at once that all our life is unholy, and that it is not at all that which we imagine it to be. If we ever are to attain to true Divine Peace and be completely united to God, all that is not absolutely necessary, either bodily or spiritually, must be cast off—everything that could interpose itself to an unlawful extent between us and Him, and lead us astray. For He alone will be Lord in our hearts, and none other; for Divine Love can admit of no rival.

A. B. SIMPSON

The Gospel of Healing

Man has a two-fold nature. He is both a material and a spiritual being. And both natures have been equally affected by the fall. His body is exposed to disease; his soul is corrupted by sin. We would therefore expect that any complete scheme of redemption would include both natures, and provide for the restoration of his physical as well as the renovation of his spiritual life. Nor are we disappointed.

The Redeemer appears among men with both hands stretched out to our misery and need. In the one He holds salvation; in the other, healing. He offers Himself to us as a complete Savior; His indwelling Spirit the life of our spirit; His resurrection body the life of our mortal flesh. He begins His ministry by healing all that had need of healing. He closes it by making on the Cross a full atonement for our sin, and then on the other side of the open tomb He passes into Heaven, leaving the double commission for "all the world," and "all the days even unto the end of the world." "Go into all the world and preach the Gospel to every creature." "He that believes and is baptized shall be saved. He that believeth not shall be damned. And these signs shall follow them that believe. In My name they shall cast out devils . . . they shall lay hands upon the sick and they shall recover."

This was "the faith once delivered unto the saints." What has become of it? Why is it not still universally taught and realized? Did it disappear with the Apostolic age? Was it withdrawn when

Peter, Paul, and John were removed? By no means. It remained in the Church for centuries and only disappeared gradually in the growing worldliness, corruption, formalism, and unbelief of the early Christian centuries. With a reviving faith, with a deepening spiritual life, with a more marked and Scriptural recognition of the Holy Spirit and the Living Christ, and with the nearer approach of the returning Master Himself, this blessed Gospel of physical redemption is beginning to be restored to its ancient place, and the Church is slowly learning to reclaim what she never should have lost.

But along with this there is also manifested such a spirit of conservative unbelief and cold, traditional, theological rationalism as to make it necessary that we should "contend earnestly for the faith once delivered unto the saints." First of all we must be sure of our Scriptural foundations. Faith must ever rest on the Divine Word, and the most important element in the "prayer of faith" is a full and firm persuasion that the healing of disease by simple faith in God is, beyond question, a part of the Gospel and a doctrine of the Scriptures.

. . . Thus have we traced the teachings of the Holy Scriptures from Exodus to Patmos. We have seen God giving His people the ordinance of healing in the very outset of their pilgrimage; we have seen it illustrated in the ancient dispensation in the sufferings of Job, the songs of David, and the sad death of Asa; we have seen Isaiah's prophetic vision of the coming Healer; we have seen the Son of Man coming to fulfill that picture to the letter; we have heard Him tell His weeping disciples of His unchanging presence with them; we have seen Him transmit His healing power to their hands; and we have seen them hand it down to us and to the permanent officers of the Church of God, until the latest ages of time.

And now what more evidence can we ask? What else can we do but believe, rejoice, receive, and proclaim this great salvation to a sick and sinking world?

THOMAS À KEMPIS

The Imitation of Christ

Blessed is he who appreciates what it is to love Jesus and who despises himself for the sake of Jesus. Give up all other love for His, since He wishes to be loved alone above all things. Affection for creatures is deceitful and inconstant, but the love of Jesus is true and enduring. He who clings to a creature will fall with its frailty, but he who gives himself to Jesus will ever be strengthened.

Love Him, then; keep Him as a friend. He will not leave you as others do, nor let you suffer lasting death. Sometime, whether you will or not, you will have to part with everything. Cling, therefore, to Jesus in life and death; trust yourself to the glory of Him who alone can help you when all others fail.

Your Beloved is such that He will not accept what belongs to another—He wants your heart for Himself alone, to be enthroned therein as King in His own right. If you but knew how to free yourself entirely from all creatures, Jesus would gladly dwell within you. You will find, apart from Him, that nearly all the trust you place in men is a total loss. Therefore, neither confide in nor depend upon a wind-shaken reed, for "all flesh is grass" (Isaiah 15:6), and all its glory, like the flower of grass, will fade away.

You will quickly be deceived if you look only to the outward appearance of men, and you will often be disappointed if you seek comfort and gain in them. If, however, you seek Jesus in all things, you will surely find Him. Likewise, if you seek yourself, you will find yourself—to your own ruin. For the man who does not seek Jesus does himself much greater harm than the whole world and all his enemies could ever do.

WILLIAM LAW

The Spirit of Prayer

But you will say, "Do not all Christians desire to have Christ to be their Savior?" Yes. But here is the deceit: all would have Christ to be their Savior *in the next world*, and to help them into Heaven when they die, by his power and merits with God. But this is not willing Christ to be your Savior. For his salvation, if it is had, must be had in this world; if he saves you, it must be done in this life by changing and altering all that is within you, by helping you to a new heart, as he helped the blind to see, the lame to walk, and the dumb to speak.

For to have salvation from Christ is nothing else but to be made like unto him; it is to have his humility and meekness, his mortification and self-denial, his renunciation of the spirit, wisdom, and honors of this world, his love of God, his desire of doing God's Will and seeking only his honor. To have these tempers formed and begotten in your heart is to have salvation from Christ. But if you will not have these tempers brought forth in you, if your faith and desire does not seek and cry to Christ for them in the same reality as the lame asked to walk and the blind to see, then you must be said to be unwilling to have Christ to be your Savior.

Consider, how was it that the carnal Jew, the deep-read Scribe, the learned Rabbi, and the religious Pharisee not only did not receive, but *crucified* their Savior? It was because they willed and desired no such Savior as he was, no such inward salvation as He offered to them. They desired no change of their own nature, no inward destruction of their own natural tempers, no deliverance from the love of themselves and the enjoyments of their passions. They liked their state, the gratifications of their old man, their long robes, their broad phylacteries and greetings in the markets. They wanted not to have their pride and self-love dethroned, their covetousness and sensuality to be subdued by a new nature from Heaven derived into them. Their only desire was the success of Judaism, to have an outward savior, a temporal prince, that should establish their law and ceremonies over all the Earth. And therefore they crucified their dear Redeemer, and would have none of his salvation, because it all consisted in a change of their nature, in a new birth from above and a Kingdom of Heaven to be opened within them by the Spirit of God.

Oh Christendom, look not only at the old Jews, but see yourself in this glass. For at this day (oh, sad truth to be told!), a Christ within us, an inward Savior raising a birth of his own nature, life, and spirit within us, is rejected as gross enthusiasm; the learned Rabbi's take counsel against it. The propagation of property, the propagation of Protestantism, the success of some particular church is the salvation which priests and people are chiefly concerned about today.

WALTER HILTON

The Song of Angels

For when a soul offers himself to Jesus truly and humbly, putting all his trust and his desire in Him, and busily keeping Him in mind, our Lord Jesus purges the affection of the soul, and fills it and feeds it with sweetness of Himself. He makes His name feel in the soul as honey, and as song, and as anything that is delectable; so that the soul evermore wants to cry Jesus, Jesus. And the soul has comfort not only in this, but also in psalms and hymns, and anthems of the holy Church. The heart sings them sweetly, devoutly, and freely, without any effort of the soul or bitterness, in the music that the holy Church uses.

This is good, and a gift of God, for the substance of this feeling lies in the love of Jesus, which is fed and illuminated by such songs. Nevertheless, in this manner of feeling, a soul may be deceived by pride—not while the affection sings to Jesus, and loves Jesus in sweetness of Him, but afterward, when it ceases and the heart cools down from the love of Jesus. Then pride may enter in.

Also, a man may be deceived in this way: he hears it said that it is good to have Jesus in his mind, or any other good word of God, so he strains his heart mightily to that name, and by habit he has it nearly always in his mind. Nevertheless, he does not feel by it sweetness in his affection or light of knowing in his reason, but only an abstract thought of God, or of Jesus, or of Mary, or of any other good word. Here may be deceit—not that it is evil to have Jesus in mind in this way, but if he holds this feeling and this thought (which is only by his own effort and habit) to be a special visitation of our Lord, he thinks it more than it is.

For note well that an abstract thought or imagination of Jesus, or of any spiritual thing, without sweetness of love in the affection, and without light of knowing in reason, is but a blindness and a way to deceit, if a man hold it to be more than it is.

CHARLES SPURGEON

The Letters of C. H. Spurgeon

My Dear Father,

Many thanks to you for your kind, instructive, and unexpected letter. My very best love to dear Mother; I hope she will soon be better.

At our last church-meeting, I was proposed. No one has been to see me yet. I hope that now I may be doubly circumspect, and doubly prayerful.

How could a Christian live happily, or live at all, if he had not the assurance that his life is in Christ, and his support, the Lord's undertaking? I am sure I would not have dared to take this great decisive step were it not that I am assured that Omnipotence will be my support, and the Shepherd of Israel my constant Protector. Prayer is to me now what the sucking of milk was to me in my infancy. Although I do not always feel the same relish for it, yet I am sure I cannot live without it.

"When by sin overwhelm'd, shame covers my face, I look unto Jesus who saves by His grace; I call on His name from the gulf of despair, And He plucks me from hell in answer to prayer. Prayer, sweet prayer! Be it ever so feeble, there's nothing like prayer."

Even the Slough of Despond can be passed by the supports of prayer and faith. Blessed be the name of the Lord, despondency has vanished like a mist before the Sun of righteousness, who has shone into my heart! "Truly, God is good to Israel." In the blackest darkness I resolved that, if I never had another ray of comfort, and even if I was everlastingly lost, yet I would love Jesus and endeavor to run in the way of His commandments: from the time that I was enabled thus to resolve, all these clouds have fled.

If they return, I fear not to meet them in the strength of the Beloved. One trial to me is that I have nothing to give up for Christ, nothing wherein to show my love to Him. What I can do is little, and what I do now is less.

The tempter says, "You don't leave anything for Christ; you only follow Him to be saved by it. Where are your evidences?" Then I tell him that I have given up my self-righteousness, and he says, "Yes, but not until you saw it was filthy rags!" All I have to answer is this: that my sufficiency is not of myself.

JULIAN OF NORWICH

Revelations of Divine Love

As truly as God is our Father, so truly is God our Mother. He revealed that in everything, especially in these sweet words where he says: "I am he." That is to say: I am he, the power and goodness of fatherhood; I am he, the wisdom and the lovingness of motherhood; I am he, the light and the grace which is all blessed love; I am he, the Trinity; I am he, the unity; I am he, the great supreme goodness of every kind of thing; I am he who makes you to love; I am he who makes you to long; I am he, the endless fulfilling of all true desires.

For where the soul is highest, noblest, and most honorable, still it is lowest, meekest, and mildest.

And from this foundation in substance we have all the powers of our sensuality by the gift of nature, without which we cannot profit. Our great Father, almighty God, who is being, knows us and loved us before time began. Out of this knowledge, in his most wonderful deep love and by the prescient eternal counsel of all the blessed Trinity, he wanted the second person to become our Mother, our brother, and our savior. From this it follows as truly as God is our Father, so truly is God our Mother. Our Father wills, our Mother works, our good Lord the Holy Spirit confirms. And therefore it is our part to love our God in whom we have our being, reverently thanking and praising him for our creation, mightily praying to our Mother for mercy and pity, and to our Lord the Holy Spirit for help and grace. For in these three is all our life:

nature, mercy, and grace, of which we have mildness, patience, pity, and hatred of sin and wickedness; for the virtues must of themselves hate sin and wickedness.

And so Jesus is our true Mother in nature by our first creation, and he is our true Mother in grace by his taking our created nature. All the lovely works and all the sweet loving offices of beloved motherhood are appropriated to the second person, for in him we have this godly will, whole and safe forever, both in nature and in grace, from his own goodness which is proper to him.

NICHOLAS OF CUSA

The Vision of God

O Jesus, End of the universe, in whom every creature finds rest, as in the Finality of perfection! You are altogether unknown to all the wise of this world because we affirm of You those most true contradictions. For You are Creator and likewise creature, the Attracting and likewise the attracted, the Infinite and likewise the finite. The wise of this world say that to believe that this is possible is foolishness. Hence, they flee from Your name; they do not receive Your light, by which You have enlightened us. Although they consider themselves wise, they will remain forever foolish, ignorant, and blind.

But were they to believe that You are the Christ, God and man, and were they to accept and ponder the words of the Gospel as words of so great a Teacher, then they would come to see the following most clearly: that in comparison to the light hidden in the Gospel in the simplicity of Your words, all else is in every respect ignorance and deepest darkness. Therefore, only humble believers obtain this enlivening and most pleasing revelation.

For as in manna, so in Your most sacred Gospel, which is food from Heaven, there is hidden all desired sweetness—sweetness which can be tasted only by one who believes and partakes. But if anyone believes and accepts, he will most truly find that You descended from Heaven and that You alone are the Teacher of truth.

TERESA OF AVILA

The Life of Saint Teresa of Jesus

What I saw was an image; it was a living image, not a dead man, but the living Christ. And He makes me see that He is God and man—not as He was in the sepulcher, but as He was when He had gone forth from it, risen from the dead. He comes at times in majesty so great that no one can have any doubt that it is our Lord Himself, especially after Communion: we know that He is then present, for faith says so. He shows Himself so clearly to be the Lord of that little dwelling-place that the soul seems to be dissolved and lost in Christ.

O my Jesus, who can describe the majesty wherein You show Yourself! How utterly You are the Lord of the whole world, and of heaven, and of a thousand other and innumerable worlds and heavens, the creation of which is possible to You! The soul understands by that majesty wherein You show Yourself that it is nothing for You to be Lord of all this.

Here it is plain, O my Jesus, how slight is the power of all the devils in comparison with You, and how he who is pleasing unto You is able to tread all hell under his feet. Here we see why the devils trembled when You went down to Limbus, and why they might have longed for a thousand hells still lower, that they might escape from Your terrible Majesty. I see it is Your will that the soul should feel the greatness of Your Majesty, and the power of Your most Sacred Humanity, united with Your Divinity.

Here, too, we see what the day of judgment will be, when we

shall behold the King in His Majesty, and in the rigor of His justice against the wicked. Here we learn true humility, imprinted in the soul by the sight of its own wretchedness, of which now it cannot be ignorant. Here, also, is confusion of face and true repentance for sins; for though the soul sees that our Lord shows how He loves it, yet it knows not where to go, and so is utterly dissolved.

D. L. MOODY

From the Sermon, "Christ in All"

Now we have seen Christ is our Savior, Redeemer, Deliverer, Leader, or Way. But He is more than all that: He is our Light. "I am the light of the world: he that follows me shall not walk in darkness, but shall have the light of life." He shall have the very "light of life." Yes, it is the privilege of every Christian to walk in an unclouded sky.

But do we walk thus in an unclouded sky? No, most Christians are often in darkness. If I were to ask this congregation if they were all walking in the light, I believe there is scarcely one, if he spoke the true feeling of his heart, but would reply, "No, I am often in darkness." Why is that? It is because we are not following Christ, and keeping close to Him. We are much in darkness when we might be in the light.

Suppose the windows of this building were all closed, and we were complaining of the darkness, what would any one say to us? Why, they would say, "Admit the light; open the windows all round, and you'll soon have plenty of light." Similarly we must let in Christ, who is the light, and open our minds to receive Him, and we shall soon walk in light. There is a great deal of darkness at the present time, even in the hearts of God's own people. But follow Him, and then you will have plenty of light. Then Christ will show to each of us that He is "The Light." And He will do more: He will set us on fire with His light, that we also may shine as lights in this dark world.

May God help His own people to shine brightly, to flash out of darkness, that men may take knowledge of us that we have been with Jesus. But remember, the world hates the light. Christ was the light of the world, and the world sought to extinguish it at Calvary. Now He has left His people to shine. "You are the light of the world." He has left us here to shine. He means us to be "living epistles, known and read of all men." The world is certain to watch, and to read you and me. If we are inconsistent, then you may be sure the world will take occasion to stumble at us.

The world finds plenty of difficulties on the way; let us see that we Christians do not add more stumbling-blocks by our un-Christlike walk.

God help us to keep our lights burning clear and brilliant! Out West a friend of mine was walking along one of the streets one dark night, and saw approaching him a man with a lantern. As he came up close to him he noticed by the bright light that the man had no eyes. He went past, but the thought struck him, "Surely that man is blind." He turned round, and said, "My friend, are you not blind?" "Yes." "Then what have you got the lantern for?" "I carry the lantern that people may not stumble over me, of course," said the blind man. Let us take a lesson from that blind man, and hold up our light, burning with the clear radiance of heaven, that men may not stumble over us.

JOHN CALVIN

Institutes of the Christian Religion

I come to the Kingly office of Christ, of which it were in vain to speak without previously reminding the reader that its nature is spiritual. Because it is from thence we learn its efficacy, the benefits it confers, its whole power and eternity. Eternity, moreover, which in Daniel an angel attributes to the office of Christ (Daniel 2:44), in Luke an angel justly applies to the salvation of his people (Luke 1:33). But this is also twofold, and must be viewed in two ways; the one pertains to the whole body of the Church, the other is proper to each member.

To the former is to be referred what is said in the Psalms: "Once have I sworn by my holiness, that I will not lie unto David. His seed shall endure forever, and his throne as the sun before me. It shall be established forever, as the moon, and as a faithful witness in heaven" (Psalm 89:35, 37). There can be no doubt that God here promises that he will be, by the hand of his Son, the eternal governor and defender of the Church. In none but Christ will the fulfillment of this prophecy be found, since immediately after Solomon's death the kingdom in great measure lost its dignity, and, with ignominy to the family of David, was transferred to a private individual. Afterwards decaying by degrees, it at length came to a sad and dishonorable end. In the same sense are we to understand the exclamation of Isaiah: "Who shall declare his generation?" (Isaiah 53:8). For he asserts that Christ will so survive death as to be connected with his members.

Therefore, as often as we hear that Christ is armed with eternal power, let us learn that the perpetuity of the Church is thus effectually secured; that amid the turbulent agitations by which it is constantly harassed, and the grievous and fearful commotions which threaten innumerable disasters, it still remains safe. Thus, when David derides the audacity of the enemy who attempts to throw off the yoke of God and his anointed, and says that kings and nations rage "in vain" (Psalm 2:2–4) because he who sits in heaven is strong enough to repel their assaults, assuring believers of the perpetual preservation of the Church, he animates them to have good hope whenever it is occasionally oppressed.

So, in another place, when speaking in the person of God, he says, "The Lord said unto my Lord, 'Sit at my right hand, until I make your enemies your footstool' " (Psalm 110:1), he reminds us that however numerous and powerful the enemies who conspire to assault the Church, they are not possessed of strength sufficient to prevail against the immortal decree by which he appointed his Son eternal King. Whence it follows that the devil, with the whole power of the world, can never possibly destroy the Church, which is founded on the eternal throne of Christ.

Then, in regard to the special use to be made by each believer, this same eternity ought to elevate us to the hope of a blessed immortality. For we see that every thing which is earthly, and of the world, is temporary and soon fades away. Christ, therefore, to raise our hope to the heavens, declares that his kingdom is not of this world (John 18:36). In fact, let each of us, when he hears that the kingdom of Christ is spiritual, be roused by the thought to entertain the hope of a better life, and to expect that as it is now protected by the hand of Christ, so it will be fully realized in a future life.

JOHN WESLEY

From the Sermon, "On the Holy Spirit"

Everything in Christianity is some kind of anticipation of something that is to be at the end of the world. If the apostles were to preach by their Master's command "that the kingdom of God drew nigh," the meaning was that from henceforth all men should fix their eyes on that happy time, foretold by the prophets, when the Messiah should come and restore all things; that by renouncing their worldly conversation, and submitting to the gospel institution, they should fit themselves for, hasten, that blessing. "Now are we the sons of God," as John tells us, and yet what he imparts to us at present will hardly justify that title without taking in that fullness of his image which shall then be displayed in us when we shall be "the children of God, by being the children of the resurrection."

True believers, then, are entered upon a life the sequel of which they know not; for it is "a life hid with Christ in God." He, the forerunner, has attained the end of it, being gone unto the Father. But we can know no more of it than appeared in him while he was upon earth. And even that, we shall not know but by following his steps—which, if we do, we shall be so strengthened and renewed day by day in the inner man that we shall desire no comfort from the present world through a sense of "the joy set before us." Even though, as to the outward man, we shall be subject to distresses and decays, and treated as the scourges of all things.

G. CAMPBELL MORGAN

Discipleship

"Disciples" is the term consistently used in the four Gospels to mark the relationship existing between Christ and His followers. Jesus used it Himself in speaking of them, and they in speaking of each other. Neither did it pass out of use in the new days of Pentecostal power. It runs right through the Acts of the Apostles. It is interesting also to remember that it was on this wise that the angels thought and spoke of these men; the use of the word in the days of the Incarnation is linked to the use of the word in the apostolic age by the angelic message to the women, "Go, tell his disciples and Peter" (Mark 16:7).

It is somewhat remarkable that the word is not to be found in the Epistles. This is to be accounted for by the fact that the Epistles were addressed to Christians in their corporate capacity as churches, and so spoke of them as members of such, and as the "saints" or separated ones of God. The term *disciple* marks an individual relationship, and though it has largely fallen out of use, it is of the utmost value still in marking that relationship, existing between Christ and each single soul and suggesting our consequent position in all the varied circumstances of everyday living. It is to that study we desire to come in this series of papers.

The word itself signifies a taught or trained one, and gives us the ideal of relationship. Jesus is the Teacher. He has all knowledge of the ultimate purposes of God for man, of the will of God concerning man, of the laws of God that mark for man the path of his progress and final crowning.

Disciples are those who gather around this Teacher and are trained by Him. Seekers after truth, not merely in the abstract, but as a life force, come to Him and join the circle of those to whom He reveals these great secrets of all true life. Sitting at His feet, they learn from the unfolding of His lessons the will and ways of God for them; and obeying each successive word, they realize within themselves the renewing force and uplifting power thereof. The true and perpetual condition of discipleship, and its ultimate issue, were clearly declared by the Lord Himself: "If ye abide in My word, then are ye truly My disciples; and ye shall know the truth, and the truth shall make you free" (John 8:31).

Before considering the glorious enduement the Teacher confers on every disciple, and the stern requirements that guard the entrance to discipleship, it is very important that we should have clearly outlined in our minds the true meaning of this phase of the relationship, which Jesus bears to His people. It is not that of a lecturer, from whose messages men may or may not deduce applications for themselves. It is not that of a prophet merely, making a Divine pronouncement and leaving the issues of the same. It certainly is not that of a specialist on a given subject, declaring his knowledge to the interest of a few, the amazement of more, and the bewilderment of most. It is none of these.

It is that of a teacher—Himself possessing full knowledge—bending over a pupil, and for a set purpose, with an end in view, imparting knowledge step by step, point by point, ever working on toward a definite end. That conception includes also the true ideal of our position. We are not casual listeners, neither are we merely interested hearers desiring information. We are disciples, looking toward and desiring the same end as the Master, and therefore listening to every word, marking every inflection of voice that carries meaning, and applying all our energy to realizing the Teacher's purpose for us. Such is the ideal.

SAMUEL RUTHERFORD

A Selection From His Letters

Grace, mercy, and peace be to you. If death, which is before you and us all, were any other thing than a friendly dissolution and a change, not a destruction of life, it would seem a hard voyage to go through such a sad and dark trance, so thorny a valley, as is the wages of sin. But I am confident that you know the way, though your foot never trod in that black shadow. The loss of life is gain to you. If Christ Jesus be the period, the end, and lodging home at the end of your journey, there is no fear; you go to a friend. And since ye have had communion with Him in this life, and He has a pawn or pledge of yours, even the largest share of your love and heart, you may look death in the face with joy.

But though He be the same Christ in the other life that you found Him to be here, yet He is so far in His excellency, beauty, sweetness, irradiations, and beams of majesty when He is seen as He is, above what He appeared here, that you shall mistake Him, and He shall appear a new Christ—as water at the fountain, apples in the orchard and beside the tree, have more of their native sweetness, taste, and beauty, than when transported to us some hundred miles.

I mean not that Christ can lose any of His sweetness in the carrying, or that He, in His Godhead and loveliness of presence, can be changed to the worse between the little spot of the earth that you are in and the right hand of the Father far above all heavens. But the change will be in you, when you shall have new senses, and the soul shall be a more deep and more capacious vessel to take in more of Christ; and when means (the chariot, the Gospel, that He is now carried in, and ordinances that convey Him) shall be removed. Surely you cannot now be said to see Him face to face, or to drink of the wine of the highest fountain, or to take in seas and tides of fresh love immediately, without vessels or messengers, at the Fountain itself—as ye will do a few days hence, when ye shall be so near as to be with Christ.

Death is but an awesome step, over time and sin, to sweet Jesus Christ, who knew and felt the worst of death. For death's teeth hurt Him. We know death has no teeth now, no jaws, for they are broken. It is a free prison; citizens pay nothing for the grave. The jailer who had the power of death is destroyed. Praise and glory be to the First-begotten of the dead!

6

PRACTICING
THE PRESENCE OF GOD

"I want the presence of God Himself,
or I don't want anything at all to do with religion. . . .
I want all that God has or I don't want any."

—*The Counselor*

BROTHER LAWRENCE

The Practice of the Presence of God

Since you desire so earnestly that I should communicate to you
the method by which I arrived at that habitual sense of God's
presence—which our Lord, of His mercy, has been pleased to
vouchsafe to me—I must tell you that it is with great difficulty
that I am prevailed on by your importunities, and now I do it
only upon the terms that you show my letter to nobody. If I knew
that you would let it be seen, all the desire that I have for your
advancement would not be able to determine me to it.

The account I can give you is this. Having found in many
books different methods of going to God, and diverse practices
of the spiritual life, I thought this would serve rather to puzzle
me than facilitate what I sought after, which was nothing but how
to become wholly God's. This made me resolve to give the all for
the All. So, after having given myself wholly to God, to make all
the satisfaction I could for my sins, I renounced, for the love of
Him, everything that was not He, and I began to live as if there
was none but He and I in the world.

Sometimes I considered myself before Him as a poor criminal
at the feet of his judge; at other times I beheld Him in my heart
as my Father, as my God. I worshipped Him as often that I could,
keeping my mind in His holy Presence and recalling it as often
as I found it wandered from Him. I found no small pain in this
exercise, and yet I continued it, notwithstanding all the difficulties that occurred, without troubling or disquieting myself when

my mind had wandered involuntarily. I made this my business, as much all the day long as at the appointed times of prayer—for at all times, every hour, every minute, even in the height of my business, I drove away from my mind everything that was capable of interrupting my thought of God.

Such has been my common practice ever since I entered into religion. And though I have done it very imperfectly, yet I have found great advantages by it. These, I well know, are to be imputed to the mere mercy and goodness of God, because we can do nothing without Him—and I still less than any. But when we are faithful to keep ourselves in His holy Presence, and set Him always before us, this not only hinders our offending Him and doing anything that may displease Him, at least willfully, but it also begets in us a holy freedom. And if I may so speak, it begets a familiarity with God wherewith we ask, and that successfully, the graces we stand in need of.

By often repeating these acts, they become habitual, and the presence of God is rendered as it were natural to us. Give Him thanks, if you please, with me, for His great goodness towards me, which I can never sufficiently admire, and for the many favors He has done to so miserable a sinner as I am. May all things praise Him. Amen.

ANONYMOUS

The Cloud of Unknowing

Lift up your heart unto God with a meek stirring of love, focusing on God Himself and none of His goods. As you do this, be loathe to think on anything but God so that nothing works its way into your wit, nor in your will, but only Himself. To achieve this is to forget all the creatures that ever God made and the works of them, so that your thoughts and desires be not directed nor stretched to any of them, neither in general nor in special. Let all created things be, and take no heed to them. This is the work of the soul that most pleases God.

All saints and angels take joy in this work, and they all hasten to help it with all their might. All fiends are furious when you do this, and they try to defeat it in every way they can. All men living in earth can be wonderfully helped by this work, though you don't understand how. Yes, even the souls in purgatory can be eased of their pain by virtue of this work. You yourself can be cleansed and made virtuous by this work more than any other, and yet it is the lightest work of all when a soul is helped with grace, and it can soon be done.

Therefore don't wait, but work at it until you clear your mind of everything but God. The first time you try this, you will find only a darkness—a "cloud of unknowing," as it were—and you won't understand what it is, except that you feel in your will a naked intent unto God. This darkness and this cloud will be, whatever you try, between you and your God, and it will allow you to neither see Him clearly by the light of understanding in your reason, nor to feel Him in the sweetness of love in your affection.

Therefore shape yourself to abide in this darkness as long as you are able, evermore crying after Him that you love. For if you ever shall feel God or see Him, as it may be here, it behooves you always to be in this cloud of darkness. And if you will busily work as I have instructed you, I trust in His mercy that you shall come to it.

WILLIAM LAW

A Collection of Letters

The first business of a clergyman awakened by God into a sensibility and love of the truths of the gospel, and of making them equally felt and loved by others, is to thankfully, joyfully, and calmly adhere to and give way to the increase of this new-risen light, and by true introversion of his heart to God, as the sole author of it, humbly beg of him that all that he feels a desire of doing to those under his cure may be first truly and fully done in himself.

Now the way to become more and more awakened, to feel more and more of this first conviction or work of God within you, is not to reflect and reason yourself into a further and deeper sensibility of it by finding out arguments to strengthen it in your mind. But the one true way is, in faith and love, to keep close to the presence and power of God, which has manifested itself within you, willingly resigned to and solely depending upon the one work of his all-creating Word and all-quickening Spirit, which is always more or less powerful in us, according as we are more or less trusting to and depending upon it.

And thus it is that by faith we are saved, because God is always ours in such proportion as we are his; as our faith is in him, such is his power and presence in us. What an error, therefore, to turn one thought from him, or cast a look after any help but his; for if we ask all of him, if we seek for all in him, if we knock only at his own door of mercy in Christ Jesus and patiently wait and abide there, God's kingdom must come, and his will must be done in us.

A. B. SIMPSON

Walking in the Spirit

What is it to live in the Spirit? It is to be born of the Spirit. It is
to have received a new spiritual life from above. "That which is
born of the flesh is flesh, that which is born of the Spirit is Spirit."
"Except a man be born of water and of the Spirit, he cannot
enter into the Kingdom of God." "If any man be in Christ, he
is a new creature; old things have passed away; behold, all things
have become new."

We may have the brightest intellectual life, the most unblem-
ished moral character, and the most amiable qualities of disposition,
and yet without the new life of the Holy Spirit in our heart, we
can no more enter Heaven than the lovely canary that sings in our
window can become a member of our family, or the gentle lamb
that our children play with can sit down at our table, and share
our domestic fellowship and enjoyment. It belongs to a different
world, and nothing but a new nature and human heart could bring
it into fellowship with our human life. The most exalted intellect,
and the most attractive, natural disposition, reach no higher than
the earthly. The Kingdom of Heaven consists of the family of
God, those who have risen to an entirely different sphere, and
received a nature as much above the intellectual and the moral as
God is above an angel.

A modern writer has finely wrought out this wonderful thought
of the difference between the various orders of life, even in the
natural world. The little tuft of moss that grows upon the granite

rock can look down from immeasurable heights upon the mass of stone on which it rests and say, "I am transcendently above you, for I have life, vegetable life, and you are an inorganic mass!" And yet, as we ascend one step, the smallest insect that crawls upon the majestic palm tree can look down upon the most beautiful production of the vegetable world and say, "I am transcendently above you, for I have animal life, and you have not even the consciousness of your own loveliness, or of the little creature that feeds upon your blossom!" Still higher we ascend, until we reach the world of mind; and the youngest child of the most illiterate peasant can say to the mightiest creations of the animal world—to the majestic lion, king of the forest; the soaring eagle of the skies; the many-tinted bird of Paradise, or the noble steed that bears his master, like the whirlwind, over the desert—"I am your lord, for I possess intellectual life, and you have neither soul nor reason, and must perish with your expiring breath, and become like the clods beneath your feet, but I shall live forever."

But there is still another step beyond all this. There is a spiritual world which is as much higher than the intellectual as that is above the physical; and the humblest and most uncultured Christian, who has just learned to pray and say, "Our Father, who art in Heaven" from the depths of a regenerate heart, is as much above the loftiest genius of the world of mind as he is above the material creation at his feet.

This is the meaning of Christianity; it is the breath of a new nature; it is the translation of the soul into a higher universe and a loftier scale of being, even introducing it into the family of God Himself and making it a part of the Divine nature. This is indeed a stupendous mystery, and a bestowment whose glory may well fill our hearts with everlasting wonder, as we cry with the adoring apostle, "Behold what manner of love the Father hath bestowed upon us, that we should be called the sons of God!"

MEISTER ECKHART

From the Sermon,
"The Nearness of the Kingdom"

Professors and theologians have often asked how it is possible for the soul to know God. It is not from severity that God demands much from men in order to obtain the knowledge of Himself. Rather, it is of His kindness that He wills the soul by effort to grow capacious of receiving much, so that He may give much.

Let no man think that to attain this knowledge is too difficult— although it may sound so, and indeed the commencement of it and the renouncement of all things is difficult. But when one attains to it, no life is easier nor more pleasant nor more lovable, since God is always endeavoring to dwell with man and teach him in order to bring him to Himself.

Indeed, no man desires anything so eagerly as God desires to bring men to the knowledge of Himself. God is always ready, but we are very unready. God is near us, but we are far from Him. God is within, and we are without. God is friendly; we are estranged. The prophet said, "God leads the righteous by a narrow path into a broad and wide place, that is into the true freedom of those who have become one spirit with God." May God help us all to follow Him that He may bring us to Himself. Amen.

JAN VAN RUYSBROECK

The Spiritual Espousals

Now, if the spirit is to contemplate God with God, without intermediary, in this divine light, three things are necessary for a person.

The first is that he must be well-ordered from without in all virtues and unhindered within—just as empty of all outward works as though he were not working. For if he is busy within by any work of virtue, then he is assailed by images. And as long as that is going on inside him, he cannot contemplate.

Secondly, he must cleave to God within by devoted intention and love, just like a kindled, blazing fire that can no longer be extinguished. During the time that he feels himself to be in this state, he can contemplate.

Thirdly, he must have lost himself in a waylessness and in a darkness in which all contemplatives wander around in enjoyment and can no longer find themselves in a creaturely way. In the abyss of this darkness, in which the loving spirit has died to itself, there begins the revelation of God and eternal life. For in this darkness there shines and is born an incomprehensible light which is the Son of God, in whom one contemplates eternal life.

And in this light one becomes seeing.

FRANCIS DE SALES

Introduction to the Devout Life

When God created the world, He commanded each tree to bear fruit after its kind. And even so He bids Christians, the living trees of His Church, to bring forth fruits of devotion—each one according to his kind and vocation. A different exercise of devotion is required of each—the noble, the artisan, the servant, the prince, the maiden, and the wife; furthermore, such practice must be modified according to the strength, the calling, and the duties of each individual.

I ask you, my child, would it be fitting that a Bishop should seek to lead the solitary life of a Carthusian? Or if the father of a family were as regardless in making provision for the future as a Capucin, or if the artisan spent the day in church like a Religious, or if the Religious involved himself in all manner of business on his neighbor's behalf, as a Bishop is called upon to do? Would not such devotion be ridiculous, ill-regulated, and intolerable? Nevertheless such a mistake is often made, and the world, which cannot or will not discriminate between real devotion and the indiscretion of those who fancy themselves devout, grumbles and finds fault with devotion (which is really nowise concerned in these errors).

No indeed, my child, the devotion which is true hinders nothing; on the contrary, it perfects everything. And that which runs counter to the rightful vocation of any person is, you may be sure, a spurious devotion. Aristotle says that the bee sucks honey from flowers without damaging them, leaving them as whole and fresh

234

as it found them. But true devotion does better still, for it not only hinders no manner of vocation or duty, but rather adorns and beautifies all. Throw precious stones into honey, and each will grow more brilliant according to its several color. And, in like manner, everybody fulfills his special calling better when subject to the influence of devotion—family duties are lighter, married love truer, service to our King more faithful, every kind of occupation more acceptable and better performed where that is the guide.

It is an error—nay more, a heresy—to seek to banish the devout life from the soldier's guardroom, the mechanic's workshop, the prince's court, or the domestic hearth. Of course, a purely contemplative devotion, such as is specially proper to the religious and monastic life, cannot be practiced in these outer vocations, but there are various other kinds of devotion well-suited to lead those whose calling is secular along the paths of perfection.

The Old Testament furnishes us examples in Abraham, Isaac, Jacob, David, Job, Tobias, Sarah, Rebecca, and Judith; and in the New Testament we read of Joseph, Lydia, and Crispus, all of whom led a perfectly devout life in their trades. We have Anne, Martha, Monica, Aquila, and Priscilla as examples of household devotion; Cornelius, Sebastian, and Maurice among soldiers; Constantine, Helena, Louis, and Edward on the throne. And we even find instances of some who fell away in solitude—usually so helpful to perfection—some who had led a higher life in the world, which seems so antagonistic to it. Saint Gregory dwells on how Lot, who had kept himself pure in the city, fell in his mountain solitude. Be sure that wherever our lot is cast we may and must aim at the perfect life.

JOHANNES TAULER

The Following of Christ

The question here occurs: What is freedom? Freedom is a complete purity and detachment that seeks the Eternal. Freedom is an isolated, withdrawn being identical with God, or entirely attached to God. Poverty is an isolated condition, an existence withdrawn from all creatures, and therefore poverty is free. A free soul dismisses all defect and all created things; it penetrates into the increate good— that is, God—and acquires it with violence. As Christ said: "The kingdom of heaven suffers violence, and the mighty take it" (Matthew 11:12). God is the kingdom of heaven to souls; if therefore a soul leaves all things and clings to God alone, she acquires God by constraint. For God cannot withhold Himself; He must give Himself to her, for it is His nature that He communicates Himself to the soul that is receptive of Him.

To a free soul all things are equal—pleasure or pain, chiding or praise, riches or poverty, weal or woe, friend or foe. A free soul does not let itself be drawn away by anything that might separate it or mediate between it and God, as Paul said: "Who shall separate us from God?" (Romans 8:35). All things rather further it to God, and she presses forward through all that intervenes to her first original.

A free soul seizes and wins all virtue—and not only virtue, but also the essence of virtue. Nothing binds it except virtue, and the most intimate and purest virtue; but this is no bond, rather is it the way of freedom. And then is the soul thoroughly free when she can only endure what is best and entirely abandon evil. For freedom does not consist in sins, but slavery. Genuine freedom is so noble that no one gives it away save God the Father, for it is a power flowing immediately from God the Father into the soul, and giving all capacity to the soul. As Paul said: "I am able to do all things in Him that strengtheneth me" (Philippians 4:13).

FRANÇOIS FÉNELON

The Inner Life

What men stand most in need of is the knowledge of God. They know, to be sure, by dint of reading, that history gives an account of a certain series of miracles and marked providences. They have reflected seriously on the corruption and instability of worldly things. They are even, perhaps, convinced that the reformation of their lives on certain principles of morality is desirable in order to their salvation. But the whole of the edifice is destitute of foundation; this pious and Christian exterior possesses no soul.

The living principle that animates every true believer—God, the all and in all, the author and the sovereign of all—is wanting. he is in all things infinite—in wisdom, power, and love—and what wonder, if everything that comes from his hand should partake of the same infinite character and set at nothing the efforts of human reason.

When he works, his ways and his thoughts are declared by the prophet to be as far above our ways and our thoughts as the heavens are above the earth. He makes no effort when he would execute what he has decreed, for to Him all things are equally easy. He speaks and causes the heavens and the earth to be created out of nothing, with as little difficulty as he causes water to descend or a stone to fall to the ground. His power is co-extensive with his will; when he wills, the thing is already accomplished.

When the Scriptures represent him as speaking in the creation of the world, it is not to be understood as signifying that it was necessary that the word of command should issue from him in order that the universe he was about to create should hear and obey his will; that word was simple and interior, neither more nor less than the thought which he conceived of what he was about to do and the will to do it. The thought was fertile, and without being rendered exterior, begat from him as the fountain of all life the sum of the things that are.

His mercy, too, is but his pure will. He loved us before the creation of the world; he saw and knew us, and he prepared his blessings for us. He loved and chose us from all Eternity. Every new blessing we receive is derived from this Eternal origin. He forms no new will respecting us; it is not he that changes, but we. When we are righteous and good, we are conformable to his will and agreeable to him. When we depart from well doing and cease to be good, we cease to be conformable to him and to please him. This is the immutable standard which the changeable creature is continually approaching and leaving. His justice against the wicked and his love towards the righteous are the same thing; it is the same quality that unites him to everything that is good, and is incompatible with everything that is evil.

Mercy is the goodness of God beholding our wickedness and striving to make us good; perceived by us in time, it has its source in the eternal love of God for his creature. From him alone proceeds true goodness. Alas! For that presumptuous soul that seeks it in itself! It is God's love towards us that gives us everything, but the richest of his gifts is that we may love him with that love which is his due.

When he is able by his love to produce that love in us, he reigns within; he constitutes there our life, our peace, our happiness, and we then already begin to taste that blissful existence which he enjoys. His love towards us is stamped with his own character of infinity. It is not like our love, bounded and constrained; when he loves, all the measures of his love are infinite. He comes down from Heaven to earth to seek the creature of clay whom he loves. He becomes creature and clay with him. He gives him his flesh to eat.

These are the prodigies of Divine love in which the Infinite outstrips all the affection we can manifest. He loves like a God, with a love utterly incomprehensible. It is the height of folly to seek to measure infinite love by human wisdom. Far from losing any element of its greatness in these excesses, he impresses upon his love the stamp of his own grandeur, while he manifests a delight in us bounded only by the infinite. Oh! How great and lovely is he in his mysteries! But we want eyes to see them, and have no desire to behold God in everything.

BROTHER LAWRENCE

The Practice of the Presence of God

There is not in the world a kind of life more sweet and delightful than that of a continual conversation with God. Those only can comprehend it who practice and experience it, yet I do not advise you to do it from that motive. It is not pleasure which we ought to seek in this exercise, but let us do it from a principle of love, and because God would have us.

Were I a preacher, I should above all other things preach the practice of the presence of God. And were I a director, I should advise all the world to do it—so necessary do I think it, and so easy, too.

Ah! Knew we but the want we have of the grace and assistance of God, we should never lose sight of Him—no, not for a moment. Believe me, make immediately a holy and firm resolution never more willfully to forget Him, and to spend the rest of your days in His sacred presence, deprived for the love of Him, if He thinks fit, of all consolations. Set heartily about this work, and if you do it as you ought, be assured that you will soon find the effects of it. I will assist you with my prayers, poor as they are. I recommend myself earnestly to yours, and those of your holy society.

AUGUSTINE OF HIPPO

Confessions

If to any man the tumult of the flesh grew silent—silent the images of earth and sea and air—and if the heavens grew silent, and the very soul grew silent to herself and by not thinking of self mounted beyond self;

If all dreams and imagined visions grew silent, and every tongue and every sign and whatsoever is transient—for indeed if any man could hear them, he should hear them saying with one voice: "We did not make ourselves, but He made us who abides forever"; but if, having uttered this and so set us to listening to Him who made them, they all grew silent, and in their silence He alone spoke to us, not by them but by Himself so that we should hear His word not by any tongue of flesh nor the voice of an angel nor the sound of thunder nor in the darkness of a parable, but that we should hear Himself whom in all these things we love, should hear Himself and not them—just as we two had but now reached forth and in a flash of the mind attained to touch the eternal Wisdom which abides over all;

And if this could continue, and all other visions so different be quite taken away, and this one should so ravish and absorb and wrap the beholder in inward joys that his life should eternally be such as that one moment of understanding for which we had been sighing—would not this be: "Enter into the joy of your Lord"?

JAN VAN RUYSBROECK

The Adornment of the Spiritual Marriage

Spiritual inebriation is this: that a man receives more sensible joy
and sweetness than his heart can either contain or desire. Spiritual
inebriation brings forth many strange gestures in men. It makes
some sing and praise God because of their fullness of joy, and
some weep with great tears because of their sweetness of heart. It
makes one restless in all his limbs, so that he must run and jump
and dance, and so excites another that he must gesticulate and clap
his hands. Another cries out with a loud voice and so shows forth
the plenitude he feels within; another must be silent and melt away
because of the rapture which he feels in all his senses.

At times he thinks that all the world must feel what he feels;
at times he thinks that none can taste what he has attained. Often
he thinks that he never could, nor ever shall, lose this well-being;
at times he wonders why all men do not become God-desiring. At
one time he thinks that God is for him alone, or for none other so
much as for him; at another time he asks himself with amazement
of what nature these delights can be, and whence they come, and
what has happened to him.

This is the most rapturous life (as regards our bodily feelings)
which man may attain upon earth. Sometimes the excess of joy
becomes so great that the man thinks that his heart must break.
And for all these manifold gifts and miraculous works, he shall,
with a humble heart, thank and praise and honor and reverence the
Lord, who can do all this, and thank Him with fervent devotion

because it is His will to do all this. And the man shall always keep in his heart and speak through his mouth with sincere intention: "Lord, I am not worthy of this; yet I have need of Your boundless goodness and of Your support." In such humility he may grow and rise into higher virtues.

TERESA OF AVILA

The Interior Castle

Therefore, sisters, I think it best for us to place ourselves in the presence of God—contemplate His mercy and grandeur and our own vileness and leave Him to give us what He will, whether water or drought, for He knows best what is good for us. Thus we enjoy peace and the devil will have less chance to deceive us.

Amongst these favors, at once painful and pleasant, Our Lord sometimes causes in the soul a certain jubilation and a strange and mysterious kind of prayer. If He bestows this grace on you, praise Him fervently for it. I describe it so that you may know that it is something real. I believe that the faculties of the soul are closely united to God, but that He leaves them at liberty to rejoice in their happiness together with the senses, although they do not know what they are enjoying nor how they do so. This may sound nonsense but it really happens. So excessive is its jubilee that the soul will not enjoy it alone, but speaks of it to all around so that they may help it to praise God, which is its one desire.

Oh, what rejoicings would this person utter and what demonstrations would she make, if possible, so that all might know her happiness! She seems to have found herself again and wishes, like the father of the prodigal son, to invite all her friends to feast with her and to see her soul in its rightful place—because, at least for the time being, she cannot doubt its security. I believe she is right, for the devil could not possibly infuse a joy and peace into the very center of her being which makes her whole delight consist in urging others to praise God. It requires a painful effort to keep silent and to dissemble such impulsive happiness.

JULIAN OF NORWICH

Showing of Love

And in this he showed me a little thing: the quantity of a hazel-nut, lying in the palm of my hand. And it was as round as any ball. I looked upon it with the eye of my understanding, and thought, *What may this be?* And it was answered generally thus: "It is all that is made." I marveled how it might last, for I thought it might suddenly have fallen to naught for littleness. And I was answered in my understanding: "It lasts and ever shall, for God loves it. And so have all things their beginning by the love of God."

In this little thing I saw three properties. The first is that God made it. The second, that he loves it. And the third, that God keeps it. But what is this to me? Truly, the Creator, the Keeper, the Lover. For until I am substantially owned to him, I may never have full rest nor true bliss. That is to say, until I be so fastened to him that there is nothing that is made between my God and me.

This little thing that is made, I thought it might have fallen to nothing for littleness. Of this we need to understand that all of the things that have been made are already nothing when compared to loving and having God, who is unmade.

This is the cause why we are not at ease in heart and soul, for we seek rest here, in this thing that is so little and where there is no rest—knowing not our God who is all mighty, all wise, and all good. For he is true rest. God will be known, and he likes us to rest in him. For all that is beneath him cannot suffice us. And this is the cause why no soul is rested until it is negated of all that is made. And when he wills to be negated for love, to have him who is all, then he is able to receive spiritual rest.

WALTER HILTON

The Song of Angels

Our Lord God is an endless being without changing; almighty without failing; supreme wisdom, light, truth without error or darkness; supreme goodness, love, peace, and sweetness. Therefore the more that a soul is united, fastened, conformed, and joined to our Lord, the more stable and strong it is; the more wise and clear, good and peaceable, loving and virtuous it is; and so it is more perfect.

For a soul that has (by the grace of Jesus and long, hard work of bodily and spiritual exercise) overcome and destroyed lusts, passions, and unreasonable impulses within itself and without in the sensuality—and is clothed all in virtues as in meekness and mildness, in patience and softness, in spiritual strength and righteousness, in continence, in wisdom, in truth, hope and charity—then it is made as perfect as it may be in this life. Much comfort it receives from our Lord, not only inwardly in its own secret nature, by virtue of the union to our Lord that lies in knowing and loving God, in illumination and spiritual burning from Him, in transforming of the soul into the Godhead; but also many other comforts, savors, sweetnesses, and wonderful feelings in various manners, because our Lord graciously visits His creatures here on earth, and because the soul profits and grows in charity.

Some souls, by virtue of the love that God gives them, are so cleansed that all creatures and everything they hear, or see, or feel by any of the senses, turns them to comfort and gladness; and the sensuality receives new savor and sweetness in all creatures. And just as previously the sensual appetites were carnal, vain, and corrupt because of the pain of original sin, so now they are made spiritual and clean, without bitterness and biting of conscience.

And this is the goodness of our Lord, that since the soul is punished in the sensuality, and the flesh shares the pain, that afterward the soul be comforted in the sensuality, and the flesh join in joy and comfort with the soul—not carnal, but spiritual, as it was a fellow in tribulation and pain.

This is the freedom and the lordship, the dignity, and the worth that a man has over all creatures, which dignity he may so recover by grace here, that every creature appear to him as it is. And that occurs when by grace he sees, he hears, he feels only God in all creatures. In this way a soul is made spiritual in the sensuality by abundance of love—that is, in the nature of the soul.

SAINT JOHN OF THE CROSS

Dark Night of the Soul

Therefore, since these proficients are still at a very low stage of progress—and follow their own nature closely in the intercourse and dealings which they have with God, because the gold of their spirit is not yet purified and refined—they still think of God as little children, and speak of God as little children, and feel and experience God as little children, even as Saint Paul says. This is because they have not reached perfection, which is the union of the soul with God. In the state of union, however, they will work great things in the spirit—even as grown men—and their works and faculties will then be Divine rather than human.

To this end God is pleased to strip them of this old man and clothe them with the new man, who is created according to God, as the apostle says (Ephesians 4:24), in the newness of sense. He strips their faculties, affections, and feelings—both spiritual and sensual, both outward and inward—leaving the understanding dark, the will dry, the memory empty, and the affections in the deepest affliction, bitterness, and constraint. This involves taking from the soul the pleasure and experience of spiritual blessings which it had before in order to make of this privation one of the principles which are requisite in the spirit so that there may be introduced into it and united with it the spiritual form of the spirit, which is the union of love.

All this the Lord works in the soul by means of a pure and dark contemplation, as the soul explains in the first stanza.

SAINT JOHN OF THE CROSS

Ascent of Mount Carmel

The reason it is necessary for the soul—in order to attain to divine union with God—to pass through this dark night of mortification of the desires and denial of pleasures in all things, is because all the affections that it has for creatures are pure darkness in the eyes of God. And when the soul is clothed in these affections it has no capacity for being enlightened and possessed by the pure and simple light of God, if it does not first cast them from it. For light cannot agree with darkness, since, as Saint John says: "The darkness could not receive the light" (John 1:5).

The reason is that two contraries cannot coexist in one person; and that darkness, which is affection set upon the creatures, and light, which is God, are contrary to each other, and have no likeness or accord between one another—even as Saint Paul taught the Corinthians, saying: "What communion can there be between light and darkness?" Therefore the light of Divine union cannot dwell in the soul if these affections do not first flee away from it.

In order that we may better prove what has been said, it must be known that the affection and attachment which the soul has for creatures renders the soul like to these creatures. And the greater its affection, the closer the equality and likeness between them; for love creates a likeness between that which loves and that which is loved. . . . Thus, he that loves a creature becomes as low as that creature—and in some ways lower, for love not only makes the lover equal to the object of his love, but even subjects him to it.

Hence in the same way it comes to pass that the soul that loves anything else becomes incapable of pure union with God and transformation in Him. For the low estate of the creature is much less capable of union with the high estate of the Creator than is darkness with light. For all things of earth and heaven, compared with God, are nothing.

MIGUEL DE MOLINOS

The Spiritual Guide
Which Disentangles the Soul

There are two kinds of darkness: some are unhappy and others happy. The first are those that arise from sin, and they are unhappy because they lead the Christian to an eternal precipice. The second are those that the Lord suffers to be in the soul in order to ground and settle it in virtue; these are happy because they enlighten the soul, fortify it, and cause greater light therein.

Therefore, you should not grieve and disturb yourself, nor be disconsolate, in seeing yourself obscure and darksome, judging that God has failed you and the light you formerly had experience of. Rather, at these times you should persevere constantly in prayer, the darkness being a manifest sign that God in his infinite mercy intends to bring you into the inward path, and to the happy way of Paradise. Oh, how happy will you be if you embrace it with peace and resignation as the instrument of perfect quiet, true light, and of all your spiritual good.

Know then that the straightest, most perfect and secure way of proficients is the way of darkness—because in it the Lord placed his own Throne. Psalm 18 says, "He made darkness his secret place." By the path of darkness, the supernatural light which God infuses into the soul grows and increases. It is amidst darkness that wisdom and strong love are found, by darkness the soul is annihilated, and by darkness that the species which hinder the right view of the divine truth are consumed. By this means God introduces the soul, by the inward way, into the Prayer of Rest, and of perfect contemplation, which so few have experienced. Finally, by darkness the Lord purges the senses and sensibility, which hinder the mystical progress.

See now if darkness should not be esteemed and embraced. What you should do in darkness, then, is to believe that you are before the Lord and in His presence. But you should do so with a sweet and quiet attention—not bringing a desire to know anything; nor to search after delicacies, tenderness, or sensible devotions; nor to do any thing except what is the good will and pleasure of God. Because otherwise you will only make circles all your lifetime, and you will not advance one step toward perfection.

JAN VAN RUYSBROECK

The Book of Supreme Truth

The most profitable stirrings which such a man can feel, and for which he is best fitted, are heavenly weal and hellish woe—and the ability to respond to these two with fit and proper works.

For heavenly weal lifts a man up above all things into an untrammelled power of praising and loving God in every way that his heart and his soul desire. After this comes hellish woe, and casts him down into a misery and into a lack of all the comfort and consolation that he experienced before. In this woe, weal sometimes shows itself and brings with it a hope which none can gainsay. And then the man falls back again into a despair in which he can find no consolation.

When a man feels God within himself with rich and full grace, this I call heavenly health; for then he is wise and clear of understanding, rich and outflowing with heavenly teachings, ardent and generous in charity, drunken and overflowing with joy, strong in feeling, bold and ever ready in all the things which he knows to be well pleasing to God—and such things without number, which may only be known by those who feel them.

But when the scale of love goes down, and God hides Himself with all His graces, then the man falls back into dereliction and torment and dark misery—as though he should never more recover. And then he feels himself to be nothing else but a poor sinner, who knows little or nothing of God. He scorns every consolation that creatures may give him, and the taste and consolation of God he does not receive. And then his reason says within him: *Where is now your God? What has become of all that you received from God?* Then his tears are his meat day and night, as the prophet says.

Now if that man is to recover from this misery, he must observe and feel that he does not belong to himself, but to God; and therefore he must freely abandon his own will to the will of God, and must leave God to work in him in time and in eternity. As soon as he can do this, with untroubled heart and with a free spirit, at that very moment he recovers his health, and brings heaven into hell, and hell into heaven. For howsoever the scales of love go up and down, all things to him are even or alike. For whatsoever love gives or takes away, he who abandons himself and loves God finds peace in all. For his spirit remains free and unmoved who lives in all pains without rebellion; and he is able to feel the unmediated union with God. For he has achieved the union through means by the richness of his virtues. And after this, because he is one aim and one will with God, he feels God within himself together with the fullness of His grace as the quickening health of his being and all his works.

MEISTER ECKHART

From the Sermon,

"The Self-Communication of God"

The soul has by nature two capacities. The first is intelligence, which may comprehend the Holy Trinity with all Its works, and may be contained by It as water is by a vessel. When the vessel is full, it has enclosed all that is contained in it, and it is united with that which it has enclosed and of which it is full. Thus intelligence becomes one with that which it has understood and comprehended. It is united therewith by grace, as the Son is one with the Father.

The second capacity is Will. That is a nobler one, and its essential characteristic is to plunge into the Unknown which is God. There the Will lays hold of God in a mysterious manner, and the Unknown God imparts His impress to the Will. The Will draws thought and all the powers of the soul after it in its train, so that the soul becomes one with God by grace, as the Holy Ghost is one with the Father and with the Son by nature. In God, the soul is more worthy to be loved than it is in itself. Therefore Augustine said that the soul is greater by its love-giving power than by its life-giving power.

If man might only abide in this union, and do all the works which have ever been done by creatures, he would be no other than God—if his higher powers so brought his lower powers under control that he could only work God-like works. That cannot be, however, and so man's highest faculty contemplates God as best it can, and so influences his lower faculties that they can discern between Good and Evil.

WILLIAM BOOTH

Purity of Heart

After trying to show you the desirability of this experience, and urging it upon your acceptance, I cannot help feeling that a few counsels bearing upon the best method of retaining the blessing of Holiness after it has been gained may be useful.

Beyond question many do find this sacred treasure of a Pure Heart, and exult in the confidence and joy it brings, who after a short season lose it again. They enter the Holy Temple and then for one reason or another desert it. They struggle with tears and prayers up on to the Highway of Holiness, and then turn aside on to some by path or other, where they become the prey once more of the doubts and fears and sins of the olden time. This is a great pity. Those who act this way are the chief sufferers; but, alas! a great injury is also inflicted upon others by their unfaithfulness.

But the failure of those who obtain the grace to keep what they have received should be no discouragement to you who have entered upon this holy path, and no argument against your persevering in it. What you have to do is to make up your minds that, having found the Pearl of Great Price, no enemy shall rob you of the treasure.

To this end my counsel is: seek till you obtain a settled conviction in your own heart that the work is done. Be content with nothing less than the assurance that God has really and truly cleansed your soul from sin. Do not allow yourselves to rest in any pleasant feelings merely, or in any hope of a future revelation on the subject. Continue to wrestle, and pray, and believe until you are satisfied that the work is accomplished.

But do you ask, "How can I tell whether God has cleansed my soul from sin?" I reply, "How did you find out that God had forgiven your sins? How did you come to know that precious fact?" For, assuredly, a precious fact it was when you were saved. I suppose that since that gracious gift was yours, you have sung over, a thousand times or more, the words: "I never shall forget the day when Jesus washed my sins away."

"How did you come to the personal assurance that you were saved?" I ask. And you reply that God spoke it to your heart. Well, the assurance of your sanctification will come in the same way. The Holy Spirit will produce a delightful persuasion in your soul that all the pride and malice and envy and selfishness have been taken away, and that God has filled you with peace and love. This precious persuasion will, no doubt, come in different forms to different individuals. To some it will appear as the "Rest of Faith," to others as the "Baptism of Fire," to others as the "Fullness of Love," and to others as the "Enthronement of Christ" come to reign in their souls supreme over an inward Kingdom, which is righteousness, peace, and joy in the Holy Ghost.

But to all alike when the work is real and complete there will be the conviction that the blood cleanses and that the heart is pure. Be content with nothing less than this, and leave to God's good pleasure the giving or the withholding of more.

BROTHER LAWRENCE

The Practice of the Presence of God

If we were well accustomed to the exercise of the presence of God, all bodily diseases would be much alleviated thereby. God often permits that we should suffer a little in order to purify our souls and oblige us to continue with Him.

Take courage, offer Him your pains incessantly, and pray to Him for strength to endure them. Above all, get a habit of entertaining yourself often with God, and forget Him the least you can. Adore Him in your infirmities; offer yourself to Him from time to time; and, in the height of your sufferings, beseech Him humbly and affectionately (as a child his father) to make you conformable to His holy will. I shall endeavor to assist you with my poor prayers.

God has many ways of drawing us to Himself. He sometimes hides Himself from us, but faith alone, which will not fail us in time of need, ought to be our support and the foundation of our confidence—which must be all in God. I know not how God will dispose of me, so I am always happy. All the world suffers, and I, who deserve the severest discipline, feel joys so continual and so great that I can scarce contain them.

I would willingly ask of God a part of your sufferings, but that I know my weakness—which is so great that if He left me one moment to myself, I should be the most wretched man alive. And yet I know not how He can leave me alone, because faith gives me as strong a conviction as sense can do that He never forsakes us till we have first forsaken Him. Let us fear to leave Him. Let us be always with Him. Let us live and die in His presence. Please do pray for me, as I for you.

ON CHRISTIAN DOCTRINE

"The Word of God well understood and religiously
obeyed is the shortest route to spiritual perfection.
And we must not select a few favorite passages to the
exclusion of others. Nothing less than a
whole Bible can make a whole Christian."

—*Of God and Men*

MARTIN LUTHER

Large Catechism

The First Commandment: You must not have other gods. That is, I must be your only God.

Question: What does this saying mean? How should we understand it? What does it mean to have a god? What is God?

Answer: To have a god means this: You expect to receive all good things from it and turn to it in every time of trouble. Yes, to have a god means to trust and to believe in Him with your whole heart. I have often said that only the trust and faith of the heart can make God or an idol. If your faith and trust are true, you have the true God, too. On the other hand, where trust is false, is evil, there you will not have the true God either. Faith and God live together. I tell you, whatever you set your heart on and rely on is really your god.

Therefore it is the intent of this commandment to require true faith and trust of the heart, which settles upon the only true God and clings to Him alone. That is as much as to say: See to it that you let Me alone be your God, and never seek another.

In other words: whatever you lack of good things, expect it of Me, and look to Me for it, and whenever you suffer misfortune and distress, creep and cling to Me. I, yes I, will give you enough and help you out of every need; only do not let your heart cleave to or rest in any other.

JAN VAN RUYSBROECK

The Spiritual Espousals

You should know that the heavenly Father—as a living ground, with all that is living in Him—is actively turned toward His Son as towards His own eternal Wisdom. And the same Wisdom and all that is living within it is actively turned back towards the Father— that is, towards the same ground whence it comes. And in this meeting there springs forth the third person, between the Father and the Son—that is, the Holy Spirit, their mutual love, who is one with them both in the same nature. And this love actively and enjoyably encompasses and pervades the Father, the Son, and everything that is living in both of them with such great richness and joy that all creatures must eternally keep silent about it.

For the incomprehensible marvel which resides in this love eternally transcends the understanding of all creatures. But where one understands and savors this marvel without astonishment, there the spirit is above itself and is one with the Spirit of God. And it tastes and sees without measure, even as God, the richness which itself is in the unity of the living ground where it possesses itself according to the way of its un-createdness.

Now, this blissful meeting, according to God's way, is actively, without cease, renewed within us. For the Father gives Himself in the Son, and the Son in the Father, in an eternal mutual complacency and in a loving embrace. And this is renewed every moment in the bond of love. For just as the Father beholds all things anew, without cease, in the birth of His Son, so all things are loved anew by the

Father and by the Son in the outflowing of the Holy Spirit. And this is the active meeting of the Father and of the Son in which we are lovingly embraced, through the Holy Spirit, in eternal love.

Now, this active meeting and this loving embrace are, in their ground, enjoyable and without way. For the unfathomable waylessness of God is so dark and so wayless that it encompasses within itself all divine ways and activity and property of the persons, in the rich embrace of the essential unity, and produces a divine enjoyment in the abyss of namelessness. And here is the enjoyable passing-over, an engulfment flowing away into essential bareness where all divine names and all ways and all life-giving ideas which are depicted in the mirror of divine truth fall without exception into this simple namelessness, without ways and without reason.

For in this fathomless whirlpool of simplicity all things are encompassed in enjoyable blessedness, whereas the ground itself remains totally uncomprehended, unless it be by essential unity. The persons and everything that is living in God must yield before this, for here there exists nothing but an eternal rest in an enjoyable embrace of loving transport—that is, in the wayless existence that all inner spirits have preferred above all things. This is the dark stillness in which all the loving are lost.

But if we could thus prepare ourselves in virtues, we would rapidly divest ourselves of the body and would fly into the wild waves of the sea; no creature could ever bring us back again. May divine love, which rebuffs no beggar, grant us that we might possess the essential unity in enjoyment and clearly contemplate oneness in threeness. Amen. Amen.

MEISTER ECKHART

From the Sermon, "The Angel's Greeting"

It is more worthy of God that He be born spiritually of every pure and virgin soul than that He be born of Mary. Hereby we should understand that humanity is, so to speak, the Son of God born from all eternity. The Father produced all creatures, and me among them, and I issued forth from Him with all creatures—and yet I abide in the Father. Just as the word which I now speak is conceived and spoken forth by me, and you all receive it, yet none the less it abides in me. Thus I and all creatures abide in the Father.

Hereto I adjoin a parable. There were a certain man and wife; the woman by accident lost an eye, and she was sorely troubled by the loss. Her husband said to her, "Wife, why are you troubled? "She answered, "It is not the loss of my eye that troubles me, but the thought that you may love me less on account of that loss." He said, "I love you all the same." Not long after he put one of his own eyes out, then he came to his wife and said, "Wife, that you may believe I love you, I have made myself like you: now I, too, have only one eye."

So men could hardly believe that God loved them till God put one of His eyes out—that is, took upon Himself human nature and was made man. Just as fire infuses its essence and clearness into the dry wood, so has God done with man. He has created the human soul and infused His glory into it, and yet in His own essence has remained unchangeable.

If you ask me, seeing that my spiritual birth is out of time, whether I am an eternal son, I answer "Yes and No." In the everlasting foreknowledge of God, I slumbered like a word unspoken. He hath brought me forth His son in the image of His eternal fatherhood, that I also should be a father and bring forth Him. It is as if one stood before a high mountain and cried, "Are you there?" The echo comes back, "Are you there?" If one cries, "Come out," the echo answers, "Come out."

JOHN BUNYAN

An Exposition of the
First Ten Chapters of Genesis

If in the Godhead there be but one, not three, then the Father, the Son, or the Spirit must needs be that one; so then, the other two are nothing. Again, if the reality of a being be neither in the Father, Son, nor Spirit, as such, but in the eternal Deity, without consideration of Father Son and Spirit as three, then neither of the three are anything but notions in us, or manifestations of the Godhead, or nominal distinctions, so related by the word. But if so, then when the Father sent the Son, and the Father and Son the Spirit, one notion sent another; one manifestation sent another. This being granted, it unavoidably follows there was no Father to beget a Son, no Son to be sent to save us, no Holy Ghost to be sent to comfort us and to guide us into all the truth of the Father and Son. At most, it amounts to but this: a notion sent a notion, a distinction sent a distinction, or one manifestation sent another.

Of this error these are the consequences: we are only to believe in notions and distinctions when we believe in the Father and the Son; and so shall have no other heaven and glory than notions and nominal distinctions can furnish us withal.

If you feel your thoughts begin to wrestle about this truth, and to struggle concerning this, one against another, take heed of admitting such a question as, "How can this be?" For here is no room for reason to make it out; here is only room to believe it is a truth. You find not one of the prophets propounding an argument to prove it, but asserting it; they let it lie for faith to take it up and embrace it.

"The grace of our Lord Jesus Christ, and the love of God, and the communion of the Holy Ghost, be with you all. Amen."

WALTER HILTON

The Scale of Perfection

The soul of a man is a life consisting of three powers—Memory, Understanding, and Will—after the image and likeness of the Blessed Trinity. The *Memory* was made strong and steadfast by the power of the Father to hold and retain God in perpetual remembrance without forgetting, distracting, or letting go of any creature, and so it has the likeness of the Father. The *Understanding* was made bright and clear, without error or darkness (as perfectly as a soul in a body unglorified could have), and so it has the likeness and image of the Son, who is infinite wisdom. The *Will* and affections were made pure and clean, burning in love towards God without sensual love of the flesh or of any creature by the sovereign goodness of God the Holy Ghost, and so it has the likeness of the Holy Ghost, which is blessed love. Whereby you may see that man's soul (which may be called a created Trinity) was in its natural state replenished in its three powers with the remembrance, sight, and love of the most blessed uncreated Trinity, which is God.

This was the dignity and worth of man's soul by nature at his first creation, which you had in Adam before the first sin. But when Adam sinned, choosing to love and delight in himself and in the creatures, he lost all his excellency and dignity. (You have done the same also, through him.) Adam fell from that Blessed Trinity into a foul, dark, wretched trinity—that is to say, he fell into the forgetting of God and ignorance of himself, and into a beastly love and liking of himself—and all this he did wittingly and willingly.

For, as David says in Psalm 49:20: "A man who is in honor, yet does not understand, is like the beasts that perish."

See then the wretchedness of your soul. For as the *Memory* was something established and fixed upon God, so now it has forgotten Him and seeks its rest in the creatures—now in one creature and then in another—and never can find full rest, having lost Him in whom is full rest. So it is with the *Understanding* and the *Will*, both of which were pure in spiritual favor and sweetness but are now turned into a foul, beastly lust and liking in itself and in the creatures and in fleshly favors. This is true both in the senses (as in gluttony and lechery) and in the imagination (as in pride, vainglory, and covetousness), so much so that you can do no good deed but it is defiled with vainglory. Nor can you easily make use of any of your five senses cleanly upon anything that is pleasant, but your heart will be taken and enflamed with a vain lust and liking of it, which puts out the love of God from your heart so that no feeling of love or spiritual favor may come into it.

Every man that lives in the spirit understands all of this well. This is the soul's wretchedness and our mischief for the first man's sin, besides all other wretchedness and sins which you have willfully added thereto. And you know well that had you never committed any sin within your body, either mortal or venial, but only this which is called "original sin" (for that is the first sin, and is nothing else but the losing of our righteousness which we were created in), you should never have been saved—had not our Lord Jesus Christ by His precious passion delivered you and restored you again.

G. CAMPBELL MORGAN

The Voice of the Devil

"Yea, hath God said?"

That is the voice of the devil. We are living in an hour in which we are very conscious that in this world of ours, and in the midst of all its affairs, hell is let loose. I resolutely use that phrase, and say hell is let loose, for hell can have no power save under the government of God; just as Satan could not touch Job until he had asked permission, just as it is true that when he desired to have the disciples to sift them as wheat, he obtained them by asking. It is always so. That is a tremendous truth, at which we may often be puzzled; but our confidence is in God, and in the assurance that when He allows the forces of hell to be loosed, there is a reason for it, and a meaning in it. It is so in the days in which we are living.

The existence of evil, spiritual principalities is granted by all those who accept the Biblical revelation. Words we have doubt-less often quoted recently to ourselves, occurring in Paul's letter to the Ephesians, are true. "Our wrestling is not against flesh and blood." That is to say that such conflict is not final. Behind it there is something else, "But against the principalities, against the powers, against the world rulers of this darkness, against the spiritual hosts of wickedness in the heavenly places."

This fact of the existence of the principalities of evil is assumed and revealed throughout the Bible; and at the head of this empire of evil is one, named variously, named Satan. We are very conscious of his power and of his deeds. It is an interesting thing to remark in hurried passing, when we open our Bible, we do not find him in the first two chapters. He does not appear. And it is equally arresting that we do not find him in the last two chapters. He is not there at the beginning or end of the Bible, though, as Browning had it, "a wide compass first be fetched."

When Paul wrote to the Corinthians, he said, "We are not ignorant of his devices." That is a suggestive word rightly understood—"devices," which might correctly be rendered, "his mental activities, his conceptions, his purpose, his thinking." We are not ignorant, said Paul, of these things. Sometimes we are inclined to say, if Paul was not, we are. Yet it is not so. As we are men and women of faith, and followers of the Lord Jesus Christ, and believers in the Biblical revelation, we can say we are not ignorant of his mental activity, of the conceptions that underlie that activity, and of the purpose that inspires that activity. Paul had what we have, the Biblical history, with its revelation of this personality, and the story of Jesus with the supreme revelation of this personality through His ministry. Paul had these things. So have we, and so we can say that we are not ignorant of his devices.

ANONYMOUS

Theologica Germanica

Mark this: when it is said that such a thing or such a deed is contrary to God, or that such a thing is hateful to God and grieves His Spirit, you must know that no creature is contrary to God, or hateful or grievous unto Him, insofar as it lives, knows, has power to do or produce, and so forth—for all of this is not contrary to God. That an evil spirit or man lives is altogether good and of God; for God is the Being of all that are, and the Life of all that live, and the Wisdom of all the wise; for all things have their being more truly in God than in themselves, and also all their powers, knowledge, life, and the rest. For if it were not so, God would not be all good; And thus all creatures are good. Now what is good is agreeable to God, and He will have it. Therefore it cannot be contrary to Him.

But what, then, can there be that is contrary to God and hateful to Him? Nothing but sin. But what is Sin? Mark this: sin is nothing else than when a creature wills otherwise than God wills, and contrary to Him. Each of us may see this in himself; for he who wills otherwise than I, or whose will is contrary to mine, is my foe; but he who wills the same as I is my friend, and I love him. It is even so with God. And he who wills, speaks, or is silent, does or leaves undone otherwise than as I will, he is contrary to me and an offence unto me. So it is also with God—when a man wills otherwise than God, or contrary to God, whatever he does or leaves undone, in short all that proceeds from him, is contrary

278

to God and is sin. As Christ said: "He who is not with Me is against me."

Hereby may each man see plainly whether or not he is without sin, and whether or not he is committing sin, and what sin is, and how sin ought to be atoned for, and wherewith it may be healed. This contradiction to God's will is what we call, and is, disobedience. And therefore Adam—the I, the Self, Self-will, Sin, or the Old Man, the turning aside or departing from God—do all mean one and the same thing.

AUGUSTINE OF HIPPO

Handbook on Faith, Hope, and Love

I shall now mention what I have often discussed before in other places in my short treatises. We sin from two causes: either from not seeing what we ought to do, or else from not doing what we have already seen we ought to do. Of these two, the first is ignorance of the evil; the second, weakness.

We must surely fight against both; but we shall as surely be defeated unless we are divinely helped, not only to see what we ought to do, but also, as sound judgment increases, to make our love of righteousness victor over our love of those things because of which—either by desiring to possess them or by fearing to lose them—we fall, open-eyed, into known sin. In this latter case, we are not only sinners—which we are even when we sin through ignorance—but also lawbreakers: for we do not do what we should, and we do what we know already we should not.

Accordingly, we should pray for pardon if we have sinned, as we do when we say, "Forgive us our debts as we also forgive our debtors." But we should also pray that God should guide us away from sin, and this we do when we say, "Lead us not into temptation"—and we should make our petitions to Him of whom it is said in the psalm, "The Lord is my light and my salvation"; that, as Light, he may take away our ignorance, as Salvation, our weakness.

MIGUEL DE MOLINOS

The Spiritual Guide
Which Disentangles the Soul

Our own nature is so base, proud, and ambitious—and so full of
its own appetites, judgments, and opinions—that if temptations
did not restrain it, it would be undone without remedy. The Lord,
seeing our misery and perverse inclination, and thereby moved to
compassion, suffers us to be assaulted by diverse thoughts against
the faith. These include horrible temptations—violent and painful
suggestions of impatience, pride, gluttony, luxury, rage, blasphemy,
cursing, despair, and an infinite number of others—so that we may
know ourselves and be humble. With these horrible temptations,
that infinite goodness humbles our pride, giving us in them the
most wholesome medicine.

"All our righteousness are as filthy rags," as Isaiah said (Isaiah
64:6), and this is through the stains of vanity, conceitedness, and
self-love. It is necessary they be purified with the fire of tribulation and temptation so that they may be clean, pure, perfect, and
agreeable to the eyes of God.

Therefore the Lord purifies the soul that he calls and will
have for himself, using the rough file of temptation—with which
he polishes it from the rust of pride, avarice, vanity, ambition,
presumption, and self-conceitedness. With the same, he humbles,
pacifies, and exercises it, making it to know its own misery. Through
these means He purifies and strips the heart with the goal that all
its operations may be pure and of inestimable value.

SAMUEL RUTHERFORD

The Trial and Triumph of Faith

There are two parts in our human will: 1) The natural frame and constitution of it, and 2) The goodness of it. The will of angels and of sinless Adam was not essentially good, for then, angels could never have turned devils. Therefore, the constitution of the will needs supervenient goodness and confirming grace, even when the will is at its best.

Grace, grace is now the only oil to our wheels. Christ has taken the castle, both in-works and out-works, when he has taken the will—the proudest enemy that Christ has out of hell. When Saul rendered his will, he rendered his weapon. This is mortification, when Christ runs away with your will. As Christ was like a man that had not a man's will, so Saul (Acts 9:6), "trembling and astonished said, 'Lord, what will You have me to do?' " It is good when the Lord tramples upon Ephraim's fair neck (Hosea 10:11).

There is no goodness in our will now, except what it has from grace. And to turn the will from evil to good is no more nature's work than we can turn the wind from the east to the west. When the wheels of the clock are broken and rusted, it cannot go. When the bird's wing is broken, it cannot fly. When there is a stone in the spring and in-work of the lock, the key cannot open the door. Christ must oil the wheels of our misordered wills, and heal them, and remove the stone, and infuse grace (which is wings to the bird). If not, the motions of our wills are all hell-ward.

JOHANNES TAULER

The Inner Way

Children, the poison of the first Fall has sunk into the very depths of our nature. We have been made and placed between the two ends: time and eternity. Time for us ought to be nothing more than a passage to the end, and eternity should be our aim and our dwelling place.

Now poor man, unhappily, because of his fallen nature and his blindness, is attacked by everything on his weakest side. He rests himself by the way and forgets his true destiny. His nature clings to everything with which it comes into contact; it clutches at whatever it may be and seeks rest therein—either bodily or spiritual, internal or external.

It is quite apparent how worldly men seek their rest and pleasure, and they will surely find out hereafter how things stand with them. But those who hide worldly hearts under a spiritual appearance, but still find rest in temporal things—whoever they may be, and whatever may be the cares which oppress them, would find, if they only knew it, what would make their hearts shrivel up in terror. God made all things that are needful, not for our satisfaction or pleasure, but for Himself alone.

JOHN MILTON

Paradise Lost

Those leaves they gathered, broad as Amazonian targe;
And, with what skill they had, together sewed,
To gird their waist; vain covering, if to hide
Their guilt and dreaded shame! O, how unlike
To that first naked glory! Such of late
Columbus found the American, so girt
With feathered cincture; naked else, and wild
Among the trees on isles and woody shores.

Thus fenced, and, as they thought, their shame in part
Covered, but not at rest or ease of mind,
They sat them down to weep; nor only tears
Rained at their eyes, but high winds worse within
Began to rise—high passions, anger, hate,
Mistrust, suspicion, discord—and shook sore
Their inward state of mind, calm region once
And full of peace, now tossed and turbulent:
For Understanding ruled not, and the Will
Heard not her lore; both in subjection now
To sensual Appetite, who from beneath
Usurping over sovereign Reason claimed superior sway.

From this distempered breast,
Adam, estranged in look and altered style,
Speech intermitted thus to Eve renewed.
"Would thou hadst hearkened to my words, and stayed
With me, as I besought thee, when that strange
Desire of wandering, this unhappy morn,

I know not whence possessed thee; we had then
Remained still happy; not, as now, despoiled
Of all our good; shamed, naked, miserable!"

Let none henceforth seek needless cause to approve
The faith they owe; when earnestly they seek
Such proof, conclude, they then begin to fail.
To whom, soon moved with touch of blame, thus Eve.
"What words have passed thy lips, Adam severe!
Imputest thou that to my default, or will
Of wandering, as thou callest it, which who knows
But might as ill have happened thou being by,
Or to thyself perhaps? Hadst thou been there,
Or here the attempt, thou couldst not have discerned
Fraud in the Serpent, speaking as he spake;
No ground of enmity between us known,
Why he should mean me ill, or seek to harm.
Was I to have never parted from thy side?
As good have grown there still a lifeless rib.
Being as I am, why didst not thou, the head,
Command me absolutely not to go,
Going into such danger, as thou saidst?
Too facile then, thou didst not much gainsay;
Nay, didst permit, approve, and fair dismiss.
Hadst thou been firm and fixed in thy dissent,
Neither had I transgressed, nor thou with me."

. . . Thus they in mutual accusation spent
The fruitless hours, but neither self-condemning;
And of their vain contest appeared no end.

JONATHAN EDWARDS

From the Discourse, "The Wisdom of God
Displayed in the Way of Salvation"

By this contrivance for our redemption, God's greatest dishonor
is made an occasion of his greatest glory. Sin is a thing by which
God is greatly dishonored; the nature of its principle is enmity
against God, and contempt of him. And man, by his rebellion,
has greatly dishonored God. But this dishonor, by the contrivance
of our redemption, is made an occasion of the greatest manifestation of God's glory that ever was. Sin, the greatest evil, is made
an occasion of the greatest good.

It is the nature of a principle of sin that it seeks to dethrone
God: but this is hereby made an occasion of the greatest manifestation of God's royal majesty and glory that ever was. By sin,
man has slighted and despised God: but this is made an occasion
of his appearing the more greatly honorable. Sin casts contempt
upon the authority and law of God: but this, by the contrivance
of our redemption, is made the occasion of the greatest honor
done to that same authority, and to that very law. It was a greater
honor to the law of God that Christ was subject to it, and obeyed
it, than if all mankind had obeyed it. It was a greater honor to
God's authority that Christ showed such great respect, and such
entire subjection to it, than the perfect obedience of all the angels
in heaven. Man by his sin showed his enmity against the holiness
of God: but this is made an occasion of the greatest manifestation

of God's holiness. The holiness of God never appeared to so great a degree as when God executed vengeance upon his own dear Son.

So has the wisdom of God contrived that those attributes are glorified in man's salvation, whose glory seemed to require his destruction. When man had fallen, several attributes of God seemed to require his destruction. The justice of God requires that sin be punished as it deserves: but it deserves no less than eternal destruction. God proclaims it as a part of the glory of his nature, that he will in no wise clear the guilty (Exodus 34:7). The holiness of God seemed to require man's destruction; for God by his holiness infinitely hates sin. This seemed to require therefore that God should manifest a proportionable hatred of the sinner; and that he should be for ever an enemy unto him. The truth of God seemed also to require man's destruction; for eternal death was what God had threatened for sin, one jot or tittle of which threatening cannot by any means pass away.

But yet so has God contrived that those very attributes not only allow of man's redemption, and are not inconsistent with it, but they are glorified in it. Even vindictive justice is glorified in the death and sufferings of Christ. The holiness of God, or his holy hatred of sin that seemed to require man's damnation, is seen in Christ's dying for sinners. So herein also is manifested and glorified the truth of God, even in the threatenings of the law.

Yes, it is so ordered now that the glory of these attributes requires the salvation of those that believe. The justice of God that required man's damnation, and seemed inconsistent with his salvation, now as much requires the salvation of those that believe in Christ as ever before it required their damnation.

CHARLES SPURGEON

Morning and Evening

As God's creatures, we are all debtors to him: to obey him with all our body, and soul, and strength. Having broken his commandments, as we all have, we are debtors to his justice, and we owe to him a vast amount which we are not able to pay. But of the Christian it can be said that he does not owe God's justice anything, for Christ has paid the debt his people owed; for this reason the believer owes the more to love.

I am a debtor to God's grace and forgiving mercy; but I am no debtor to his justice, for he will never accuse me of a debt already paid. Christ said, "It is finished!" and by that he meant, that whatever his people owed was wiped away forever from the book of remembrance. Christ, to the uttermost, has satisfied divine justice; the account is settled; the handwriting is nailed to the cross; the receipt is given, and we are debtors to God's justice no longer.

But then, because we are not debtors to our Lord in that sense, we become ten times more debtors to God than we should have been otherwise. Christian, pause and ponder for a moment. What a debtor you are to divine sovereignty! How much you owe to his disinterested love, for he gave his own Son that he might die for you. Consider how much you owe to his forgiving grace, that after ten thousand affronts he loves you as infinitely as ever. Consider what you owe to his power; how he has raised you from your death in sin; how he has preserved your spiritual life; how he has kept you from falling; and how, though a thousand enemies have beset your path, you have been able to hold on your way. Consider what you owe to his immutability. Though you have changed a thousand times, he has not changed once.

You are as deep in debt as you can be to every attribute of God. To God you owe yourself and all you have. Yield yourself as a living sacrifice—it is but thy reasonable service.

FREDERICK FABER

Tracts on the Church and Her Offices

Thus we gain one great principle in Christian education: It is all made to depend upon Baptism. It is the education of a baptized soul. Now, it is not too much to say that there are very few of us who give this prominence to Baptism in the education of our children. The little ones tell us that they were made in their Baptism "members of Christ, children of God, and inheritors of the kingdom of Heaven;" and moreover they "heartily thank God their heavenly Father, that He *has* called them to this state of salvation."

Yet we educate them as if we did not believe a word of all this. Alas! Many among us do not believe it. We bring them up as if they were one day to be Christians, not as if they were so already; as much as we ourselves are. A jewel of great price, even the Cross of Christ, has been given into their charge—a jewel which there is a fearful chance of our losing from the evil, the inherited evil, of our nature; a jewel which, when once lost, is well nigh irretrievable. Yet we do not tell them of all this. They grow up: and in many cases they know nothing about Baptism, neither what it is nor that they have received it, till the near approach of Confirmation obliges us to give them views and notions of some sort or other about it.

The Church, when she educates her children in the Catechism, is ever teaching them to look back. We, on the contrary, are always making them look forward. She gives them great thoughts and tries to make them careful, jealous, and obedient, because they are

Christians. We educate their minds and inform them with high principles of action, because they may be Christians and ought to be Christians. In a word, with the Church Baptism is a gift and a power; with us it is a theory and a notion.

If, then, what is called religious education keeps failing and turning out ill on all sides of us, it might not be amiss if we return to the guidance of our Church in this matter. Her rule ought at least to have the benefit of a trial. The primitive Christians seem in the main to have been far holier men than ourselves, and one very striking difference between us and them is their frequent reference to their Baptism. The Church is the prodigal's home. Christ may be there, waiting to bless, while we have sought Him sorrowing among the waysides leading from Jerusalem.

A. B. SIMPSON

The Fourfold Gospel

Sanctification is separation from sin. That is the root idea of the word. The sanctified Christian is separated from sin, from an evil world, even from his own self, and from anything that would be a separating cause between him and Christ in the new life. It does not mean that sin and Satan are to be destroyed. God does not yet bring the millennium, but He puts a line of demarcation between the sanctified soul and all that is unholy.

The great trouble with Christians is that they try to destroy evil. They think if sin could be really decapitated and Satan slain, they would be supremely happy. It is a surprise to many of them after conversion that God still lets the devil live. He has nowhere promised that He will kill Satan, but He has promised to put a broad, deep Jordan between the Christian and sin.

The only thing to do with it is to repudiate it and let it alone. There is sin enough in the world to destroy us all, if we take it in. The air is full of it, as the air in some of our Western States is full of soot from the soft coal that is burned there. It will be so to the end of time, but God means you and me, beloved, to be separated from it in our spirit.

Next, sanctification means dedication to God. That is the root idea of the word also. It is separation from sin and dedication unto God. A sanctified Christian is wholly yielded to God to please Him in every particular. His first thought is always, "Your will be done"; his one desire that he may please God and do His holy will. This is the thought expressed by the word *consecration*. In the Old Testament all things which were set apart to God were called sanctified, even if there had been no sin in them before. The Tabernacle was sanctified; it had never sinned, but it was dedicated to God. In the same sense all the vessels of the Tabernacle were sanctified. They were set apart to a holy use.

Dear friends, God expects something more of us than simply to be separated from sin. That is only negative goodness. He expects that we shall be wholly dedicated to Him, having it the supreme wish of our heart to love and honor and please Him. Are we fulfilling His expectations in this?

Next, sanctification includes conformity to the likeness of God. We are to be in His image, and stamped with the impress of Jesus Christ. Sanctification also means conformity to the will as well as the likeness of God. A sanctified Christian is submissive and obedient. He desires the Divine will above everything else in life as kinder and wiser for him than anything else can be. He is conscious that he misses something if he misses it. He knows it will promote his highest good far more than his own will, crying instinctively, "Thy will be done."

Finally, sanctification means love—supreme love to God and all mankind. This is the fulfilling of the law. It is the spring of all obedience, the fountain from which all right things flow. We cannot be conformed to the image of God without love, for God is Love.

This is, perhaps, the strongest feature in a truly sanctified life. It clothes all the other virtues with softness and warmth. It takes the icy peaks of a cold and naked consecration and covers them with mosses and verdure. It sends bright sunlight into the heart, making everything warm and full of life, which would otherwise be cold and desolate. The savage was able to stand before his enemies and be cut to pieces with stoical firmness that disdained to cry, but his indifference was like some stony cliff. It was not the warm, tender love of the heart of Jesus, which made Him bow meekly to His painful death because it was His Father's will. It was the spontaneous, glad outflowing of His loving heart.

Dear friends, if we are so filled with love to God, it will flow out to others, and we shall love our neighbors as we love ourselves.

MEISTER ECKHART

From the Sermon, "Sanctification"

Although God is Almighty, He can only work in a heart when
He finds readiness or makes it. He works differently in men than
in stones. For this we may take the following illustration: if we
bake in one oven three loaves of barley-bread, of rye-bread, and
of wheat, we shall find the same heat of the oven affects them
differently. When one is well-baked, another will be still raw, and
another yet more raw. That is not due to the heat, but to the variety
of the materials.

Similarly, God works in all hearts not alike, but in proportion
as He finds them prepared and susceptible. If the heart is to be
ready for the highest, it must be vacant of all other things.

If I wish to write on a white tablet, whatever else is written
on the tablet, however noble its purport, is a hindrance to me. If
I am to write, I must wipe the tablet clean of everything, and the
tablet is most suitable for my purpose when it is blank. Similarly,
if God is to write on my heart, everything else must come out of
it until it is really sanctified. Only so can God work His highest
will, and so the sanctified heart has no outward object at all.

ANONYMOUS

Theologica Germanica

Again, when we read of the old man and the new man, we must mark what that means. The old man is Adam and disobedience—the Self, the Me, and so forth. But the new man is Christ and true obedience—a giving up and denying oneself of all temporal things, and seeking the honor of God alone in all things.

And when dying and perishing and the like are spoken of, it means that the old man should be destroyed and not seek its own either in spiritual or in natural things. For where this is brought about in a true divine light, there the new man is born again. In like manner, it has been said that man should die unto himself—that is, to earthly pleasures, consolations, joys, appetites, the I, the Self, and all that is thereof in man, to which he clings and on which he is yet leaning with content. Whether it be the man himself, or any other creature, whatever it be, it must depart and die if the man is to be brought aright to another mind, according to the truth. This is why Paul exhort us, saying: "Put off concerning the former conversation the old man, which is corrupt according to the deceitful lusts . . . and put on the new man, which after God is created in righteousness and true holiness" (Ephesians 4:22, 24).

Now, he who lives to himself after the old man is called and is truly a child of Adam; and though he may give diligence to the ordering of his life, he is still the child and brother of the Evil Spirit. But he who lives in humble obedience and in the new man which is Christ, he is, in like manner, the brother of Christ and the child of God.

Behold! Where the old man dies and the new man is born, there is that second birth of which Christ said, "Except a man be born again, he cannot enter into the kingdom of God" (John 3:3). Likewise Paul said, "As in Adam all die, even so in Christ shall all be made alive" (1 Corinthians 15:22). That is to say, all who follow Adam in pride, in lust of the flesh, and in disobedience are dead in soul and never will or can be made alive but in Christ. And for this cause, so long as a man is an Adam or his child, he is without God. Christ said, "He who is not with Me is against Me" (Matthew 12:30).

Now he who is against God is dead before God, and so it follows that all Adam's children are dead before God. But he who stands with Christ in perfect obedience, he is with God and lives.

MEISTER ECKHART

From the Sermon, "Outward and Inward Morality"

As God can only be seen by His own light, so He can only be loved by His own love. The merely natural man is incapable of this, because nature by itself is incapable of responding to the Divine Love and is confined within its own circle. Therefore it is necessary for Grace, which is a simple supernatural power, to elevate the natural faculties to union in God above the merely temporal objects of existence. The possibility of love to God is grounded in the relative likeness between man and God. If the soul is to reach its moral goal—which is God-likeness—it must become inwardly like God through grace, and through a spiritual birth which is the spring of true morality.

The inner work that man has to do is the practical realization of Grace: without this, all outward work is ineffectual for salvation. Virtue is never mere virtue; it is either from God, or through God, or in God. All the soul's works which are to inherit an everlasting recompense must be carried on in God. They are rewarded by Him in proportion as they are carried on in Him, for the soul is an instrument of God whereby He carries on His work.

The essence of morality is inwardness, the intensity of will from which it springs, and the nobleness of the aim for which it is practiced. When a good work is done by a man, he is free of it, and through that freedom is more like and more near his Original than he was before.

NICHOLAS OF CUSA

On Being a Son of God

But in order that you may be led by an illustration, I propose the following: You are not ignorant, I know, of the fact that visible forms that are equal in straight mirrors appear to be less than equal in curved mirrors. Therefore, suppose that there is a most lofty Reflection of our Beginning, which is the glorious God—a Reflection in which God Himself appears. Think of this Reflection as a "Mirror of Truth" that is without blemish, completely straight, most perfect, and without bounds. And think of all other creatures as mirrors with different degrees of contraction and differently curved. Among these creatures, think of those with intellectual natures as living mirrors that are straighter and more clearly reflecting than the others. And since these intellectual mirrors are alive and intellectual and free, conceive them to be of such kind that they can curve themselves, straighten themselves, and clean themselves.

I say, then: There is One and the same reflected brightness that appears variously in all of the mirror reflections. And in the brightness of the first, the "Mirror of Truth," all the other mirrors appear as they truly are. (This occurrence can be observed in the case of material mirrors turned toward one another in a facing circle.) But in each of the other mirrors, which are contracted and curved, all the other mirrors appear not as they truly are, but in accordance with the condition of the receiving mirror—in other words, with some diminishment because of the receiving mirror's deviation from straightness.

Therefore, when any intellectual, living mirror is brought before that first and straight Mirror of Truth—in which all other mirrors appear truly and accurately as they are—then the Mirror of Truth reflects itself, along with all that it has received from all the mirrors, into the intellectual, living mirror. And the intellectual mirror receives unto itself that mirror ray from the Mirror of Truth, which Mirror has within itself the truth of all the mirrors. However, the mirror receives this ray in its own manner.

And that intellectual, living mirror, upon receiving the first Mirror's reflected light, in the same moment of eternity beholds itself as it really is, and beholds all the other mirrors in its own manner. For the more simple and less contracted—the more bright, clean, straight, just, and true—the intellectual mirror is, the more clearly, joyously, and truly it will behold within itself God's glory and in all other mirrors. Therefore, in that first Mirror, the Mirror of Truth (which can be said to be God's Word, Logos, or Son), the intellectual mirror obtains sonship so that (1) it is all things in all things, and (2) all things are in it, and (3) its kingdom is the possession, in glorious life, of God and all things.

MARTIN LUTHER

An Introduction to
Saint Paul's Letter to the Romans

Faith is not what some people think it is. Their human dream is a delusion. Because they observe that faith is not followed by good works or a better life, they fall into error, even though they speak and hear much about faith. "Faith is not enough," they say, "You must do good works, you must be pious to be saved."

They think that, when you hear the gospel, you start working, creating by your own strength a thankful heart which says, "I believe." That is what they think true faith is. But, because this is a human idea, a dream, the heart never learns anything from it, so it does nothing and reform doesn't come from this "faith," either.

Instead, faith is God's work in us that changes us and gives new birth from God (John 1:13). It kills the Old Adam and makes us completely different people. It changes our hearts, our spirits, our thoughts and all our powers. It brings the Holy Spirit with it. Yes, it is a living, creative, active and powerful thing, this faith. Faith cannot help doing good works constantly. It doesn't stop to ask if good works ought to be done, but before anyone asks, it already has done them and continues to do them without ceasing. Anyone who does not do good works in this manner is an unbeliever. He stumbles around and looks for faith and good works, even though he does not know what faith or good works are. Yet he gossips and chatters about faith and good works with many words.

Faith is a living, bold trust in God's grace, so certain of God's favor that it would risk death a thousand times trusting in it. Such confidence and knowledge of God's grace makes you happy, joyful and bold in your relationship to God and all creatures. The Holy Spirit makes this happen through faith. Because of it, you freely, willingly and joyfully do good to everyone, serve everyone, suffer all kinds of things, love and praise the God who has shown you such grace. Thus, it is just as impossible to separate faith and works as it is to separate heat and light from fire! Therefore, watch out for your own false ideas and guard against good-for-nothing gossips, who think they're smart enough to define faith and works, but really are the greatest of fools. Ask God to work faith in you, or you will remain forever without faith, no matter what you wish, say or can do.

A. B. SIMPSON

A Larger Christian Life

Why should God make all things dependent on our faith? Because the ruin of the race began with the loss of faith, and its recovery must come through the exercise of faith. The poison Satan injected into the blood of Eve was a question of God's faithfulness, and the one prescription that the Gospel gives to unsaved sinners is, "Believe on the Lord Jesus Christ and you shall be saved."

Faith is the law of Christianity, the vital principle of the Gospel dispensation. The law of faith the apostle calls it in distinction from the law of works. The Lord Jesus expressed it in the simple formula which has become the standard of answered prayers and every blessing that we receive through the name of Jesus. God is, therefore, bound to act according to our faith and also according to our unbelief.

Faith is the only way known to us by which we can accept a gift from God, and inasmuch as all the blessings of the Gospel are the gifts of grace, they must come to us through faith and in the measure of our faith, if they come at all.

Faith is necessary as a subjective influence to prepare our own hearts for the reception of God and His grace. How can the Father communicate His love to a timid, trembling heart? How can God come near to a frightened child? I have seen a little bird die of terror in my hand, when I intended it no harm but tried in vain to caress it and win its love. And so the individual heart without faith would die in the presence of God in absolute terror, and be unable to receive the overflowing love of the Father which it could not understand.

Faith is an actual, spiritual force. It is, no doubt, one of the attributes of God Himself. We find it exemplified in Jesus in all His miracles. He explains to His disciples that it was the very power by which He withered the fig tree, and the power by which they could overcome and dissolve the mightiest obstacles in their way. There is no doubt that while the soul is exercising through the power of God the faith that commands what God commands, that a mighty force is operating at that very moment upon the obstacle, a force as real as the currents of electricity or the power of dynamite. God has really put into our hands one of His own implements of omnipotence and permitted us to use it in the name of Jesus according to His will and for the establishment of His Kingdom.

FRANÇOIS FÉNELON

Maxims of the Saints

One great point of difference between the First Covenant (or the covenant of works, which said to men, "Do this and live") and the Second Covenant (or the covenant of grace, which says, "Believe and live") is this: The first covenant did not lead men to anything that was perfect. It showed men what was right and good, but it failed in giving them the power to fulfill what the covenant required. Men not only understood what was right and good; they knew what was evil. But, in their love and practice of depravity, they had no longer power of themselves to flee from it.

The new or Christian covenant of grace not only prescribes and commands, but gives also the power to fulfill. In the practical dispensations of divine grace, there are a number of principles which it may be important to remember.

1. God being Love, it is a part of His nature to desire to communicate Himself to all moral beings, and to make Himself one with them in a perfect harmony of relations and feelings. The position of God is that of giver; the position of man is that of recipient. Harmonized with man by the blood and power of the Cross, he has once more become the infinite fullness, the original and overflowing fountain, giving and ever ready to give.

2. Such are the relations between God and man, involved in the fact of man's moral agency, that man's business is to receive.

3. Souls true to the grace given them will never suffer any diminution of it. On the contrary, the great and unchangeable condition of continuance and of growth in grace is cooperation with what we now have. This is the law of growth, not only deducible from the Divine nature, but expressly revealed and declared in the Scriptures: "For everyone who has will be given more, and he will have an abundance. Whoever does not have, even what he has will be taken from him" (Matthew 25:29).

4. A faithful cooperation with grace is the most effectual preparation for attracting and receiving and increasing grace. This is the great secret of advancement to those high degrees which are permitted; namely, a strict, unwavering, faithful cooperation moment by moment.

5. It is important to correctly understand the doctrine of cooperation. A disposition to cooperate is not more opposed to the sinful indolence which falls behind, than to the hasty and unrighteous zeal which runs before. It is in the excess of zeal, which has a good appearance but in reality has unbelief and self at the bottom, that we run before God.

6. Cooperation, by being calm and peaceable, does not cease to be efficacious. Souls in this purified but tranquil state are souls of power; watchful and triumphant against self; resisting temptation; fighting even to blood against sin. But it is, nevertheless, a combat free from the turbulence and inconsistencies of human passion—because they contend in the presence of God, who is their strength, in the spirit of the highest faith and love and under the guidance of the Holy Ghost, who is always tranquil in His operations.

AUGUSTINE OF HIPPO

Handbook on Faith, Hope, and Love

And now regarding love, which the apostle says is greater than the other two—that is, faith and hope—for the more richly it dwells in a man, the better the man in whom it dwells. For when we ask whether someone is a good man, we are not asking what he believes, or hopes, but what he loves.

Now, beyond all doubt, he who loves aright believes and hopes rightly. Likewise, he who does not love believes in vain, even if what he believes is true; he hopes in vain, even if what he hopes for is generally agreed to pertain to true happiness—unless he believes and hopes for this: that he may through prayer obtain the gift of love. For, although it is true that he cannot hope without love, it may be that there is something without which, if he does not love it, he cannot realize the object of his hopes. An example of this would be if a man hopes for life eternal—and who is there who does not love that?—and yet does not love righteousness, without which no one comes to it.

Now this is the true faith of Christ which the apostle commends: faith that works through love. And what it yet lacks in love it asks that it may receive, it seeks that it may find, and knocks that it may be opened unto it (Matt. 7:7). For faith achieves what the law commands. And, without the gift of God—that is, without the Holy Spirit, through whom love is shed abroad in our hearts—the law may bid but it cannot aid. Moreover, it can make of man a transgressor, who cannot then excuse himself by pleading ignorance. For appetite reigns where the love of God does not.

FRANCIS DE SALES

Introduction to the Devout Life

Love alone leads to perfection, but the three chief means for acquiring it are obedience, chastity, and poverty. Obedience is a consecration of the heart, chastity of the body, and poverty of all worldly goods to the love and service of God. These are the three members of the Spiritual Cross, and all three must be raised upon the fourth, which is humility. . . . Let us endeavor to practice these three virtues according to our several vocations, for although we are not thereby called to a state of perfection, we may attain through them to perfection itself, and of a truth we are all bound to practice them—although not all after the same manner.

There are two kinds of obedience: one necessary and the other voluntary. The first includes a humble obedience to your ecclesiastical superiors, whether Pope, Bishop, Curate, or those commissioned by them. You are likewise bound to obey your civil superiors, king, and magistrates; as also your domestic superiors, father, mother, master, or mistress. Such obedience is called necessary because no one can free himself from the duty of obeying these superiors, God having appointed them severally to bear rule over us.

Therefore obey their commands as of right, but if you would be perfect, follow their counsels and even their wishes as far as charity and prudence will allow. Obey as to things acceptable, as when they bid you eat, or take recreation, for although there may be no great virtue in obedience in such a case, there is great harm in disobedience. Obey in things indifferent, as concerning questions of dress, coming and going, singing or keeping silence, for herein is a very laudable obedience. Obey in things hard, disagreeable, and inconvenient, and therein lies a very perfect obedience. Moreover, obey quietly, without answering again; promptly, without delay; cheerfully, without reluctance; and, above all, render a loving obedience for His sake who became obedient even to the death of the Cross for our sake—who, as Saint Bernard says, chose rather to resign His life than His obedience.

If you would acquire a ready obedience to superiors, accustom yourself to yield to your equals, giving way to their opinions where nothing wrong is involved, without arguing or peevishness. Adapt yourself easily to the wishes of your inferiors as far as you reasonably can, and forbear the exercise of stern authority so long as they do well.

Voluntary obedience is such as we undertake by our own choice, and which is not imposed by others. Persons do not choose their own King, or Bishop, or parents—often not even their husband. But most people choose their confessor or director. And whether a person takes a vow of obedience to him (as Saint Theresa, beyond her formal vow to the Superior of her Order, bound herself by a simple vow to obey Father Gratian), or without any vow they resolve to obey their chosen spiritual guide, all such obedience is voluntary because it depends upon our own will.

Obedience to lawful superiors is regulated by their official claims. Thus, in all public and legal matters, we are bound to obey our King; in ecclesiastical matters, our Bishop; in domestic matters, our father, master or husband; and in personal matters which concern the soul, our confessor or spiritual guide. Seek to be directed in your religious exercises by your spiritual father, because thereby they will have double grace and virtue—that which is inherent in that they are devout, and that which comes by reason of the spirit of obedience in which they are performed. Blessed indeed are the obedient, for God will never permit them to go astray.

JOHN BUNYAN

The Groans of a Damned Soul

Consider what a happy state you are in that has gotten the faith of
the Lord Jesus into your soul—but be sure you have it, I say—how
safe, how sure, how happy you are! For when others go to hell,
you must go to heaven; when others go to the devil, you must go
to God; when as others go to prison, you must be set at liberty, at
ease, and at freedom; when others must roar for sorrow of heart,
then you shall also sing for the joy of heart.

Consider you must have all your well-spent life to follow you
instead of all your sins, and the glorious blessings of the gospel
instead of the dreadful curses and condemnations of the law; the
blessing of the father instead of a fiery sentence from the judge.

Let dissolution come when it will; it can do you no harm. For
it will be but only a passage out of a prison into a palace; out of
a sea of troubles into a haven of rest; out of a crowd of enemies,
to an innumerable company of true, loving, and faithful friends;
out of shame, reproach, and contempt, into exceeding great and
eternal glory. For death shall not hurt you with his sting, nor bite
you with his soul-murdering teeth; but shall be a welcome guest
to you, even to your soul, in that it is sent to free you from your
troubles which you are in while here in this world, dwelling in the
tabernacle of clay.

JOHN KNOX

The Scots Confession

We most surely believe that God preserved, instructed, multiplied, honored, adorned, and called from death to life his Church in all ages since Adam until the coming of Christ Jesus in the flesh.

For he called Abraham from his father's country, instructed him, and multiplied his seed; he marvelously preserved him, and more marvelously delivered his seed from the bondage and tyranny of Pharaoh. To them he gave his laws, constitutions, and ceremonies; to them he gave the land of Canaan; after he had given them judges, and afterwards Saul, he gave David to be king, to whom he gave promise that of the fruit of his loins should one sit forever upon his royal throne. To this same people from time to time he sent prophets to recall them to the right way of their God, from which sometimes they strayed by idolatry.

And although, because of their stubborn contempt for righteousness, he was compelled to give them into the hands of their enemies—as had previously been threatened by the mouth of Moses, so that the holy city was destroyed, the temple burned with fire, and the whole land desolate for seventy years—yet in mercy he restored them again to Jerusalem, where the city and the temple were rebuilt. And they endured against all temptations and assaults of Satan till the Messiah came according to the promise.

JOHN CALVIN

On the Christian Life

But, most strange to say, many who boast of being Christians, instead of thus longing for death, are so afraid of it that they tremble at the very mention of it as a thing ominous and dreadful. We cannot wonder, indeed, that our natural feelings should be somewhat shocked at the mention of our dissolution. But it is altogether intolerable that the light of piety should not be so powerful in a Christian breast as with greater consolation to overcome and suppress that fear.

For if we reflect that this our tabernacle—unstable, defective, corruptible, fading, pining, and putrid—is dissolved in order that it may forthwith be renewed in sure, perfect, incorruptible, in fine, in heavenly glory, will not faith compel us eagerly to desire what nature dreads? If we reflect that by death we are recalled from exile to inhabit our native country, a heavenly country, shall this give us no comfort?

But everything longs for permanent existence. I admit this, and therefore contend that we ought to look to future immortality, where we may obtain that fixed condition which nowhere appears on the earth. For Paul admirably enjoins believers to hasten cheerfully to death, not because they would be unclothed, but clothed upon (2 Corinthians 5:2). Shall the lower animals and inanimate creatures themselves, even wood and stone, as conscious of their present vanity, long for the final resurrection that they may with the sons of God be delivered from vanity (Romans 8:19), and shall we, endued with the light of intellect—and more than intellect, enlightened by the Spirit of God—when our essence is in question rise no higher than the corruption of this earth?

. . . This let us hold as fixed: that no man has made much progress in the school of Christ who does not look forward with joy to the day of death and final resurrection (2 Timothy 4:18; Titus 2:13), for Paul distinguishes all believers by this mark. And the usual course of Scripture is to direct us thither whenever it would furnish us with an argument for substantial joy. "Look up," says our Lord, "and lift up your heads: for your redemption draws near" (Luke 21:28). Is it reasonable, I ask, that what he intended to have a powerful effect in stirring us up to alacrity and exultation should produce nothing but sadness and consternation? If it is so, why do we still glory in him as our Master?

Therefore, let us come to a sounder mind. And how repugnant so ever the blind and stupid longing of the flesh may be, let us doubt not to desire the advent of the Lord—not in wish only, but with earnest sighs, as the most propitious of all events. He will come as a Redeemer to deliver us from an immense abyss of evil and misery, and to lead us to the blessed inheritance of his life and glory.

D. L. MOODY

Heaven

To me it is very sad to think that so many professed Christians look upon death as they do. I received some time ago a letter from a friend in London, and I thought, as I read it, I would take it and show it to other people and see if I could not get them to look upon death as this friend does. He lost his beloved mother.

In England it is a very common thing to send out cards in memory of the departed ones, and they put upon them great borders of black—sometimes a quarter of an inch of black border—but this friend had put on a gold border. He did not put on black at all; his mother had gone to the golden city, and so he put on a golden border. And I think it is a good deal better than black. I think when our friends die, instead of putting a great black border upon our memorials to make them look dark, it would be better for us to put on gold.

It is not death at all; it is life. Some one said to a person dying; "Well, you are in the land of the living yet." "No," said he, "I am in the land of the dying yet, but I am going to the land of the living; they live there and never die." This is the land of sin and death and tears, but up yonder they never die. It is perpetual life; it is unceasing joy.

CHARLES SPURGEON

From the Sermon, "The Death of the Christian"

There are two funerals for every Christian: the funeral of the body
and the funeral of the soul. Funeral, did I say, of the soul? No, I
meant not so. It is a marriage of the soul. For as soon as it leaves
the body, the angel reapers stand ready to carry it away. They may
not bring a fiery chariot as they had for Elijah, but they have their
broad spreading wings.

I rejoice to believe that angels will come as convoys to the soul
across the ethereal plains. Lo! angels at the head support the ascending
saint and lovingly they look upon his face as they bear him upwards;
and angels at the feet assist in wafting him up yonder through the
skies. And as the husbandmen come out from their houses and cry,
"A joyous harvest home," so will the angels come forth from the gates
of heaven and say, "Harvest home! Harvest home! Here is another
shock of corn fully ripe gathered in to the garner."

. . . Oh! Methinks there is a shout that comes from heaven
whenever a Christian enters it, louder than the noise of many
waters. The thundering acclamations of a universe are drowned,
as if they were but a whisper, in that great shout which all the
ransomed raise when they cry, "Another, and yet another comes."
And the song is still swelled by increasing voices as they chant,
"Blessed husbandman, blessed husbandman, your wheat is coming
home; shocks of corn fully ripe are gathering into your garner."
Well, wait a little, beloved. In a few years more you and I shall be
carried through the ether on the wings of angels.

Methinks I die, and the angels approach. I am on the wings of cherubs. Oh, how they bear me up—how swiftly and yet how softly. I have left mortality with all its pains. Oh, how rapid is my flight! Just now I passed the morning star. Far behind me now the planets shine. Oh, how swiftly do I fly, and how sweetly! Cherubs! What sweet flight is yours, and what kind arms are these I lean upon. And on my way you kiss me with the kisses of love and affection. You call me brother. Cherubs, am I your brother? I who just now was captive in a tenement of clay—am I your brother? "Yes!" they say. Oh, hark! I hear music strangely harmonious! What sweet sounds come to my ears! I am nearing Paradise. Do not spirits approach with songs of joy? "Yes!" they say. And before they can answer, behold they come—a glorious convoy! I catch a sight of them as they are holding a great review at the gates of Paradise.

And, ah! There is the golden gate. I enter in, and I see my blessed Lord. I can tell you no more. All else were things unlawful for flesh to utter. My Lord! I am with you—plunged into you—lost in you just as a drop is swallowed in the ocean; as one single tint is lost in the glorious rainbow! Am I lost in you, glorious Jesus? And is my bliss consummated? Is the wedding day come at last? Have I really put on the marriage garments? And am I yours? Yes! I am. There is nothing else now for me. In vain your harps, you angels. In vain all else. Leave me a little while. I will know your heaven by-and-bye. Give me some years—yes give me some ages to lean here on this sweet bosom of my Lord; give me half eternity and let me bask myself in the sunshine of that one smile.

Yes; give me this. Did you speak, Jesus? "Yes, I have loved you with an everlasting love, and now you are mine! You are with me." Is not this heaven? I want nothing else. I tell you once again, you blessed spirits, I will see you by-and-bye. But with my Lord I will now take my feast of loves. Oh, Jesus! Jesus! Jesus! You are heaven! I want nothing else. I am lost in you!

ANSELM

Saint Anselm's Book of
Meditations and Prayers

For there is no mourning there—no weeping, no sorrow, and no fear. There is no sadness there, no difference, no envy, no distress, no temptation, no changefulness and no unhealthiness of clime; no suspicion, no pretence, no flattery, no detraction, no sickness, no age, no death, no poverty, no night, no gloom; no need of eating, of drinking, or of sleeping; and no fatigue.

What good, then, will be found there? For surely where there is neither mourning nor weeping nor sorrow nor sadness, what can there be but perfect joy? Where there is neither trial nor distress nor change of seasons nor unhealthiness of clime; no summer too fierce, no winter too severe; what can there be but a certain perfect temperature of the elements and true and uttermost tranquility both of body and of mind? Where there is no cause for fear, what can there be but uttermost security? When neither envy nor estrangement, what but real and perfect love? Where no unsightliness, what but real and consummate beauty? Where no poverty, what but perfect fullness? Where neither labor nor exhaustion, what but uttermost repose and fullest strength? Where there is nothing to oppress or burden, what can there be but plenitude of happiness? And where old age and disease are never expected, never feared, what but truest health? Where no night is, and no darkness, what but perfect light? Where death and mortality are altogether swallowed up, what is there but eternal life?

And what more can we require? Yes, indeed, we may ask for more—for something that transcends all this. I mean the vision, the knowledge, and the love of the Creator. He shall be seen in Himself, and seen in all His creatures; ruling all things, but without solicitude; sustaining all things, but without exertion; communicating Himself in some strange way to each according to his capacity, but without diminution of Himself and without division of Himself. That Face shall be seen inviting all love and every longing, the Face that angels long to gaze into; and the meaning, the light, the sweetness of that Face, who shall tell them? The Father shall be seen in the Son, and the Son in the Father, and in each of Them the Holy Ghost. For He shall be seen as He is, the promise fulfilled in which He says, "He that loves Me shall be loved by My Father; and I will love him, and will manifest Myself to him" (John 14:21).

And from this vision proceeds the knowledge of God, of which He Himself says: "This is life everlasting, that they may know You, the only true God" (John 17:3).

MEISTER ECKHART

From the Sermon,
"The Nearness of the Kingdom"

Our Lord said that the Kingdom of God is near us. Yes, the
Kingdom of God is within us, as Paul said: "For now our salvation is nearer than when we first believed." Now, we should know
in what manner the Kingdom of God is near us. Therefore let us
pay diligent attention to the meaning of the words. If I were a
king, and did not know it, I should not really be a king. But if I
were fully convinced that I was a king, and all mankind coincided
in my belief, and I knew that they shared my conviction, I should
indeed be a king and all the wealth of the king would be mine.
But, if one of these three conditions were lacking, I should not
really be a king.

In similar fashion, our salvation depends upon our knowing
and recognizing the Chief Good which is God Himself. I have
a capacity in my soul for taking in God entirely. I am as sure
as I live that nothing is so near to me as God. God is nearer to
me than I am to myself; my existence depends on the nearness
and presence of God. He is also near things of wood and stone,
but they know it not. If a piece of wood became as aware of the
nearness of God as an archangel is, the piece of wood would be
as happy as an archangel. For this reason man is happier than the
inanimate wood, because he knows and understands how God is
near him. His happiness increases and diminishes in proportion to
the increase and decrease in his knowledge of this. His happiness

does not arise from the knowledge that God is near him, and in him, and that he possesses God. Rather, it comes from this: that he knows the nearness of God, and loves Him, and is aware that "the Kingdom of God is near."

So, when I think on God's Kingdom, I am compelled to be silent because of its immensity, because God's Kingdom is none other than God Himself with all His riches. God's Kingdom is no small thing: we may survey in imagination all the worlds of God's creation, but they are not God's Kingdom. In whichever soul God's Kingdom appears, and which knows God's Kingdom, that soul needs no human preaching or instruction; it is taught from within and assured of eternal life. Whoever knows and recognizes how near God's Kingdom is to him may say with Jacob, "God is in this place, and I knew it not" (Genesis 28:17).

God is equally near in all creatures. A wise man said, "God has spread out His net over all creatures, so that whosoever wishes to discover Him may find and recognize Him in each one." Another said, "He knows God rightly who recognizes Him alike in all things." To serve God with fear is good; to serve Him out of love is better; but to fear and love Him together is best of all. To have a restful or peaceful life in God is good; to bear a life of pain in patience is better; but to have peace in the midst of pain is the best of all.

FREDERICK FABER

The Unfulfilled Glory of the Church

It troubles worldly men and frightens faithless men to think that they are living in a state of miracles, that a miraculous dispensation is going on all round them, and that disclosures and appearances of it may be expected at any moment. It disturbs their peace and comfort to imagine that they are so near such great things, from the presence and (it may so happen) from the sight of which they cannot escape.

They are like the Gadarenes, whose hearts failed them when they besought Jesus that He would depart out of their coasts. They have not the cause of the Church at heart, except where it does not interfere with themselves—where it does not call on them to labor and suffer hardness, to make sacrifices, and to go heavily as one that mourns for his mother. They are not anxious to see all nations and kingdoms who will not serve the Church perish, because they know the victory involves trouble and unquietness in which they themselves will be concerned; and so they "see that rest is good, and the land that it is pleasant; and bow their shoulders to bear, and become servants unto tribute" (Genesis 49:15).

They do not see any miracles, and it is not likely they will believe what they do not see when they are so anxious to disbelieve; and thus, however unconsciously to themselves, they use the very language of unbelief. "Since the fathers fell asleep, all things continue as they were from the beginning" (2 Peter 3:4). But St. Peter warns us distinctly that the "Lord is not slack concerning

His promise, as some men count slackness" (2 Peter 3:9). We know then that He has made the Church great promises of glory; we see that those promises are not yet fulfilled, and so we believe they will be fulfilled very soon because St. Peter tells us "the Lord is not slack concerning His promise."

But worldly men have not set their hearts upon this glory. They are not earnest about it. They do not feel at all unhappy about the Church. They have forgotten Jerusalem in their mirth. They have not remembered her captivity. They are afraid of the trouble and noise which may accompany the bringing in of this glory, and so they do not like to be told that they are living under a dispensation of miracles.

FRANCIS DE SALES

Treatise on the Love of God

Here is what God has said: "I am the Lord your God, a jealous God" (Deuteronomy 5:9); "The Lord whose name is jealous" (Exodus 34:14). God is jealous, then, but what is His jealousy?

Truly it seems at first to be a jealousy of cupidity, such as is that of husbands for their wives. For He will have us so to be his, that He will in no sort have us to be any other's but His. "No man," He says, "can serve two masters" (Matthew 6:24). He demands all our heart, all our soul, all our mind, and all our strength. For this very reason He calls Himself our spouse, and our souls His spouses; and names all sorts of separations from Him—all sorts of fornications adulteries.

And high reason indeed has this great God, all singularly good, to exact most rigorously our whole heart. For ours is a little heart, which cannot supply love enough worthily to love the divine goodness. Is it not therefore reasonable that, since we cannot give Him such measure of love as were requisite, that at least we should love Him all we can? The good which is sovereignly lovable, ought it not to be sovereignly loved? Now to love sovereignly, is to love totally.

However, God's jealousy of us is not truly a jealousy of cupidity, but of sovereign friendship. For it is not in His interest that we should love Him, but ours. Our love is useless to Him, but to us a great gain; and if it be agreeable to Him, it is because it is profitable to us. For, being the sovereign good, He takes pleasure in communicating Himself by love, without any kind of profit that can return to Him thereby. And from there He cries out, making His complaint of sinners by way of jealousy: "They have forsaken me, the fountain of living water, and have dug for themselves cisterns, broken cisterns, that can hold no water" (Jeremiah 2:13). Consider a little, I pray you, how delicately this divine Lover expresses the nobility and generosity of His jealousy: "They have left me," says He, "who am the fountain of living water."

As if he said: I complain not that they have forsaken Me because of any injury their forsaking can cause Me, for what the worse is a living spring if men do not draw water at it? Will it therefore cease to run, or to flow out on the earth? But I grieve for their misfortune that, having left Me, they have chosen for themselves wells that have no water. And if, by supposition of an impossible thing, they could have met with some other fountain of living water, I would lightly bear their departure from Me, since I aim at nothing in their love but their own good. But to forsake Me to perish—to fly from Me to fall headlong—is what astonishes and offends Me in their folly.

It is then for the love of us that He desires we should love Him, because we cannot cease to love Him without beginning to be lost. And whatever part of our affections we take from Him, we lose.

MEISTER ECKHART

From the Sermon, "The Angel's Greeting"

If I am in a higher place and say to someone, "Come up here," that might be difficult for him. But if I say, "Sit down," that would be easy. Thus God deals with us.

When man humbles himself, God cannot restrain His mercy; He must come down and pour His grace into the humble man, and He gives Himself most of all, and all at once, to the least of all. It is essential to God that He give, for His essence is His goodness, and His goodness is His love. Love is the root of all joy and sorrow. Slavish fear of God is to be put away. The right fear is the fear of losing God.

If the earth flees downward from heaven, it finds heaven beneath it. If it flees upward, it comes again to heaven. The earth cannot flee from heaven: whether it flee up or down, heaven rains its influence upon it, stamps its impress upon it, and makes it fruitful—whether the earth be willing or not. God does the same with men: whoever thinks to escape Him flies into His bosom, for every corner is open to Him. God brings forth His Son in you whether you like it or not, whether you are asleep or awake. God works His own will.

That man is unaware of it is man's fault, for his taste is so spoilt by feeding on earthly things that he cannot relish God's love. If we had love to God, we should relish God, and all His works; we should receive all things from God and work the same works as He works.

God created the soul after the image of His highest perfection. He issued forth from the treasure-house of the everlasting Fatherhood in which He had rested from all eternity. Then the Son opened the tent of His everlasting glory and came forth from His high place to fetch His Bride, whom the Father had espoused to Him from all Eternity, back to that heaven from which she came. Therefore He came forth rejoicing as a bridegroom and suffered the pangs of love. Then He returned to His secret chamber in the silence and stillness of the everlasting Fatherhood. As He came forth from the Highest, so He returned to the Highest with His Bride, and revealed to her the hidden treasures of His Godhead.

The first beginning is for the sake of the last end. God Himself does not rest because He is the beginning, but because He is the end and goal of all creation. This end is concealed in the darkness of the everlasting Godhead and is unknown, and never was known, and never will be known. God Himself remains unknown; the light of the everlasting Father shines in darkness, and the darkness comprehended it not. May the truth of what we have spoken lead us to the truth. Amen.

8

ON LIVING THE CHRISTIAN LIFE

*"There is scarcely anything so dull and meaningless
as Bible doctrine taught for its own sake.
Truth divorced from life is not truth in its Biblical sense,
but something else and something less."*

—*Of God and Men*

CHARLES SPURGEON

From the Sermon, "Ebenezer!"

It is certainly a very delightful thing to mark the hand of God in
the lives of ancient saints. How profitable an occupation to observe
God's goodness in delivering David out of the jaw of the lion and
the paw of the bear; his mercy in passing by the transgression,
iniquity, and sin of Manasseh; his faithfulness in keeping the covenant made with Abraham; or his interposition on the behalf of
the dying Hezekiah.

But, beloved, would it not be even more interesting and profitable for us to remark the hand of God in our own lives? Ought
we not to look upon our own history as being at least as full of
God, as full of his goodness and of his truth, as much a proof of
his faithfulness and veracity as the lives of any of the saints who
have gone before? I think we do our Lord an injustice when we
suppose that he wrought all his mighty acts in days of yore, and
showed himself strong for those in the early time, but does not
perform wonders or lay bare his arm for the saints that are now
upon the earth.

Let us review, I say, our own diaries. Surely in these modern
pages we may discover some happy incidents, refreshing to ourselves
and glorifying to our God. Have you had no deliverances? Have you
passed through no rivers, supported by the Divine presence? Have
you walked through no fires unharmed? Have you not been saved
in six troubles? Yea, in seven has not Jehovah helped you? Have
you had no manifestations? The God that spoke to Abraham at

Mamre, has he never spoken to you? The angel that wrestled with Jacob at Peniel, has he never wrestled with you? He that stood in the fiery furnace with the three holy children, has he never trodden the coals at your side?

O beloved, he has manifested himself unto us as he does not unto the world. Forget not these manifestations; fail not to rejoice in them. Have you had no choice favors? The God that gave Solomon the desire of his heart, has he never listened to you and answered your requests? That God of lavish bounty, of whom David sang, "Who satisfies your mouth with good things, so that thy youth is renewed like the eagle's," has he never satiated you with fatness? Have you never been made to lie down in green pastures? Have you never been led by the still waters?

Surely, beloved, the goodness of God of old has been repeated unto us. The manifestations of his grace to those gone to glory have been renewed to us, and delivering mercies as experienced by them are not unknown even to us, upon whom the ends of the world are come.

JOHN CALVIN

On the Christian Life

I don't insist that the life of the Christian shall breathe nothing but the perfect Gospel, though this is to be desired, and ought to be attempted. I insist not so strictly on evangelical perfection as to refuse to acknowledge as a Christian any man who has not attained it. In this way all would be excluded from the Church, since there is no man who is not far removed from this perfection—while many who have made but little progress would be undeservedly rejected.

What then? Let us set this before our eye as the end at which we ought constantly to aim. Let it be regarded as the goal towards which we are to run. For you cannot divide the matter with God, undertaking part of what his word enjoins, and omitting part at pleasure. For, in the first place, God uniformly recommends integrity as the principal part of his worship, meaning by integrity real single-ness of mind, devoid of gloss and fiction. And to this is opposed a double mind; as if it had been said that the spiritual commencement of a good life is when the internal affections are sincerely devoted to God, in the cultivation of holiness and justice.

But seeing that, in this earthly prison of the body, no man is supplied with strength sufficient to hasten in his course with due alacrity, while the greater number are so oppressed with weakness that hesitating, and halting, and even crawling on the ground, they make little progress, let every one of us go as far as his humble ability enables him, and prosecute the journey once begun. No one will travel so badly as not daily to make some degree of progress.

This, therefore, let us never cease to do, that we may daily advance in the way of the Lord; and let us not despair because of the slender measure of success. How little the success may correspond with our wish, our labor is not lost when today is better than yesterday, provided with true singleness of mind we keep our aim, and aspire to the goal, not speaking flattering things to ourselves, nor indulging our vices, but making it our constant endeavor to become better, until we attain to goodness itself. If during the whole course of our life we seek and follow, we shall at length attain it, when relieved from the infirmity of flesh we are admitted to full fellowship with God.

JOHN WESLEY

A Plain Account of Christian Perfection

A Methodist is one who loves the Lord his God with all his heart, with all his soul, with all his mind, and with all his strength. God is the joy of his heart, and the desire of his soul, which is continually crying, "Whom have I in heaven but you? and there is none upon earth whom I desire besides you." My God and my all! "You are the strength of my heart, and my portion for ever." He is therefore happy in God; yes, always happy, as having in him a well of water springing up unto everlasting life, and overflowing his soul with peace and joy. Perfect love living now casting out fear, he rejoices evermore. Yes, his joy is full, and all his bones cry out, "Blessed be the God and Father of our Lord Jesus Christ, who, according to his abundant mercy, has begotten me again unto a living hope of an inheritance incorruptible and undefiled, reserved in heaven for me."

And he, who has this hope, thus full of immortality, in everything gives thanks, as knowing this (whatsoever it is) is the will of God in Christ Jesus concerning him. From him therefore he cheerfully receives all, saying, "Good is the will of the Lord"; and whether he gives or takes away, equally blessing the name of the Lord. Whether in ease or pain, whether in sickness or health, whether in life or death, he gives thanks from the ground of the heart to Him who orders it for good; into whose hands he has wholly committed his body and soul, "as into the hands of a faithful Creator." He is therefore anxiously careful for nothing, as having "cast all his care on Him that cares for him"; and in all things resting on him, after making his request known to him with thanksgiving.

For indeed he "prays without ceasing"; at all times the language of his heart is this: "Unto you is my mouth, though without a voice; and my silence speaks unto you." His heart is lifted up to God at all times, and in all places. In this he is never hindered, much less interrupted, by any person or thing. In retirement or company, in leisure, business, or conversation, his heart is ever with the Lord. Whether he lies down, or rises up, "God is in all his thoughts": He walks with God continually, having the loving eye of his soul fixed on him, and everywhere "seeing Him that is invisible."

And loving God, he "loves his neighbor as himself"; he loves every man as his own soul. He loves his enemies, yes, and the enemies of God. And if it be not in his power to "do good to them that hate" him, yet he ceases not to "pray for them," though they spurn his love, and still persecute him.

For he is "pure in heart." Love has purified his heart from envy, malice, wrath, and every unkind temper. It has cleansed him from pride, and he has now "put on bowels of mercies, kindness, humbleness of mind, meekness, long-suffering." And indeed all possible ground for contention, on his part, is cut off. For none can take from him what he desires, seeing he "loves not the world, nor any of the things of the world"; but "all his desire is unto God, and to the remembrance of his name."

CHARLES SPURGEON

Around the Wicket Gate

Friends, if you have begun to trust the Lord, trust him out and out. Let your faith be the most real and practical thing in your whole life. Don't trust the Lord in mere sentiment about a few great spiritual things; trust him for everything, for ever, both for time and eternity, for body and for soul. See how the Lord hangs the world upon nothing but his own Word! It has neither prop nor pillar. The great arch of heaven stands without a buttress or a wooden center. The Lord can and will bear all the strain that faith can ever put upon him. The greatest troubles are easy to his power, and the darkest mysteries are clear to his wisdom. Trust God up to the hilt. Lean, and lean hard; yes, lean all your weight and every other weight upon the Mighty God of Jacob.

The future you can safely leave with the Lord, who ever lives and never changes. The past is now in your Savior's hand, and you shall never be condemned for it, whatever it may have been, for the Lord has cast your iniquities into the midst of the sea. Believe at this moment in your present privileges. You are saved! If you are a believer in the Lord Jesus, you have passed from death unto life, and you are saved.

In the old slave days a lady brought her black servant on board an English ship, and she laughingly said to the Captain, "I suppose if I and Aunt Chloe were to go to England she would be free?" "Madam," said the Captain, "she is now free. The moment she came on board a British vessel she was free." When the negro woman knew this, she did not leave the ship—not she. It was not the hope of liberty that made her bold, but the fact of liberty. So you are not now merely hoping for eternal life, but "He that believeth in him hath everlasting life." Accept this as a fact revealed in the sacred Word, and begin to rejoice accordingly.

Do not reason about it, or call it in question; believe it and leap for joy.

WALTER HILTON

The Scale of Perfection

Now I have told you of the end you should set in your desire and draw as close to it as you can. I have also told what is needful for you to have in the beginning of your journey—namely humility, firm faith, and an entire and strong will and purpose. Upon that ground you shall build your spiritual house by prayer and meditation and other spiritual virtues.

Furthermore, when you pray or meditate, or when you undertake any other good deed or exercise—be it either good by grace or defective through your own frailty; or whatever you see, feel, hear, smell, or taste, either outwardly by your bodily senses or inwardly by your imagination—bring it all within the truth and the rules of holy Church. Cast it all into the mortar of humility and break it small with the pestle of the fear of God. Then throw the powder of all this into the fire of desire, and so offer it up to God. And I tell you the truth that this offering shall be well pleasing in the sight of our Lord Jesus, and sweet shall the smoke of that fire smell before His face.

The sum is this: draw all that you see and intend within the truth of holy Church, and break yourself by humility. Offer up the desire of your heart only to your Lord Jesus, to have Him and nothing else but Him. If you do this, I hope by the grace of Christ that you shall never be overcome by your enemy. This is what Paul teaches us when he says: "whether you eat or drink, or whatever you do, do it all for the glory of God"—forsaking yourselves and offering all up to Him. And the means that you shall use to this purpose are prayer and meditation.

JOHN CALVIN

Institutes of the Christian Religion

The pious mind does not devise for itself any kind of God, but looks alone to the one true God; nor does it feign for him any character it pleases, but is contented to have him in the character in which he manifests himself—always guarding, with the utmost diligence, against transgressing his will and wandering, with daring presumptions, from the right path.

He by whom God is thus known, perceiving how he governs all things, confides in him as his guardian and protector, and casts himself entirely upon his faithfulness. He perceives God to be the source of every blessing and, if he is in any strait or feels any want, he instantly recurs to his protection and trusts to his aid; persuaded that God is good and merciful, he reclines upon him with sure confidence and doubts not that, in the divine clemency, a remedy will be provided for his every time of need. Acknowledging God as his Father and his Lord, he considers himself bound to have respect for his authority in all things, to reverence his majesty, aim at the advancement of his glory, and obey his commands.

Regarding God as a just judge, armed with severity to punish crimes, he keeps the Judgment seat always in his view. Standing in awe of it, he curbs himself, and fears to provoke God's anger. Nevertheless, he is not so terrified by an apprehension of Judgment as to wish he could withdraw himself, even if the means of escape lay before him; nay, he embraces God not less as the avenger of wickedness than as the rewarder of the righteous, because he perceives that it equally appertains to his glory to store up punishment for the one and eternal life for the other. Besides, it is not the mere fear of punishment that restrains him from sin. Loving and revering God as his Father, honoring and obeying him as his master, although there were no hell, he would revolt at the very idea of offending him.

Such is pure and genuine religion: namely, confidence in God coupled with serious fear—fear, which both includes in it willing reverence and brings along with it such legitimate worship as is prescribed by the law. And it ought to be more carefully considered that all men promiscuously do homage to God, but very few truly reverence him. On all hands there is abundance of ostentatious ceremonies, but sincerity of heart is rare.

NICHOLAS OF CUSA

On Being a Son of God

I do not think we become sons of God in such way that we will be then something essentially "other" than what we are now. Instead, then we will be in another manner than we are in our present manner. For the intellectual power—which receives the actual divine light, through which light the intellectual power is enlivened—draws, by faith upon that light's continual influence, so that it may grow into a perfect man.

But manliness does not belong to the world of boyhood, where the human being is still developing. Rather, it belongs to the world of full development. The boy is the same individual as the grown man, but sonship does not appear in the boy, who is counted among the servants. Sonship appears at the adult age, when the son co-reigns with the father. The one who is now in school, in order to progress, is the same one who later obtains the mastery.

In this present world we are learning; in the next world we will have mastery. But we study, as the theologian John says, in the following way: we receive reason's word from a teacher, whom we believe, for he is a truthful teacher and teaches us rightly, and we are confident of being able to progress. And because we receive his word and believe, we will be teachable by God. Hereby there arises in us the power to be able to attain unto that mastery which is sonship.

JONATHAN EDWARDS

From the Sermon, "Christian Knowledge"

Consider yourselves as scholars or disciples put into the school of Christ, and therefore be diligent to make proficiency in Christian knowledge. Content not yourselves with this: that you have been taught your catechism in your childhood, and that you know as much of the principles of religion as is necessary to salvation—or else you will be guilty of what the apostle warns against, which is going no further than laying the foundation of repentance from dead works.

You are all called to be Christians, and this is your profession. Endeavor, therefore, to acquire knowledge in things which pertain to your profession. Let not your teachers have cause to complain that while they spend and are spent to impart knowledge to you, you take little pains to learn. It is a great encouragement to an instructor to have such students to teach as those that make a business of learning, bending their minds to it. This makes teaching a pleasure, when otherwise it will be a very heavy and burdensome task.

You all have by you a large treasure of divine knowledge, in that you have the Bible in your hands; therefore be not contented in possessing but little of this treasure. God has spoken much to you in the Scriptures; labor to understand as much of what he says as you can. God has made you all reasonable creatures, therefore let not the noble faculty of reason or understanding lie neglected. Don't be content with having so much knowledge as is thrown in your way, and receive in some sense unavoidably by the frequent inculcation of divine truth in the preaching of the word, of which you are obliged to be hearers, or accidentally gain in conversation. But let it be very much your business to search for it, and to do so with that same diligence and labor with which men are wont to dig in mines of silver and gold.

Especially I would advise those who are young to employ themselves in this way. Men are never too old to learn, but the time of youth is especially the time for learning; it is peculiarly proper for gaining and storing up knowledge.

WILLIAM BOOTH

Letters to Salvationists on
Religion for Every Day

My Dear Comrades,

I desire to offer you some counsel about the Bible. You will all know that the Bible is a very important Book, and I have no doubt you set great store by it; indeed, I am pleased to learn that, of late, more thought is being given to its pages than ever throughout the Salvation Army. But still, I am afraid that the precious Book does not receive the attention that it demands.

Let me try to say a word or two that will be likely to better impress upon you its great value. The Bible is a very wonderful book. Its very name signifies this, for the word Bible simply means "the book," so that when we say the Bible, we mean that it is *The Book*, the book which, above every other, a man should know, treasure, and obey. If a wise man were offered the Bible on the one hand, or all the books in the world on the other, he would choose the Bible. . . . Oh, precious Book! What a priceless blessing it has been to The Salvation Army.

Now, my comrades, I want to ask this question: What ought you to do with the Bible? Ought you to neglect it—pass it over for the newspaper, the story book, or other rubbish? By no means. That is how the godless world around you deals with the precious treasure. What, then, ought you to do? I will tell you.

The very least that you can do with the Bible is to read it. If I, your General, sent you a letter, you could not do less than read it over, try to understand it, and strive to do what I requested in it. The Bible is a letter from your Heavenly Father; you cannot do less with His letter than you would do with one from the general.

Next, read it alone. Read a few verses at a time; read them on your knees; read them as you walk the streets, while you take your midday meal, when you rise in the morning, when you retire at night; and read the blessed book in your spare moments. Read it in your families. Impress its precious truths on your children, if you are parents. Explain them to the ignorant—make them understand.

See to it that you experience in your own hearts the blessings the Bible offers you. Remember, it will be little better than a curse to you if you only know the Word, and do not possess and live in the spirit of it. If you only believe it with your head, and do not enjoy the things that it describes and accept the mercy, wash in the fountain, receive the Holy Ghost, and live and die in the light and joy of its good tidings, it will only add to your condemnation and guilt.

In the same way, fulfill the duties it commands. It is the doers of the Word who are blessed. Make it the guide of your life: at home, abroad, in your Corps, in sickness and health, in joy and sorrow, everywhere and all the time. And publish the salvation of the Bible wherever you go—in the streets, in the barracks, in your home, at your work—everywhere tell the glad tidings.

Oh, my Comrades, do not let the Bible rise up in judgment against you, as it surely will if you either neglect it, or if reading and knowing about the salvation and victory of which it tells, you do not enjoy that salvation and experience that victory.

FRANÇOIS FÉNELON

The Inner Life

There is a time for everything in our lives, but the maxim that governs every moment is this: that there should be none useless; that they should all enter into the order and sequence of our salvation; that they are all accompanied by duties which God has allotted with his own hand, and of which he will demand an account. For from the first instant of our existence to the last, he has never assigned us a barren moment, nor one which we can consider as given up to our own discretion. The great thing is to recognize his will in relation to them.

This is to be effected not by an eager and restless seeking, which is much more likely to spoil everything than to enlighten us as to our duty, but by a true submission to those whom God has set over us, and a pure and upright heart which seeks God in its simplicity and heartily opposes all the duplicity and false wisdom of self as fast as it is revealed. For we misemploy our time not only when we do wrong or do nothing, but also when we do something else than what was incumbent on us at the moment, even though it may be the means of good. We are strangely ingenious in perpetually seeking our own interest, and what the world does nakedly and without shame, those who desire to be devoted to God do also, but in a refined manner, under favor of some pretext which serves as a veil to hide from them the deformity of their conduct.

The best general means to ensure the profitable employment of our time is to accustom ourselves to living in continual dependence upon the Spirit of God and his law—receiving, every instant, whatever he is pleased to bestow; consulting him in every emergency requiring instant action, having recourse to him in our weaker moments when virtue seems to fail; and invoking his aid and raising our hearts to him whenever we are solicited by objects of the senses and find ourselves surprised and estranged from God, and far from the true road. Happy is the soul that commits itself, by a sincere self-abandonment, into the hands of its Creator, ready to do all his will and continually crying, "Lord, what would You have me to do? Teach me to do Your will, for You are my God!" (Psalm 143:10).

During our necessary occupations, we need only pay a simple attention to the leadings of Divine Providence. As they are all prepared for us, and presented by him, our only care should be to receive them with a child-like spirit and submit everything absolutely to him—our temper, our own will, our scruples, our restlessness, our self-reflections, our overflowing emotions of hurry, vain joy, or other passions which assault us according as we are pleased or displeased with the different events of the day. Let us be careful, however, not to suffer ourselves to be overwhelmed by the multiplicity of our exterior occupations, be they what they may.

Let us endeavor to commence every enterprise with a pure view to the glory of God, continue it without distraction, and finish it without impatience.

CHARLES SPURGEON

The Sword and the Trowel

Two learned doctors are angrily discussing the nature of food, and allowing their meal to lie un-tasted, while a simple countryman is eating as heartily as he can of that which is set before him. The religious world is full of quibblers, critics, and skeptics who, like the doctors, fight over Christianity without profit either to themselves or others. Those are far happier who imitate the farmer and feed upon the Word of God, which is the true food of the soul.

Luther's prayer was, "From nice questions the Lord deliver us." Questioning with honesty and candor is not to be condemned when the object is to "prove all things, and hold fast that which is good;" but to treat revelation as if it were a football to be kicked from man to man is irreverence, if not worse. Seek the true faith, by all manner of means, but do not spend a whole life in finding it, lest you be like a workman who wastes the whole day in looking for his tools. Hear the true Word of God; lay hold upon it and spend your days not in raising hard questions, but in feasting upon precious truth.

It is, no doubt, very important to settle the point of General or Particular Redemption; but for unconverted men, the chief matter is to look to the Redeemer on the cross with the eye of faith. Election is a doctrine about which there is much discussion, but he who has made his election sure finds it a very sweet morsel. Final perseverance has been fought about in all time; but he who by grace continues to rest in Jesus to the end knows the true enjoyment of it.

Reader, argue if you please, but remember that believing in the Lord Jesus gives infinitely more enjoyment than disputing can ever afford you. If you are unsaved, your only business is with the great command, "Believe!" and even if you have passed from death unto life, it is better to commune with Jesus than to discuss doubtful questions. When Melancthon's mother asked him what she must believe amidst so many disputes, he, knowing her to be trusting to Jesus in a simple-hearted manner, replied, "Go on, mother, to believe and pray as you have done, and do not trouble yourself about controversy." So say we to all troubled souls: "Rest in the Lord, and wait patiently for him."

ANSELM

The Devotions of Saint Anselm

In your kind love towards me, you request of me, my very dear daughters, that I should send you a letter of admonition to instruct you and incite you to goodness of life; although you have with you my dear son Robert, into whose heart God has put it to care for you in the things of God, and who instructs you daily by word and example how you ought to live. Yet since I ought, if I can, to do what you ask me, I will try to write to you a few words such as you desire.

My very dear daughters, every action, whether it deserves praise or blame, deserves it according to the intention of the doer. For the will is the root and principle of all actions that are in our own power, and though we cannot do what we will, yet every one of us is judged before God according to His will. Do not therefore consider what you *do*, but what you *will*; take more heed what your will is than what your works are. For every action which is right is right because of the righteousness of the will from which it proceeded; from the righteousness of his will is a man called righteous, and from the unrighteousness of his will unrighteous.

If, then, you wish to live a good life, keep watch over your will continually in great and small things alike—both in those things which are in your own control, and in things which are not—lest it swerve in any degree from the right way. But if you wish to know when your will is right, it is certainly right when it is subject to the will of God.

And so when you decide to do or think of doing anything of importance, say in your hearts, *Does God will me to will this or no?* If your conscience answers, *Yes, God does will me to will this, and my will herein is pleasing to Him;* then, whether you can carry out your will or no, cleave to it. But if your conscience witnesses to you that God does not will you to have this will, then turn away your heart from it with all your might; and if you wish to drive it quite away, put it out of your head and forget it so far as you can.

But as to the way in which you may rid yourselves of an evil thought or will, consider and observe this advice which I give you. Do not wrangle with wicked thoughts or wicked wishes. But when they beset you, do your utmost to occupy your mind with some useful thought or wish, until the others disappear. For no thought or wish is ever driven away, except by some other thought or wish which is inconsistent with it. Conduct yourselves then thus towards unprofitable thoughts and wishes, so that by attending with all your might to profitable ones, your mind may come to refuse any recollection or notice to the unprofitable.

When you wish to pray, or to engage in any other good meditation, if these thoughts which you ought not to entertain are importunate with you, never consent to give up on their account the good design upon which you have entered, lest the devil who suggests them should rejoice in having made you desist from a good work once begun. Rather, overcome them by despising them in the manner I have described. Do not grieve or vex yourselves because they beset you, so long as by despising them in the way I have shown you, you yield no assent to them; otherwise they may take occasion from your vexation with them to come back into your mind and renew their old importunity. For it is habitual with the human mind for whatever either pleases or vexes it to come back into one's head more frequently than that which it feels or thinks should be neglected.

FRANÇOIS FÉNELON

Spiritual Letters

Live in peace, my dear young lady, without any thought for the future. Perhaps there will be none for you. You have no present, even, of your own—for you must only use it in accordance with the designs of God, to whom it truly belongs. Continue the good works that occupy you, since you have an attraction that way and can readily accomplish them. Avoid distractions and the consequences of your excessive vivacity, and, above all things, be faithful to the present moment and you will receive all necessary grace.

It is not enough to be detached from the world; we must become lowly also. In detachment, we renounce the things without; in lowliness, we abandon self. Every shadow of perceptible pride must be left behind, and the pride of wisdom and virtue is more dangerous than that of worldly fortune, as it has a show of right and is more refined.

We must be lowly-minded in all points and appropriate nothing to ourselves, our virtue and courage least of all. You rest too much in your own courage, disinterestedness, and uprightness. The babe owns nothing; it treats a diamond and an apple alike. Be a babe. Have nothing of your own; forget yourself; give way on all occasions; let the smallest be greater than you.

Pray simply from the heart, from pure love, and not from the head, from the intellect alone. Your true instruction is to be found in deep recollection and silence of the whole soul before God—in renouncing your own spirit in the love of lowliness, obscurity, feebleness, and annihilation. This ignorance is the accomplished teacher of all truth; knowledge cannot attain to it and can reach it but superficially.

SAINT JOHN OF THE CROSS

Dark Night of the Soul

Some of these persons make friendships of a spiritual kind with others, which oftentimes arise from luxury and not from spirituality. This may be known to be the case when the remembrance of that friendship causes not the remembrance and love of God to grow, but occasions remorse of conscience. For, when the friendship is purely spiritual, the love of God grows with it. And the more the soul remembers it, the more it remembers the love of God, and the greater the desire it has for God; so that, as the one grows, the other grows also.

For the spirit of God has this property: that it increases good by adding to it more good, inasmuch as there is likeness and conformity between them. But, when this love arises from the vice of sensuality aforementioned, it produces the contrary effects; for the more the one grows, the more the other decreases, and the remembrance of it likewise. If that sensual love grows, it will at once be observed that the soul's love of God is becoming colder, and that it is forgetting Him as it remembers that love. There comes to it, too, a certain remorse of conscience.

And, on the other hand, if the love of God grows in the soul, that sensual love becomes cold and is forgotten; for, as the two are contrary to one another, not only does the one not aid the other, but the one which predominates quenches and confounds the other and becomes strengthened in itself. Wherefore Our Savior said in the Gospel: "That which is born of the flesh is flesh, and that which is born of the Spirit is spirit" (John 3:6). That is to say, the love which is born of sensuality ends in sensuality, and that which is of the spirit ends in the spirit of God and causes it to grow. This is the difference that exists between these two kinds of love, whereby we may know them.

When the soul enters the dark night, it brings these kinds of love under control. It strengthens and purifies the one—namely that which is according to God—and the other it removes and brings to an end.

FRANCIS DE SALES

Introduction to the Devout Life

My child, love everyone with the pure love of charity, but have no friendship save with those whose interaction is good and true. And the purer the bond which unites you, so much higher will your friendship be. If your friendship is based on science, it is praiseworthy; still more if it arises from a participation in goodness, prudence, justice, and the like. But if the bond of your mutual liking be charity, devotion, and Christian perfection, God knows how very precious a friendship it is! Precious because it comes from God, because it tends to God, because God is the link that binds you, and because it will last for ever in Him.

Truly it is a blessed thing to love on earth as we hope to love in Heaven, and to begin that friendship here which is to endure for ever there. I am not now speaking of simple charity, a love due to all mankind, but of that spiritual friendship that binds souls together, leading them to share devotions and spiritual interests, so as to have but one mind between them. Such as these may well cry out, "Behold, how good and joyful a thing it is, brethren, to dwell together in unity!" (Psalm 133:1). Even so, for the "precious ointment" of devotion trickles continually from one heart to the other, so that truly we may say that to such friendship the Lord promises His blessing and life for evermore.

To my mind, all other friendship is but as a shadow with respect to this—its links mere fragile glass compared to the golden bond of true devotion. Form no other friendships. I say "form" because you have no right to cast aside or neglect the natural bonds which draw you to relations, connections, benefactors, or neighbors. My rules apply to those you deliberately choose to make.

There are some who will tell you that you should avoid all special affection or friendship as likely to engross the heart, distract the mind, excite jealousy, and what not. But they are confusing things. They have read in the works of saintly and devout writers that individual friendships and special intimacies are a great hindrance in the religious life, and therefore they suppose it to be the same with all the world, which is not at all the case. Whereas in a well-regulated community everyone's aim is true devotion, there is no need for individual relationships, which might exceed due limits; in the world, those who aim at a devout life require to be united one with another by a holy friendship, which excites, stimulates, and encourages them in well-doing. Just as men traversing a plain have no need to hold one another up, as they have who are amid slippery mountain paths, so perfectly religious do not need the stay of individual friendships. But those who are living in the world require such for strength and comfort amid the difficulties that beset them. In the world all have not one aim, one mind, and therefore we must take to us congenial friends; nor is there any undue partiality in such attachments, which are but as the separation of good from evil, the sheep from the goats, the bee from the drone—a necessary separation. . . .

So we see that the highest grace does not lie in being without friendships, but in having none which are not good, holy and true.

BERNARD OF CLAIRVAUX

On Loving God

The eternal law of righteousness ordains that he who will not submit to God's sweet rule shall suffer the bitter tyranny of self. But he who wears the easy yoke and light burden of love (Matthew 11:30) will escape the intolerable weight of his own self-will. Wondrously and justly does that eternal law retain rebels in subjection, so that they are unable to escape. They are subject to God's power, yet deprived of happiness with Him—unable to dwell with God in light and rest and glory everlasting. O Lord my God, "Why then do You not pardon my transgression, and take away my iniquity?" (Job 7:21).

When freed from the weight of my own will, I can breathe easily under the light burden of love. I shall not be coerced by fear, nor allured by mercenary desires; for I shall be led by the Spirit of God, that free Spirit whereby Your sons are led, which bears witness with my spirit that I am among the children of God (Romans 8:16).

So shall I be under that law which is Yours; and as You are, so shall I be in the world. Whosoever does what the apostle bids, "Owe no man anything, but to love one another" (Romans 13:8), are doubtless even in this life conformed to God's likeness—they are neither slaves nor hirelings, but sons.

JONATHAN EDWARDS

Religious Affections

This has, very unreasonably of late, been looked upon as an argument against the religious affections which some have had: that they spend so much time in reading, praying, singing, hearing sermons, and the like. It is plain from Scripture that it is the tendency of true grace to cause persons to delight in such religious exercises.

True grace had this effect on Anna the prophetess: "She departed not from the temple, but served God with fastings and prayers night and day" (Luke 2:27). And grace had this effect upon the primitive Christians in Jerusalem: "And they continuing daily with one accord in the temple, and breaking bread from house to house, did eat their meat with gladness and singleness of heart, praising God" (Acts 2:46–47). Grace made Daniel delight in the duty of prayer and solemnly attend to it three times a day, as it also did David: "Evening, morning, and at noon will I pray" (Psalm 55:17). Grace makes the saints delight in singing praises to God: "Sing praises unto his name, for it is pleasant" (Psalm 135:3). It also causes them to delight to hear the word of God preached: it makes the gospel a joyful sound to them (Psalm 89:15), and makes the feet of those who publish these good tidings to be beautiful (Isaiah 52:7). It makes them love God's public worship: "Lord, I have loved the habitation of thy house, and the place where your honor dwells" (Psalm 26:8). And 27:4: "One thing have I desired of the Lord, that will I seek after, that I may dwell in the house of the Lord all the days of my life, to behold the beauty of the Lord, and to inquire in his temple."

This is the nature of true grace. But yet, on the other hand, persons' being disposed to abound and to be zealously engaged in the external exercises of religion, and to spend much time in them, is no sure evidence of grace; because such a disposition is found in many that have no grace.

So it was with the Israelites of old, whose services were abominable to God. They attended the "new moons, and Sabbaths, and calling of assemblies, and spread forth their hands, and made many prayers" (Isaiah 1:12–15). So it was with the Pharisees; they "made long prayers, and fasted twice a week." That religion which is not spiritual and saving may cause men to delight in religious duties and ordinances: "Yet they seek me daily, and delight to know my ways, as a nation that did righteousness, and forsook not the ordinance of their God: they ask of me the ordinances of justice: they take delight in approaching to God" (Isaiah 58:2). It may cause them to take delight in hearing the word of God preached, as it was with Ezekiel's hearers: "And they come unto you as the people come, and they sit before you as my people, and they hear your words, but they will not do them: for with their mouth they show much love, but their heart goes after their covetousness. And lo, you are unto them as a very lovely song of one that hath a pleasant voice, and can play well on an instrument: for they hear your words, but they do them not" (Ezekiel 33:31–32). So it was with Herod; he heard John the Baptist gladly (Mark 6:20). So it was with others of his hearers: "For a season they rejoiced in his light" (John 5:35). So the stony ground hearers heard the word with joy.

THOMAS À KEMPIS

The Imitation of Christ

Shun the gossip of men as much as possible, for discussion of worldly affairs, even though sincere, is a great distraction inasmuch as we are quickly ensnared and captivated by vanity. Many a time I wish that I had held my peace and had not associated with men. Why, indeed, do we converse and gossip among ourselves when we so seldom part without a troubled conscience? We do so because we seek comfort from one another's conversation and wish to ease the mind wearied by diverse thoughts. Hence, we talk and think quite fondly of things we like very much or of things we dislike intensely. But, sad to say, we often talk vainly and to no purpose; for this external pleasure effectively bars inward and divine consolation.

Therefore we must watch and pray lest time pass idly. When the right and opportune moment comes for speaking, say something that will edify.

Bad habits and indifference to spiritual progress do much to remove the guard from the tongue. Devout conversation on spiritual matters, on the contrary, is a great aid to spiritual progress— especially when persons of the same mind and spirit associate together in God.

FREDERICK FABER

Tracts on the Church and Her Offices

There is nothing we dislike so much in other people as selfishness; and, if we are honest with ourselves, there is nothing to which we ourselves are more liable. Everybody will acknowledge this, so I will not waste time in proving it, nor in showing what must be obvious—how it keeps us back in our way to Heaven and does us all manner of harm here as well as hereafter, on earth as well as elsewhere.

Let us rather look at what God has done for us, and how He has placed us so as to protect us from this miserable sin. We are not set down in the world by ourselves. We cannot move about independent of our neighbor. We cannot live alone. We cannot love ourselves, except as we are reflected in the love of others. We do not like to think of dying alone. Our peace and health and happiness all depend upon our neighbor. They are more in his power than they are in our own. We see this in many ways. Our neighbor can vex and annoy us every day; he can stand in the way of our getting on; he can say ill-natured things of us; and, in a word, if he chooses to act wickedly and maliciously towards us, he can make the world very wretched and miserable to us.

Nay more than this, we cannot even keep our souls safe from the harm which our neighbor may do them. Our very souls are put in one another's power. He may do harm to us by not praying for us, by setting an evil example to our children, by frightening us from confessing Christ bravely and openly before men, and the like. His sin may hinder many a blessing which would otherwise have fallen on the city or parish where he dwells. Thus do all we can to keep to ourselves and by ourselves, and try to get to Heaven of ourselves and alone—it is impossible. God has so mixed us up with our neighbors, He has so entangled our concerns with their concerns, that we cannot act and live and feel alone.

Thus selfishness is made difficult by the law of the world, and by God's arrangement of it. He has so ordered the world that our natural conscience might tell us how unnatural selfishness was—and not the world only, for this is the point I have been all along bringing you to. He has put down among us the Church of Christ to help us in this very thing: to be a refuge to us from our own selfishness, to be a protection to us against the selfishness of others, and to destroy selfishness from one end of the world to the other.

RICHARD ROLLE

The Mending of Life

What is turning to God but turning from the world and from sin;
from the fiend and from the flesh? What is turning from God but
turning from unchangeable good to changeable good; to the liking
beauty of creatures; to the works of the fiend; to lust of the flesh
and the world? Not with going of feet are we turned to God, but
with the change of our desires and manners.

Turning to God is also done while we direct the sharpness of
our minds to Him, and evermore think of His counsel and His
commandments, that they may be fulfilled by us. And wherever
we be, sitting or standing, the dread of God passes not from our
hearts. I speak not of dread that has pain, but that which is in
charity, with which we give reverence to the presence of so great a
Majesty, and always we dread that we offend not in any little thing.
Certainly, thus disposed, to God we are truly turned because we
are turned from the world.

To be turned from the world is nothing else but to put away
all lust, and to suffer the bitterness of this world gladly for God;
and to forget all idle occupations and worldly errands, in so much
that our soul, wholly turned to God, dies pithily to all things
loved or sought in the world. Therefore, being given to heavenly
desires, they have God evermore before their eyes, as if they should
unwearily behold Him, as the holy prophet bears witness: "In my
sight I saw our Lord evermore before me."

. . . By this is showed that, except that our inward eyes be unwearily raised to Christ, we may not escape the snares of temptation. And there are many things that keep the eyes of our heart from being fixed on God, of which we indulge in some: abundance of riches, flattering of women, the fairness and beauty of youth. This is the threefold rope that scarcely may be broken; and yet it behooves to be broken and despised that Christ may be loved.

Certainly he that desires to truly love Christ, not only without heaviness but with a joy unmeasured, casts away all things that may hold him down. And in this case he spares neither father nor mother, nor himself; he receives no man's cheer; he does violence to all his letters; and he breaks through all obstacles. Whatever he can do seems little to him so that he may love God. He flees from vices as a brainless man and looks not to worldly solace, but is certainly and wholly directed to God; he has nearly forgotten his sensuality. He is gathered all inward and all lifted up into Christ, so that when he seems to men as if heavy, he is wonderfully glad.

JOHN BUNYAN

Pilgrim's Progress

"Now," said Christian, "let me go on."

"No, stay," said the Interpreter, "until I have showed you a little more, and after that you shall go on your way." So he took him by the hand again and led him into a very dark room, where there sat a man in an iron cage. Now the man to look on seemed very sad. He sat with his eyes looking down to the ground, his hands folded together, and he sighed as if he would break his heart.

Then said Christian, "What means this?" At which the Interpreter bid him talk with the man.

Then said Christian to the man, "What art you?" The man answered, "I am what I was not once."

CHRISTIAN: "What were you once?"

The man said, "I was once a fair and flourishing professor, both in mine own eyes and also in the eyes of others; I once was, as I thought, fair for the celestial city and had then even joy at the thoughts that I should get there."

CHRISTIAN: "Well, but what are you now?"

MAN: "I am now a man of despair, and am shut up in it as in this iron cage. I cannot get out; oh, now I cannot."

CHRISTIAN: "But how did you earn this condition?"

MAN: "I left off to watch and be sober; I laid the reins upon the neck of my lusts; I sinned against the light of the word and the goodness of God; I have grieved the Spirit, and he is gone; I tempted the devil, and he is come to me; I have provoked God to anger, and he has left me; I have so hardened my heart that I cannot repent."

Then said Christian to the Interpreter, "But is there no hope for such a man as this?" "Ask him," said the Interpreter.

Then said Christian, "Is there no hope but you must be kept in the iron cage of despair?"

MAN: "No, none at all."

CHRISTIAN: "Why? The Son of the Blessed is very merciful."

MAN: "I have crucified him to myself afresh; I have despised his person, I have despised his righteousness, I have counted his blood an unholy thing. I have done despite to the Spirit of grace, therefore I have shut myself out of all the promises, and there now remains to me nothing but threatenings, dreadful threatenings, fearful threatenings of certain judgment and fiery indignation which shall devour me as an adversary."

CHRISTIAN: "For what did you bring yourself into this condition?"

MAN: "For the lusts, pleasures, and profits of this world, in the enjoyment of which I did then promise myself much delight; but now every one of those things also bites me and gnaws me like a burning worm."

CHRISTIAN: "But can you not repent and turn?"

MAN: "God has denied me repentance. His word gives me no encouragement to believe; yes, he himself has shut me up in this iron cage: nor can all the men in the world let me out. O eternity, eternity! How shall I grapple with the misery that I must meet with in eternity?"

Then said the Interpreter to Christian: "Let this man's misery be remembered by you, and be an everlasting caution to you."

MARTIN LUTHER

Concerning Christian Liberty

Christian faith has appeared to many an easy thing; nay, not a few even reckon it among the social virtues, as it were. And this they do because they have not made proof of it experimentally, and have never tasted of what efficacy it is. For it is not possible for any man to write well about it, or to understand well what is rightly written, who has not at some time tasted of its spirit under the pressure of tribulation. While he who has tasted of it, even to a very small extent, can never write, speak, think, or hear about it sufficiently. For it is a living fountain, springing up unto eternal life, as Christ calls it in the 4th chapter of St. John.

Now, though I cannot boast of my abundance, and though I know how poorly I am furnished, yet I hope that after having been vexed by various temptations I have attained some little drop of faith, and that I can speak of this matter, if not with more elegance, certainly with more solidity than those literal and too subtle disputants who have hitherto discoursed upon it without understanding their own words. That I may open, then, an easier way for the ignorant—for these alone I am trying to serve—I first lay down these two propositions concerning spiritual liberty and servitude.

A Christian man is the most free lord of all, and subject to none; a Christian man is the most dutiful servant of all, and subject to every one.

Although these statements appear contradictory, yet, when they are found to agree together, they will be highly serviceable to my purpose. They are both the statements of Paul himself, who says: "Though I be free from all men, yet have I made myself servant unto all" (1 Corinthians 9:19), and: "Owe no man anything, but to love one another" (Romans 8:8). Now love is by its own nature dutiful and obedient to the beloved object. Thus even Christ, though Lord of all things, was yet made of a woman; made under the law; at once free and a servant; at once in the form of God and in the form of a servant.

MEISTER ECKHART

From the Sermon,
"Outward and Inward Morality"

Grace is from God, and it works in the depth of the soul whose powers it employs. It is a light which issues forth to do service under the guidance of the Spirit. The Divine Light permeates the soul and lifts it above the turmoil of temporal things to rest in God. The soul cannot progress except with the light which God has given it as a nuptial gift; love works the likeness of God into the soul. The peace, freedom, and blessedness of all souls consist in their abiding in God's will.

Towards this union with God, for which it is created, the soul strives perpetually. Fire converts wood into its own likeness, and the stronger the wind blows, the greater grows the fire. Now by the fire understand love, and by the wind the Holy Spirit. The stronger the influence of the Holy Spirit, the brighter grows the fire of love—not all at once, but gradually as the soul grows. Light causes flowers and plants to grow and bear fruit; in animals it produces life, but in men blessedness. This comes from the grace of God, Who uplifts the soul. For if the soul is to grow God-like it must be lifted above itself.

To produce real moral freedom, God's grace and man's will must cooperate. As God is the Prime Mover of nature, so also He creates free impulses towards Himself and to all good things. Grace renders the will free that it may do everything with God's help, working with grace as with an instrument which belongs

370

to it. So the will arrives at freedom through love—nay, becomes itself love, for love unites with God. All true morality, inward and outward, is comprehended in love, for love is the foundation of all the commandments.

All outward morality must be built upon this basis, not on self-interest. As long as man loves something else than God, or outside God, he is not free, because he has not love. Therefore there is no inner freedom which does not manifest itself in works of love. True freedom is the government of nature in and outside of man through God; freedom is essential existence unaffected by creatures. But love often begins with fear; fear is the approach to love. Fear is like the awl which draws the shoemaker's thread through the leather.

As for outward works, they are ordained for this purpose: that the outward man may be directed to God. But the inner work, the work of God in the soul, is the chief matter; when a man finds this within himself, he can let go of externals. No law is given to the righteous because he fulfils the law inwardly, and bears it in himself, for the least thing done by God is better than all the work of creatures. But this is intended for those who are enlightened by God and the Holy Scriptures.

SAINT JOHN OF THE CROSS

Ascent of Mount Carmel

The fifth way in which desires harm the soul is by making it luke-warm and weak, so that it has no strength to follow after virtue and to persevere therein. For the strength of the desire, when it is set upon several different aims, is less than if it were set wholly on one thing alone. And the more aims upon which the desire is set, the less of it there is for each of them—for this cause philosophers say that virtue in union is stronger than if it be dispersed.

Therefore it is clear that, if the desire of the will be dispersed among other things than virtue, it must be weaker as regards virtue. And thus the soul whose will is set upon various trifles is like water that, because of a hole in its container, never rises; and such a soul has no profit. For this cause the patriarch Jacob compared his son Ruben to water poured out, because in a certain sin he had given rein to his desires. And he said: "Unstable as water, you shall not excel" (Genesis 49:4, NKJV). As though he had said: Since you are poured out like water as to the desires, you shall not grow in virtue.

And thus, as hot water, when uncovered, readily loses heat, and as aromatic spices, when they are unwrapped, gradually lose the fragrance and strength of their perfume, even so the soul that is not recollected in one single desire for God loses heat and vigor in its virtue. This was well understood by David when he said, speaking with God, "I will keep my strength for You" (Psalm

59:9). That is, concentrating the strength of my desires upon You alone. . . .

From this it is clear that the desires bring no good to the soul, but rather take from it that which it has; and, if not mortified, they will not cease till they have wrought in it that which the children of the viper are said to work in their mother—who, as they are growing within her womb, consume her and kill her, and they themselves remain alive at her cost. Just so the desires that are not mortified grow to such a point that they kill the soul with respect to God because it has not first killed them. And they alone live in it.

MIGUEL DE MOLINOS

The Spiritual Guide
Which Disentangles the Soul

Know that you cannot fetch one step in the way of the Spirit until you endeavor to conquer this fierce Enemy: your own judgment. And more, the soul that will not know this hurt can never be cured.

A sick man that knows his disease is certain that, though his throat is dry, yet it is not good for him to drink, and that the medicine prescribed him, though bitter, yet is profitable for him: Therefore he believes not his appetite nor trusts in his own judgment, but yields himself up to a skillful physician, obeying him in everything as the means of his recovery and cure: The knowledge that he is sick helps him not to trust to himself, but to follow the wise judgment of his doctor.

Likewise, we are all sick of the disease of self love, and of our own judgment. We are all full of our selves, we are always desiring things hurtful to us, and that which does us good is unpleasant and irksome to us.

Therefore it is necessary for him that is sick to use the means of recovery, which is not to believe our own judgments and distempered sentiments, but the wise judgment of the spiritual and skillful Physician. And we must do so without reply or excuse, despising the seeming reasons of self-love. If we obey, we shall certainly recover. And this love of ours, which is the enemy of our ease and peace and perfection, and of the Spirit, will be overcome.

How often will your own judgment deceive you? And how

much will you change your judgment with shame when you have trusted to your own self? If any man should deceive you twice or thrice, would you ever trust him more? Why, therefore, do you retain confidence in your own judgment, which has so often cozened you? Oh blessed soul, believe no more, believe not. Subject yourself with true submission to your Physician and follow Him with blind obedience.

D. L. MOODY

Heaven

It does not take long to tell where a man's treasure is. In 15 minutes' conversation with most men you can tell whether their treasures are on the earth or in heaven. Talk to a patriot about the country, and you will see his eyes light up; you will find he has his heart there. Talk to some business men, and tell them where they can make a thousand dollars, and see their interest; their hearts are there. You talk to fashionable people who are living just for fashion, of its affairs, and you will see their eyes kindle. They are interested at once; their hearts are there. Talk to a politician about politics, and you see how suddenly he becomes interested. But talk to a child of God, who is laying up treasures in heaven, about heaven and about his future home, and see what enthusiasm. "Where your treasure is, there will your heart be also."

Now, it is just as much a command for a man to "lay up treasure in heaven" as it is that he should not steal. Some people think all the commandments are in those ten that were given on Sinai, but when Jesus Christ was here, He gave us many other commandments. There is another commandment in this Sermon on the Mount: "Seek first the kingdom of God and His righteousness, and all these things shall be added unto you." Here is a command that we are to lay up treasure in heaven and not on earth. The reason there are so many broken hearts in this land, the reason there are so many disappointed people, is because they have been laying up their treasures down here.

The worthlessness of gold, for which so many are striving, is illustrated by a story that Dr. Arnot used to tell. A ship bearing a company of emigrants has been driven from her course and wrecked on a desert island, far from the reach of man. There is no way of escape; but they have a good stock of food. The ocean surrounds them, but they have plenty of seeds, a fine soil, and a genial sun, so there is no danger. Before the plans are laid, an exploring party discovers a gold mine. There the whole party goes to dig. They labor day after day and month after month. They get great heaps of gold. But spring is past, and not a field has been cleared, not a grain of seed put into the ground. The summer comes and their wealth increases; but their stock of food grows small. In the fall they find that their heaps of gold are worthless. Famine stares them in the face. They rush to the woods, they fell trees, dig up the roots, till the ground, sow the seed. It is too late! Winter has come and their seed rots in the ground. They die of want in the midst of their treasures.

This earth is the little isle, eternity the ocean round it, and on this shore we have been cast. There is a living seed, but the mines of gold attract us. We spend spring and summer there; winter overtakes us in our toil; we are without the Bread of Life, and we are lost. Let us then who are Christians value all the more the home which holds the treasures that no one can take away.

FRANCIS DE SALES

Introduction to the Devout Life

The Enemy makes use of sadness to try good men with his temptations. Just as he tries to make bad men merry in their sin, so he seeks to make the good sorrowful amid their works of piety; and while making sin attractive so as to draw men to it, he strives to turn them from holiness by making it disagreeable. The Evil One delights in sadness and melancholy, because they are his own characteristics. He will be in sadness and sorrow through all eternity, and he would prefer to have all others the same.

The "sorrow of the world" disturbs the heart, plunges it into anxiety, stirs up unreasonable fears, disgusts it with prayer; it overwhelms and stupefies the brain; it deprives the soul of wisdom, judgment, resolution, and courage, weakening all its powers. In a word, it is like a hard winter, blasting all the earth's beauty and numbing all animal life; for it deprives the soul of sweetness and power in every faculty.

Should you, my daughter, ever be attacked by this evil spirit of sadness, make use of the following remedies. "Is any among you afflicted?" says James, "let him pray" (James 5:13). Prayer is a sovereign remedy; it lifts the mind to God, who is our only Joy and Consolation. But when you pray, let your words and affections, whether interior or exterior, all tend to love and trust in God. "O God of Mercy, most Loving Lord, Sweet Savior, Lord of my heart, my Joy, my Hope, my Beloved, my Bridegroom."

Vigorously resist all tendencies to melancholy, and although you may seem to do this coldly, wearily, and indifferently, do not give in. The Enemy strives to make us languid in doing good by depression, but when he sees that we do not cease our efforts to work, and that those efforts become all the more earnest by reason of their being made in resistance to him, he leaves off troubling us.

Make use of hymns and spiritual songs; they have often frustrated the Evil One in his operations, as was the case when the evil spirit that possessed Saul was driven forth by music and psalmody. It is well also to occupy yourself in external works, and that with as much variety as may lead us to divert the mind from the subject which oppresses it, and to cheer and kindle it—for depression generally makes us dry and cold. Use external acts of fervor, even though they are tasteless at the time; embrace your crucifix, clasp it to your breast, kiss the feet and hands of your dear Lord, raise hands and eyes to heaven, and cry out to God.

Moderate bodily discipline is useful in resisting depression because it rouses the mind from dwelling on itself. And frequent communion is especially valuable; the Bread of Life strengthens the heart and gladdens the spirits.

Lay bare all the feelings, thoughts and longings which are the result of your depression to your confessor or director, in all humility and faithfulness; seek the society of spiritually-minded people, and frequent such as far as possible while you are suffering. And, finally, resign yourself into God's Hands, endeavoring to bear this harassing depression patiently, as a just punishment for past idle mirth. Above all, never doubt but that, after He has tried you sufficiently, God will deliver you from the trial.

JONATHAN EDWARDS

Discourse on the Preciousness of Time

Time is very short, which is another thing that renders it very precious. The scarcity of any commodity occasions men to set a higher value upon it, especially if it be necessary and they cannot do without it. Thus when Samaria was besieged by the Syrians, and provisions were exceedingly scarce, "an ass's head was sold for fourscore pieces of silver, and the fourth part of a cab of dove's dung for five pieces of silver" (2 Kings 6:25).

So time is the more to be prized by men, because a whole eternity depends upon it; and yet we have but a little of time. "When a few years are come, then I shall go the way whence I shall not return" (Job 16:22). "My days are swifter than a post. They are passed away as the swift ships; as the eagle that hastes to the prey" (Job 9:25–26). It is but as a moment to eternity. Time is so short, and the work which we have to do in it is so great, that we have none of it to spare. The work which we have to do to prepare for eternity, must be done in time, or it never can be done; and it is found to be a work of great difficulty and labor, and therefore that for which time is the more requisite.

Time ought to be esteemed by us very precious, because we are uncertain of its continuance. We know that it is very short, but we know not how short. We know not how little of it remains—whether a year, or several years, or only a month, a week, or a day. We are every day uncertain whether that day will not be the last, or whether we are to have the whole day. There is nothing that experience does more verify than this. If a man had but little provision laid up for a journey or a voyage, and at the same time knew that if his provision should fail, he must perish by the way, he would be the more selective of it. How much more would many men prize their time if they knew that they had but a few months, or a few days, more to live! And certainly a wise man will prize his time the more, as he knows not but that it will be so for himself.

This is the case with multitudes now in the world who at present enjoy health, and see no signs of approaching death: many such, no doubt, are to die the next month, many the next week—yes, many probably tomorrow, and some this night; yet these same persons know nothing of it, and perhaps think nothing of it, and neither they nor their neighbors can say that they are more likely soon to be taken out of the world than others. This teaches us how we ought to prize our time, and how careful we ought to be, that we lose none of it.

FRANÇOIS FÉNELON

Spiritual Letters

I am not in the least surprised to learn that your impression of death becomes more lively in proportion as age and infirmity bring it nearer. I experience the same thing. There is an age at which death is forced upon our consideration more frequently, by more irresistible reflections, and by a time of retirement in which we have fewer distractions. God makes use of this rough trial to undeceive us in respect to our courage, to make us feel our weakness, and to keep us in all humility in his own hands.

Nothing is more humiliating than a troubled imagination in which we search in vain for our former confidence in God. This is the crucible of humiliation, in which the heart is purified by a sense of its weakness and unworthiness. In his sight shall no man living be justified (Psalm 143:2); yea, the heavens are not clean in his sight (Job 15:15), and in many things we offend all (James 3:2). We behold our faults and not our virtues—which latter it would be even dangerous to behold, if they are real.

We must go straight on through this deprivation without interruption, just as we were endeavoring to walk in the way of God before being disturbed. If we should perceive any fault that needs correction, we must be faithful to the light given us, but do it carefully, lest we be led into false scruples. We must then remain at peace, not listening to the voice of self-love mourning over our approaching death, but detach ourselves from life, offering it in sacrifice to God, and confidently abandon ourselves to him.

St. Ambrose was asked, when dying, whether he was not afraid of the judgments of God. "We have a good master," said he, and so must we reply to ourselves. We need to die in the most impenetrable uncertainty, not only as to God's judgment upon us, but as to our own characters. We must, as St. Augustine has it, be so reduced as to have nothing to present before God but our wretchedness and his mercy. Our wretchedness is the proper object of his mercy, and his mercy is all our merit. In your hours of sadness, read whatever will strengthen your confidence and establish your heart. "Truly God is good to Israel, even to such as are of a clean heart" (Psalm 123:1). Pray for this cleanness of heart, which is so pleasing in his sight and which renders him so compassionate to our failings.

MARTIN LUTHER

"A Mighty Fortress Is Our God"

1. A mighty fortress is our God,
   A bulwark never failing;
   Our helper He, amid the flood
   Of mortal ills prevailing;
   For still our ancient foe
   Doth seek to work us woe;
   His craft and power are great,
   And armed with cruel hate,
   On Earth is not his equal.

2. Did we in our own strength confide,
   Our striving would be losing;
   Were not the right Man on our side,
   The Man of God's own choosing;
   Dost ask who that may be?
   Christ Jesus, it is He;
   Lord Sabaoth, His name,
   From age to age the same,
   And He must win the battle.

3. And though this world, with devils filled,
   Should threaten to undo us,
   We will not fear, for God hath willed
   His truth to triumph through us;
   The Prince of Darkness grim,
   We tremble not for him;
   His rage we can endure,
   For lo, his doom is sure,
   One little word shall fell him.

4. That word above all earthly powers,
   No thanks to them, abideth.
   The Spirit and the gifts are ours
   Through Him who with us sideth;
   Let goods and kindred go,
   This mortal life also;
   The body they may kill;
   God's truth abideth still,
   His kingdom is forever.

JOHN BUNYAN

Grace Abounding

Of all the temptations that ever I met with in my life, to question the being of God and the truth of His gospel is the worst, and the worst to be borne; when this temptation comes, it takes away my girdle from me and removes the foundations from under me. Oh, I have often thought of that word, "Have your loins girt about with truth"; and of that, "When the foundations are destroyed, what can the righteous do?"

Sometimes when, after sin committed, I have looked for sore chastisement from the hand of God, the very next that I have had from Him has been the discovery of His grace. Sometimes, when I have been comforted, I have called myself a fool for my so sinking under trouble. And then, again, when I have been cast down, I thought I was not wise to give such way to comfort. With such strength and weight have both these been upon me. . . .

I have sometimes seen more in a line of the Bible than I could well tell how to stand under, and yet at another time the whole Bible has been to me as dry as a stick. Or rather, my heart has been so dead and dry unto it that I could not conceive the least drachma of refreshment, though I have looked it all over.

Of all tears, they are the best that are made by the blood of Christ; and of all joy, that is the sweetest that is mixed with mourning over Christ. Oh! It is a goodly thing to be on our knees, with Christ in our arms, before God. I hope I know something of these things.

I find to this day seven abominations in my heart: (1) Inclinings to unbelief. (2) Suddenly to forget the love and mercy that Christ has manifested. (3) A leaning to the works of the law. (4) Wanderings and coldness in prayer. (5) To forget to watch for what I pray for. (6) Apt to murmur because I have no more, and yet ready to abuse what I have. (7) I can do none of those things which God commands me, but my corruptions will thrust in themselves— "When I would do good, evil is present with me."

These things I continually see and feel, and am afflicted and oppressed with; yet the wisdom of God does order them for my good. (1) They make me abhor myself. (2) They keep me from trusting my heart. (3) They convince me of the insufficiency of all inherent righteousness. (4) They show me the necessity of fleeing to Jesus. (5) They press me to pray unto God. (6) They show me the need I have to watch and be sober. (7) And provoke me to look to God, through Christ, to help me, and carry me through this world. Amen.

JOHN MILTON

Paradise Lost

Descended, Adam to the bower, where Eve
Lay sleeping, ran before; but found her waked;
And thus with words not sad she him received.
"Whence thou return, and whither went, I know;
For God is also in sleep; and dreams advise,
Which he hath sent propitious, some great good
Presaging, since with sorrow and heart's distress
Wearied I fell asleep: But now lead on;
In me is no delay; with thee to go,
Is to stay here; without thee here to stay,
Is to go hence unwilling; thou to me
Art all things under Heaven, all places thou,
Who for my willful crime art banished hence.
This further consolation yet secure
I carry hence; though all by me is lost,
Such favor I unworthy am vouchsafed,
By me the Promised Seed shall all restore."

So spake our mother Eve; and Adam heard
Well pleased, but answered not: For now, too nigh
The Arch-Angel stood; and, from the other hill
To their fixed station, all in bright array
The Cherubim descended; on the ground
Gliding meteorous, as evening-mist
Risen from a river o'er the marish glides,
And gathers ground fast at the laborer's heel
Homeward returning. High in front advanced,
The brandished sword of God before them blazed,

Fierce as a comet; which with torrid heat,
And vapor as the Libyan air adust,
Began to parch that temperate clime; whereat
In either hand the hastening Angel caught
Our lingering parents, and to the eastern gate
Led them direct, and down the cliff as fast
To the subjected plain; then disappeared.

They, looking back, all the eastern side beheld
Of Paradise, so late their happy seat,
Waved over by that flaming brand; the gate
With dreadful faces thronged, and fiery arms:
Some natural tears they dropt, but wiped them soon;
The world was all before them, where to choose
Their place of rest, and Providence their guide:
They, hand in hand, with wandering steps and slow,
Through Eden took their solitary way.

D. L. MOODY

From the Sermon, "Hell"

I remember a few years ago, while the Spirit of God was working in my Church, I closed the meeting one night by asking any that would like to become Christians to rise. And to my great joy, a man arose who had been anxious for some time. . . .

While I talked with him he was trembling from head to foot, and I believe the Spirit was striving earnestly with him. He came back the next night, and the next, and the next; the Spirit of God strove with him for weeks; it seemed as if he came to the very threshold of Heaven, and was almost stepping over into the blessed world. I never could find out any reason for his hesitation, except that he feared his old companions would laugh at him.

At last the Spirit of God seemed to leave him; conviction was gone. Six months from that time I got a message from him that he was sick and wanted to see me. I went to him in great haste. He was very sick, and thought he was dying. He asked me if there was any hope. Yes, I told him, God had sent Christ to save him; and I prayed with him.

Contrary to all expectations, he recovered. One day I went down to see him. It was a bright, beautiful day, and he was sitting out in front of his house. "You are coming out for God now, aren't you? You will be well enough soon to come back to our meetings again."

"Mr. Moody," said he, "I have made up my mind to become a Christian. My mind is fully made up to that, but I won't be one just now. I am going to Michigan to buy a farm and settle down, and then I will become a Christian."

"But you don't know yet that you will get well."

"Oh," said he, "I shall be perfectly well in a few days. I have got a new lease of life."

I pleaded with him, and tried every way to get him to take his stand. At last he said, "Mr. Moody, I can't be a Christian in Chicago. When I get away from Chicago, and get to Michigan, away from my friends and acquaintances who laugh at me, I will be ready to go to Christ."

"If God has not Grace enough to save you in Chicago, he has not in Michigan" I answered.

At last he got a little irritated and said, "Mr. Moody, I'll take the risk," and so I left him.

I well remember the day of the week—Thursday, about noon, just one week from that very day—when I was sent for by his wife to come in great haste. I hurried there at once. His poor wife met me at the door, and I asked her what was the matter.

"My husband," she said, "has had a relapse; I have just had a council of physicians here, and they have all given him up to die."

. . . I went in, and he at once fixed his eyes upon me. I called him by name, but he was silent. I went around to the foot of the bed and looked in his face and said, "Won't you speak to me?", and at last he fixed that terrible deathly look upon me and said: "Mr. Moody, you need not talk to me any more. It is too late. You can talk to my wife and children; pray for them; but my heart is as hard as the iron in that stove there. My damnation is sealed, and I shall be in hell in a little while."

I tried to tell him of Jesus' love and God's forgiveness, but he said, "Mr. Moody, I tell you there is no hope for me." And as I fell on my knees, he said, "You need not pray for me. My wife will soon be left a widow and my children will be fatherless; they need your prayers, but you need not pray for me."

I tried to pray, but it seemed as if my prayers didn't go higher than my head, and as if Heaven above me was like brass. The next day, his wife told me, he lingered until the sun went down, and from noon until he died all he was heard to say was, "The harvest is past, the summer is ended, and I am not saved."

He lived a Christless life, he died a Christless death—we wrapped him in a Christless shroud and bore him away to a Christless grave. Are there some here that are almost persuaded to be Christians? Take my advice and don't let any thing keep you away. Fly to the arms of Jesus this hour. You can be saved if you will.

CHARLES SPURGEON

All of Grace

He who spoke and wrote this message will be greatly disappointed if it does not lead many to the Lord Jesus. It is sent forth in childlike dependence upon the power of God the Holy Ghost to use it in the conversion of millions, if so He pleases. No doubt many poor men and women will take up this little volume, and the Lord will visit them with grace. To answer this end, the very plainest language has been chosen and many homely expressions have been used. But if those of wealth and rank should glance at this book, the Holy Ghost can impress them also; since that which can be understood by the unlettered is none the less attractive to the instructed. Oh that some might read it who will become great winners of souls!

Who knows how many will find their way to peace by what they read here? A more important question to you, dear reader, is this: Will you be one of them?

A certain man placed a fountain by the wayside, and he hung up a cup near to it by a little chain. He was told some time after that a great art critic had found much fault with its design. "But," said he, "do many thirsty persons drink at it?" Then they told him that thousands of poor people, men, women, and children, slaked their thirst at this fountain; he smiled and said that he was little troubled by the critic's observation, only he hoped that on some sultry summer's day the critic himself might fill the cup, and be refreshed, and praise the name of the Lord.

Here is my fountain, and here is my cup: find fault if you please, *but do drink of the water of life*. I only care for this. I had rather bless the soul of the poorest crossing sweeper or rag gatherer, than please a prince of the blood and fail to convert him to God.

AUTHOR BIOGRAPHIES

Albert Benjamin Simpson (1843–1919)

A popular preacher and author in his time, A. B. Simpson resigned as pastor of a prestigious New York City church in order to develop an interdenominational fellowship devoted to world missions and evangelism—now known as the Christian and Missionary Alliance. Simpson was also the founder of Nyack College and Alliance Theological Seminary.

Anselm of Canterbury (1033–1109)

Recognized as a Saint by Pope Clement XI, Anselm began his ministry as a Benedictine monk and rose to serve as Archbishop of Canterbury for more than fifteen years. He wrote several books and is best known as the originator of the ontological argument for the existence of God.

Augustine of Hippo (354–430)

Considered one of the most prolific authors in Christian history, Saint Augustine wrote more than 40 books, including *Confessions* and *City of God*. Recognized as a Doctor of the Church by Pope Boniface VIII, Augustine remains one of the most influential thinkers of Western Christianity.

Bernard of Clairvaux (1090–1153)

As the abbot of a Cistercian order of monks, Bernard remained in cloister for more than 40 years—most notably at the abbey he founded in Clairvaux. Canonized by Pope Alexander III, Bernard was eventually named a Doctor of the Church by Pope Pius VIII.

Brother Lawrence (1614–1691)

Best known as the author of *The Practice of the Presence of God* (compiled posthumously from his letters and writings), Brother Lawrence served as a lay brother in a Carmelite monastery outside of Paris for most of his life. Most of that time was spent as a kitchen worker, and later as a repairer of sandals.

Charles Haddon Spurgeon (1834–1892)

One of the most famous preachers in history, Spurgeon became the pastor of London's New Park Street Church at the age of twenty. As his ministry grew, Spurgeon frequently preached to more than ten thousand listeners at a time. He is the author of several books, including *The Treasury of David* and *Around the Wicket Gate*.

Dwight L. Moody (1837–1899)

An important figure in American Christianity, D. L. Moody is the founder of Moody Church, the Northfield Mount Hermon School, Moody Bible Institute, and Moody Publishers. After beginning his ministry in Chicago, he became an influential evangelist throughout much of Europe later in his life.

Francis of Assisi (1181–1226)

The son of a wealthy Italian merchant, Francis renounced his inheritance as a young man and embraced a life of poverty and service to the poor. He is the founder of the Order of Friars Minor, more commonly known as the Franciscans, and was canonized in 1228 by Pope Gregory IX.

Francis de Sales (1567–1622)

Canonized by Pope Alexander VII and made a Doctor of the Church by Pius IX, Francis spent most of his ministry as the Bishop of Geneva. He is best known as the author of several books on spiritual formation, including *Introduction to the Devout Life* and *Treatise on the Love of God*.

François Fénelon (1651–1715)

Fénelon served in many posts over the course of his life, including as Archbishop of Cambrai and as a missionary to the Huguenots. He also served in the court of Louis XIV. Fénelon was a respected writer and poet, and is also known as an advocate for the mystical practices known as Quietism.

Frederick William Faber (1814–1863)

Best known as a British theologian and hymn writer, Faber also served as a country pastor before joining the Catholic Church. At the end of his life he founded a religious community known as St. Wilfrid's in the Archdiocese of Birmingham.

G. Campbell Morgan (1863–1945)

At the age of ten, G. Campbell Morgan heard D. L. Moody preach on one of his trips to England. At the age of thirteen, Morgan preached his own first sermon, and at the age of twenty-three he embarked on his lifelong journey as a preacher and minister of God's Word. Morgan was also a prolific author during the course of his life, writing more than twenty books.

George Mueller (1805–1898)

George Mueller was an evangelist and social worker who changed the landscape of nineteenth-century England. Over the course of his life he founded and directed several orphanages, leading to the care of more than ten thousand orphans. Mueller also established over a hundred schools, which provided a Christian education to more than 120,000 children, combined.

Jan van Ruysbroeck (1293–1381)

One of the Flemish mystics, van Ruysbroeck served as a Catholic priest in Brussels for more than twenty-five years before founding an Augustinian abbey at Groenendaal. He is the author of several influential books, including *The Spiritual Espousals* and *The Seven Steps of the Ladder of Spiritual Love*.

Johannes Tauler (1300–1361)

An influential scholar and mystic, Tauler produced some of the most famous and respected sermons in the German language. He was heavily influenced by Meister Eckhart, a contemporary, and his writings went on to influence generations of preachers, including Martin Luther.

John Bunyan (1628–1688)

John Bunyan was an English preacher and author. He was incarcerated for more than twelve years because of his refusal to stop preaching and attend an Anglican parish. It was during these years that he wrote *The Pilgrim's Progress*, which quickly became one of the most popular and beloved books of all time.

John Calvin (1509–1564)

An influential theologian and leader during the Protestant Reformation, John Calvin is one of the most respected thinkers in Western Christianity. His efforts to reform the church in the city

of Geneva were ultimately unsuccessful, but his prolific writings—
including several commentaries and the *Institutes of the Christian Religion*—laid the foundation for the system of theology later called Calvinism.

John Knox (1510–1572)

A beloved figure in Scottish history, John Knox was a clergyman, religious reformer, and political advocate. He is also known as the founder of Presbyterianism. He wrote several books and served under both King Edward VI of England and Mary, Queen of Scots.

John Milton (1608–1674)

John Milton is a famous poet and statesman who lived and wrote during the tumultuous period of England's Civil War. Milton served as a spokesman for Oliver Cromwell during the Commonwealth of England, but was removed from the court after Charles II reclaimed the throne. It was during this time that Milton, completely blind, wrote his most famous works—including the epic poem *Paradise Lost*.

John Wesley (1703–1791)

Founder of the Methodist movement (along with his brother Charles), John Wesley is one of the most influential men in the history of Christianity. He was an accomplished preacher, a gifted writer and theologian, and an early proponent of the abolition of slavery.

Jonathan Edwards (1703–1758)

Born in Connecticut, Jonathan Edwards is recognized as one of America's most important theologians. He was also a noted revivalist, a missionary to Native Americans, and the author of several famous sermons—most notably "Sinners in the Hands of an Angry God."

Julian of Norwich (1342–1416)
Julian is the author of *Revelations of Divine Love*, which, written in 1393, may be the first book authored by a woman in the English language. Julian was an anchoress at the Church of Saint Julian in Norwich, and is considered one of the most important of the English mystics.

Madame Guyon (1648–1717)
Jeanne Marie Bouvier de la Motte Guyon was a French mystic and outspoken proponent of the value of Quietism—a system of beliefs declared heretical by the Catholic Church. She is the author of several books, including *A Short and Easy Method of Prayer*.

Martin Luther (1483–1546)
Recognized as one of the most influential people in Western history, Martin Luther was a German priest who initiated the Protestant Reformation. He also translated the Bible into the language of the common people (as opposed to Latin) and is the author of several beloved hymns.

Meister Eckhart (1260–1327)
Eckhart von Hochheim was a German theologian and mystic who influenced several other thinkers of his day, including Johannes Tauler. Eckhart was a monk of the Dominican order and a prominent preacher and teacher.

Miguel de Molinos (1628–1696)

An influential author and priest during his day, Miguel de Molinos is among the best-known representatives of the Quietist movement in Spain. He wrote *A Spiritual Guide*, which became quite popular throughout Europe; however, as with many of the Quietists, he was accused of heresy by the Roman Catholic Church and eventually sentenced to a life of penitential imprisonment.

Nicholas of Cusa (1401–1464)

Recognized as one of the great geniuses of the fifteenth century, Nicholas of Cusa was a philosopher, mathematician, astronomer, and cardinal of the Catholic Church. He was also a popular author and wrote authoritatively on many subjects.

Richard Rolle (1290–1349)

Rolle was a mystical writer and hermit who lived in England during the fourteenth century. He was educated at Oxford and Paris before choosing a life of solitude. His written works maintained a wide popularity even after his death, the most notable being *The Fire of Love*.

Saint John of the Cross (1542–1591)

A Spanish mystic and friend of Teresa of Avila, John joined the Carmelite order of monks as a young man. He was persecuted for his belief in an ordered life of prayer, and was imprisoned by the Carmelites for several months before escaping. He spent the rest of his life sharing his experiences of the deep and profound love of God, in addition to writing *Dark Night of the Soul* and several other books.

Samuel Rutherford (1600–1661)

Samuel Rutherford was a Scottish minister and professor who became embroiled in the Episcopal and political controversies of his day. He was a beloved pastor, preacher, and author, but his defense of Calvinism and arguments for limiting the divine right of kings resulted in several instances of persecution.

Teresa of Avila (1515–1582)
A popular Spanish mystic whose writings are still prevalent today, Teresa was a reformer of the Carmelite Order within the Catholic Church. She is the author of several books, including *The Interior Castle*. Teresa was canonized by Pope Gregory XV in 1622 and named a Doctor of the Church in 1970 by Pope Paul VI.

Thomas à Kempis (1380–1471)
Born in Germany, Thomas à Kempis lived a life of obscurity as a priest, monk, and writer. He has become one of the most famous authors in Christendom, however, as the immense popularity of *The Imitation of Christ* continues to grow through the centuries.

Walter Hilton (1345–1396)
Walter Hilton spent time as both a lawyer and a religious hermit before joining the Augustinian friars at the end of the fourteenth century. He is the author of several mystical books, including *Ladder of Perfection*.

William Booth (1829–1912)
A British Methodist preacher, William Booth is the founder and first General of the Salvation Army. He was adept at several skills, and throughout the course of his life he wrote a number of books, published magazines, authored hymns, and steered the course for one of the most influential organizations in recent centuries.

William Law (1686–1761)
William Law was an eighteenth-century theologian who, like many other religious personalities of his time, was caught up in the

political machinations of the English monarchy. Law served as a professor, curate, tutor, and spiritual director throughout his life, in addition to writing *A Serious Call to a Devout and Holy Life* and several other books.

EXCERPTS TAKEN FROM . . .

A. B. Simpson: *A Larger Christian Life*
The Fourfold Gospel
The Gospel of Healing
Walking in the Spirit

Anonymous: *The Cloud of Unknowing*
Theologica Germanica

Anselm: *Saint Anselm's Book of Meditations
and Prayers*
The Devotions of Saint Anselm

Augustine of Hippo: *Confessions*
*Handbook on Faith, Hope,
and Love*
On Christian Doctrine

Bernard of Clairvaux: *On Loving God*

Brother Lawrence: *The Practice of the Presence of God*

Charles Spurgeon: *All of Grace*
Around the Wicket Gate
Morning and Evening
The Letters of C. H. Spurgeon
The Sword and the Trowel

D. L. Moody: *Heaven*
The Ten Commandments
The Way to God

Francis of Assisi:	*Admonitions* *Prayers of Saint Francis* *The Canticle of the Sun*
Francis de Sales:	*Introduction to the Devout Life* *Treatise on the Love of God*
François Fénelon:	*Maxims of the Saints* *Spiritual Letters* *The Inner Life*
Frederick Faber:	*Church Doctrine, a Witness Against* *Worldly Times* *The Unfulfilled Glory of the Church* *Tracts on the Church and Her Offices*
G. Campbell Morgan:	*Discipleship* *The Spirit of God* *The Teaching of Christ* *The Voice of the Devil*
George Mueller:	*Answers to Prayer* *The Life of Trust*
Jan van Ruysbroeck:	*The Adornment of the Spiritual* *Marriage* *The Book of Supreme Truth* *The Spiritual Espousals*
Johannes Tauler:	*The Following of Christ* *The Inner Way* *Light, Life, and Love*
John Bunyan:	*An Exposition on the First Ten* *Chapters of Genesis* *A Treatise on the Fear of God* *Christ a Complete Savior* *Grace Abounding* *Israel's Hope Encouraged* *Pilgrim's Progress*

| John Bunyan: | *Solomon's Temple Spiritualized* |
| (continued) | *The Groans of a Damned Soul* |

| John Calvin: | *Institutes of the Christian Religion* |
| | *On the Christian Life* |

| John Knox: | *The Scots Confession* |

| John Milton: | *Paradise Lost* |

| John Wesley: | *A Plain Account of Christian Perfection* |
| | *Sermons on Several Occasions* |

Jonathan Edwards:	*Religious Affections*
	Treatise on Grace
	Works of Jonathan Edwards, Volume I
	Works of Jonathan Edwards, Volume II

| Julian of Norwich: | *Showing of Love* |
| | *Revelations of Divine Love* |

| Madame Guyon: | *A Short and Easy Method of Prayer* |
| | *The Autobiography of Madame Guyon* |

Martin Luther:	*Concerning Christian Liberty*
	Disputation on the Divinity and Humanity of Christ
	Large Catechism
	Luther's Little Instruction Book
	Small Catechism

| Meister Eckhart: | *Meister Eckhart's Sermons* |

| Miguel de Molinos: | *The Spiritual Guide Which Disentangles the Soul* |

Nicholas of Cusa:	*On Being a Son of God*
	On Loving God
	The Vision of God
Richard Rolle:	*The Mending of Life*
Saint John of the Cross:	*Ascent of Mount Carmel*
	Dark Night of the Soul
	Spiritual Canticle of the Soul and the Bridegroom of Christ
Samuel Rutherford:	*A Selection From His Letters*
	The Trial and Triumph of Faith
Teresa of Avila:	*The Interior Castle*
	The Life of Saint Teresa of Jesus
	The Way of Perfection
Thomas à Kempis:	*The Imitation of Christ*
Walter Hilton:	*The Scale of Perfection*
	The Song of Angels
William Booth:	*Letters to Salvationists on Religion for Every Day*
	Purity of Heart
William Law:	*A Collection of Letters*
	A Serious Call to a Devout and Holy Life
	The Spirit of Prayer

Author Index

JAMES STUART BELL is a Christian publishing veteran and the owner of Whitestone Communications, a literary development agency. He is the editor of many story collections, including the CUP OF COMFORT, LIFE SAVORS, and EXTRAORDINARY ANSWERS TO PRAYER series and the coauthor of numerous books in THE COMPLETE IDIOT'S GUIDE series. He and his family live in West Chicago, Illinois.